CONTENTS

INDEX TAB

The Index Tab on the right hand margin of each double-page spread is designed to help you get to the facts as quickly as possible. The upper index lists the main chapters of the guide, the middle index lists the main sections of the current chapter, and the bottom index lists the sub-sections.

USING ...

The ... ne detailed
maps ... nfolded
so th ... nd while
using ...

D1206482

GAME

1ST CHAPTER

The world has never been a more dangerous place, and you're right there in the heat of the action, facing down the horror and giving it back to 'em with both barrels. The battle rages around you, bullets screaming overhead, but inside you remain cool. Ice cool. What it all comes down to, right here, right now, is that millions of lives may ultimately depend on your actions. It runs far deeper in the blood and bones than mere bravery. It's about duty and destiny, and failure is unthinkable.

In your role as Specter, leader of a crack U.S. Navy SEALs team, you must draw on every ounce of courage, skill, determination and experience. When your finger's pressed against the cold hard trigger, you'd better be aiming the right weapon at the right target.

In this first chapter, you'll find all you need to know about operational basics in SOCOM 3 such as how to control your team, what equipment they have at their disposal, and what tactics will best help you ace every mission and get your unit back to base safe and sound.

BASICS

HOW TO PLAY

So, you're about to get started on your first mission, all fired up to hunt down General Heydar Mahmood and his North African Patriotic Front (NAPF). Before you get down and dirty in the desert, take a few minutes to familiarize yourself with the basic controls and onscreen displays of SOCOM 3 as described in the following pages. The enemy you face is both ruthless and resourceful, so it pays to be well-informed before entering the fray.

CONTROLS

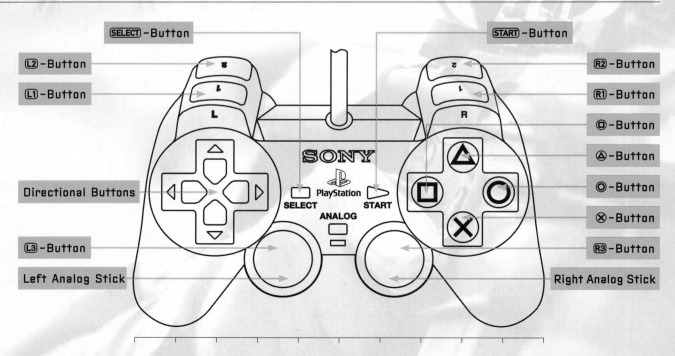

SELECT – Button

START – Button

L2 – Button

L1 – Button

R2 – Button

R1 – Button

□ – Button

△ – Button

Directional Buttons

○ – Button

⊗ – Button

L3 – Button

R3 – Button

Left Analog Stick

Right Analog Stick

Please note that this layout is for the default 'Precision Shooter' control system.

PRECISION SHOOTER CONTROL SCHEME

COMMANDS	ON FOOT	IN MENUS	ON BOARD VEHICLES
Left Analog Stick	Move, swim	Navigate menu/highlight item	Steer
Directional Buttons	Peek round corners/toggle Special Action icons (◈/◈) Cycle between first and third-person perspective and weapon scope (◈/◈) Cycle through teammates during online play (◈/◈)	Navigate menu/highlight item	Hotswap seats left and right
SELECT-Button	Access Tactical Map		Access Tactical Map
START-Button	Pause/unpause, open Pause Menu	Toggle weapon info in the Armory	Access Pause Menu
Right Analog Stick	Aim weapon/look around	Look around the room in the Armory	Aim weapon (when manning turret gun) Look around (when driving)
□-Button	Jump	Select default weapons in the Armory	
○-Button	Access Team Command Menu (tap)/ access Voice Chat (hold, with headset)		Access TCM (tap)/ Voice Chat (hold)
△-Button	Change body position (stand/go prone/crouch)-press hard to go prone Drop equipment (Inv.) Submerge/surface (tap when swimming)	Cancel/previous screen/ return to Main Menu	Brake (when driving) Cancel selection
✕-Button	Activate Special Action icons	Select weapon/equipment/ menu item Open Team Command submenu	Mount/dismount vehicle (when Special Action icon appears)
L3-Button*	Toggle rates of fire (hold)		
L2-Button	Perform Team Command Action (see details on page 12)		
L1-Button	Quickswap primary/secondary weapons (tap)		Reverse (when driving)
R3-Button*	Reload (hold)		Reset camera
R2-Button	Access Inventory (hold) Change/customize weapon during online play (when out of action)		
R1-Button	Fire/throw/deploy weapon		Accelerate (when driving)/ fire mounted weapon

Press down analog stick until you hear a click.

GAME BASICS

WALKTHROUGH

MULTIPLAYER

EXTRAS

INDEX

HOW TO PLAY

HOW TO WIN

EQUIPMENT

CONTROLS

ONSCREEN DISPLAY

OBJECTIVES

MENUS

COMMANDS

ACTIONS

ONSCREEN DISPLAY

The in-game onscreen display (Fig. 1) offers a wealth of information to help you carry out your mission.

Crosshairs: Extremely useful aiming devices that turn red when they are pointing at an enemy, and green when they are pointing at an ally. Their default color is orange. The crosshairs are also used to indicate bullet spread: the closer the lines are together around the center reticle, the more accurate your shooting will be and vice versa. Naturally, your accuracy is higher when you are standing still, crouching, or lying on the ground, and lower when you are running around.

Noise Detector: Every time you are hit by enemy fire, the outer edge of the targeting reticle will flash red in the direction from which you were hit, enabling you to quickly ascertain the enemy shooter's location.

Compass: Essential for guiding you through a mission. The 'N' on the compass stands for 'North', so glance at it often to check your bearings. Your teammates will frequently call out compass reference points to alert you to approaching enemies. Remember that you are always shown in the middle of the compass as an orange dot. Your teammates appear as light blue dots, escortees as dark blue dots and enemies as red dots. Neutral vehicles appear as white rectangles, allied appear as blue, while enemy vehicles appear as red. Once you have mounted a vehicle, it will appear as an orange rectangle. Nav Points appear on the compass as yellow chevrons, mission objectives as gold stars, and completed objectives and secondary objectives as white stars. Your line of sight is also represented on the compass as a fan-like shading, spreading out from the centre dot. The extraction zone is represented by a blue cross.

Team Member Status: All you need to know about the current status of your team can be found on the bottom right of the screen. Next to each team member's name you will see an icon showing their current activity, eg, 'following'. The thin green line underneath their name indicates the health of each team member. When the line turns red, it means that the SEAL is seriously injured. When the line disappears completely, it means that they are totally incapacitated. You will also see a small white icon to the right of the team member's name when a Satchel charge is equipped. Note that your own character icon shows your current stance (standing, crouching or prone). When swimming and submerged, a small green bar will appear next to the appropriate team member's name. As the team member's air runs out, the bar slowly changes to red. When the bar is completely red, the team member will resurface to breathe.

Weapon: Your currently equipped weapon, as well as details of its maximum ammo capacity, remaining loaded ammo, remaining magazines and present weapon fire mode, is shown in the bottom left corner of your screen.

Special Action Icon: These orange icons indicate when you can perform a Special Action. Press ⊗ to activate. See pages 17-19 to learn more about Special Actions.

Team Command Action Icon: When you see this blue icon in the bottom half of the screen, you can press L2 to execute a Team Command Action. See page 12 for more details on Team Command Actions.

Information: Various text messages will flash up in a window in the top left corner of the screen, informing you of key points in the mission, including your current mission objective, completion of an objective, and when you have reached a checkpoint.

GAME BASICS

6

OBJECTIVES

TACTICAL MAP

The Tactical Map, or TacMap, contains all the information that you need to know about your mission objectives and your current position in the game. If you're stuck or confused about where to go next, the TacMap will usually have the solution. Press (SELECT) to access the TacMap during gameplay. Press △ to return to the game. Use the left analog stick to move around the map, and the right analog stick to zoom in and out. Press ⊡ to snap to your current location, and ◎ to snap to your current objective. A very useful green arrowed-line indicates the most direct route to reach your next objective (Fig. 2). The color and symbol code is the same as for the compass.

MISSION OBJECTIVES

The Mission Objectives list appears on the left-hand side of the TacMap screen. It is updated constantly, as your objectives change depending on how the mission pans out. Should you fail one of the primary objectives, the mission will be over instantly. Killing an ally also means immediate mission failure. Secondary objectives are indented slightly to the right of the list. Failing a secondary objective does not jeopardize the mission: it simply lowers your final mission rating (and the objective turns red). Active objectives are shown in white, and turn green when highlighted by using ⊕ and ⊕ on the directional buttons. When you complete a Bonus Objective, it will be highlighted in dark blue. When you complete Primary and Secondary Objectives, they will be highlighted in yellow. Press ⊗ to learn more about any objectives on the list (Fig. 3).

MISSION SUCCESS/MISSION FAILURE

At the end of each mission, provided that you have fulfilled the Primary Objectives, you will be presented with the Mission Success screen (Fig. 4). This features a detailed breakdown of your mission stats, such as Stealth, Accuracy and Teamwork percentage ratings, number of kills achieved, and how many Bonus and Crosstalk Missions you have completed. You will also be given an alphabetical rating for your performance in the mission, with 'A' being the best, of course! If you choose to abort the mission at any time, or if you fail the mission for any reason, you will be presented with the Mission Failure screen, which has the same stats as the Mission Success screen, but always gives you a rating of 'Unsatisfactory'. Hopefully you won't be seeing too much of this particular screen!

MENUS

When playing SOCOM 3 you will use four basic menus: OCN (Operations Control Network) Main Menu, OCN Mission Briefing Menu, Team Command Menu (TCM) and the Pause Menu.

OCN MAIN MENU

When you start to play SOCOM 3: U.S. Navy SEALs for the first time, the game will detect that you have no relevant data on your memory card. When prompted, press ⊗ to continue. The Title Screen will then load, and you will be prompted to press ⊗ to access the Main Menu of the Operations Control Network system (OCN), where headquarters will provide you with mission-critical intel, allow you to re-equip and resupply, and view your statistics and mission briefings. Note that if you already have SOCOM 3 data on your memory card, you will also see the Quick Deploy option when you access the Title Screen. Here you can press ◎ to resume your game directly from your last save point.

Let's assume that you're starting SOCOM 3 for the first time. After pressing ⊗ to access the OCN, you will see four login slots. Specter is the default profile name, but you can enter your own name using the onscreen keyboard if you like. Simply highlight Specter, then press ◎ and select either Rename Profile or Delete Profile. On the right of the OCN screen you will see various game stats, such as details of when your login was created, Total Time Deployed and Current Single Player ranking (Fig. 1). When you are ready to continue, press ⊗ to select your chosen profile and access the OCN Main Menu, consisting of Campaign, Multiplayer and Profile options.

Campaign

New Campaign: Select this option to start a single-player game. You can choose from five difficulty levels: Ensign, Lieutenant, Commander, Captain and Admiral, with Ensign being the lowest, and Admiral the highest. When you first start the game you will only be able to select Ensign, Lieutenant or Commander. To unlock the other difficulty levels, game progression starts at the Commander difficulty up until the Admiral difficulty. Select any of these and you will be presented with two more options: Training Mission and Start Campaign. If this is your first time playing SOCOM 3, or indeed any SOCOM game, it's a good idea to start with the Training Mission, in order to familiarize yourself with the controls. After selecting either option, you will access the OCN Mission Briefing screen (see page 10).

Resume Campaign: You can access this option only when you have SOCOM 3 save data on your memory card. It enables you to resume from your last saved checkpoint. Note that you may save your game at certain checkpoints in each mission. You will also be prompted to save your game at the end of each mission.

Mission Redeploy: Replay a mission that you have previously completed.

Load Saved Game: Load your previously saved game.

Multiplayer

The Multiplayer option will only be available in the Main Menu if your console is set up for internet access or LAN Mode (for which you need a broadband adaptor and/or a hub). To find out all you need to know about Multiplayer Mode, turn to the Multiplayer chapter starting on page 112.

```
OCN            OPERATIONS CONTROL NETWORK

OCN v1.0 Aug 30 2005              Login Created
                                        9.8.05
      SPECTER                        Last Used
                                       9.10.05
      EMPTY               Total Time Deployed
                                    0:07:42:36
      EMPTY              Time in Single Player
                                    0:07:42:36
      EMPTY                      Current Ran
                                   LIEUTENA

  SPECTER         ◎ OPTIONS  ⊗ SELECT  △ BACK

                                            01
```

SOCOM3 U.S. NAVY SEALS

GAME BASICS

WALKTHROUGH

MULTIPLAYER

EXTRAS

INDEX

HOW TO PLAY

HOW TO WIN

EQUIPMENT

CONTROLS

ONSCREEN DISPLAY

OBJECTIVES

MENUS

COMMANDS

ACTIONS

Profile

Return to Login: Takes you back to the Login screen.

Career Stats: All your single-player stats, including percentage of missions completed, Player Hit Percentage and Enemies Downed are shown here.

Extras: Here you can see details of the Weapons, Characters, Movies, Jukebox music and Crosstalk that you've unlocked in the game (Fig. 2). Please see pages 186-187 in the Extras chapter to learn more about Crosstalk.

Options: Here you can set up all the game options, as outlined below:

Audio Options	
Sound Output	Choose from Stereo, Mono or Dolby Pro Logic II.
Music Volume	Use the directional buttons to increase or decrease the background music volume.
Sound Volume	Use the directional buttons to increase or decrease the sound effects volume.
Dialog Volume	Use the directional buttons to increase or decrease the in-game dialog volume.
Headset Volume	Use the directional buttons to increase or decrease the headset volume.
Movie Volume	Use the directional buttons to increase or decrease the sound level of the cutscenes.
Restore Defaults	Reset all those audio options that you've just carefully adjusted.
Save Changes	Save your changes to your memory card.

Video Options	
Brightness	Use the directional buttons to increase or decrease screen brightness.
Video Mode	Choose from Interlaced or Progressive Scan (480p).
Display Mode	Choose from Full Screen or Wide Screen.
Help Windows	Toggle on or off.
Head Bob	Toggle on or off realistic movement of the head in first-person view.
Screen Position	Select, then use the direc tional buttons to center the screen.
Restore Defaults	Undo any previous changes.
Save Changes	Save any changes to your memory card.

Control Options	
Vibration	Toggle controller vibration on or off.
Aim Assist	Toggle on or off. When activated, enables you to lock onto your target.
Pitch	Choose between Normal or Invert camera control.
Presets	Choose from Recruit, Sailor, SEAL or Custom. Each preset determines the degree of Look Speed, Acceleration and Dead Zone.
Look Speed	Determines how quickly the camera pans. Can only be changed manually by selecting the Custom preset.
Acceleration	Determines how quickly the crosshairs move from stationary to full speed. Can only be adjusted manually by selecting the Custom preset.
Dead Zone	Determines how much you must move the right analog stick before the crosshairs start moving. Can only be adjusted manually by selecting the Custom preset.
Restore Defaults	Puts everything back just the way you found it.
Save Changes	Record your changes on your memory card.

Control Schemes

Use the directional buttons to cycle through the Precision Shooter (default), Scout, Commando and Frogman controller configurations. Press ⊗ to make your selection. Press (START) to toggle vehicle control information.

Deploy: Lock and load! The planning stage is over, so highlight and select the Deploy icon when you're ready to go get the bad guys.

TEAM COMMAND MENU

During gameplay, tap ◎ to access the Team Command Menu (TCM). Use the left analog stick or directional buttons to navigate around the menu and press ⊗ to select the recipient of the command. Choose from Fireteam, Escortee, Friendly, Able and Bravo (Fig. 4). You will then access a submenu, where you can issue commands to your chosen teammates or allies. If you have a headset, you may use it here to issue commands (see page 12 to learn more about the headset). Not all commands will always be available, depending on the circumstances. Available commands are shown in green, unavailable ones in white. Turn to page 11 for a detailed list and explanation of all team commands.

OCN MISSION BRIEFING MENU

You will access the Mission Briefing Menu after selecting Training Mission or Start Campaign from the Main Menu. Here, you will make your final battle preparations and study all relevant mission data, before being deployed in the field. The Mission Briefing Menu consists of the following sections:

Briefing: Includes a brief description of the mission, a basic map, and details about the location of the mission, including temperature and weather conditions.

Mission Info: More details about the mission, provided by intelligence agencies and field personnel. Also includes a numbered list of your mission objectives. SOCOM will notify you of any additional objectives that may arise when you're in the field.

Intel Database: A dossier containing various pieces of intel relating to the mission, including satellite photographs, maps, and terrorist or VIP profiles.

Armory: A screen detailing every single weapon and piece of equipment for each of the four team members. If you decide to change some of your gear, you can select a SEAL and view each weapon or piece of equipment individually. Use the directional buttons or left analog stick to highlight the item, then press ⊗ to select (Fig. 3). Press (START) to find out more information about a particular item. Press ◎ to return to the default weapons and equipment settings for each SEAL, or for the whole fireteam. See page 25 to learn more about selecting equipment for a mission.

PAUSE MENU

Press (START) to display the Pause Menu during a mission, then use the directional buttons to highlight, and ⊗ to select, one of the following options:

Resume: Resume gameplay. (You can also press (START) to resume gameplay.)

Abort Mission: Leave the mission and return to the debriefing screen. An aborted mission will be indicated as a Mission Failure.

Restart Mission: Messed up? Start over from the insertion point.

Restart from Checkpoint: Restart from the last checkpoint.

Save Checkpoint Status: Save your current checkpoint status to your memory card.

Aim Pitch: Choose from Inverted or Normal aim pitch.

Controller Vibration: Toggle vibration on or off.

Aim Assist: Turn aim assist on or off.

Subtitles: Turn subtitles on or off.

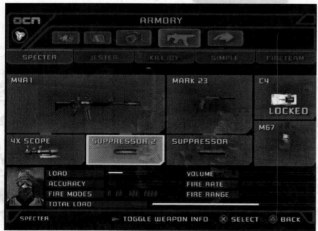

COMMANDS

Issuing commands is a very important aspect of SOCOM 3. As well as directly controlling your main character (see pages 12 to 16), you must indeed issue commands to other members of your fireteam, as well as a variety of different operatives and allies that you may meet during your mission. You can issue commands via the Team Command Menu, or directly using Team Command Actions.

TEAM COMMAND MENU
Issuing Commands

After tapping ◎ to access the TCM (or holding down ◎ if you are using the headset), use the directional buttons or left analog stick to highlight the recipient of your command from the following list:

Fireteam: All three members of your team.

Escortee: Someone who is being escorted by your team.

Friendly: A civilian.

Able: Your partner, Jester: you will only be able to send him a certain distance. One of his main duties is to cover you, though, so he will seldom stray far from your side. Should you move too far away from him, he will start following you. And you thought he only stuck so close because he liked you!

Bravo: Your remaining two teammates: they operate as a pair, and can be sent almost anywhere on the field of operations.

Command List

Once you have highlighted the teammate or ally that you wish to deploy, press ⊗ to access the command submenu for that character. Possible actions will be highlighted in green, unavailable actions will be highlighted in white (Fig. 5). Choose from the following commands:

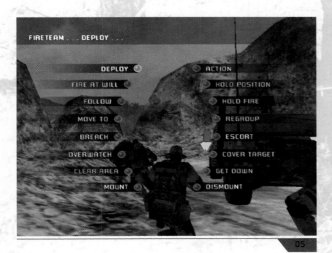

FIRETEAM . . . DEPLOY . . .

DEPLOY	ACTION
FIRE AT WILL	HOLD POSITION
FOLLOW	HOLD FIRE
MOVE TO	REGROUP
BREACH	ESCORT
OVERWATCH	COVER TARGET
CLEAR AREA	GET DOWN
MOUNT	DISMOUNT

05

DEPLOY: Use explosives, depending on what equipment your teammates are carrying. (See page 37 to learn more about the different types of explosives available to you.)

FIRE AT WILL: Your team will open fire on any enemy that you meet.

FOLLOW: You take point, and your team will follow accordingly and copy your stance. Eg, if you crouch, they will also crouch.

MOVE TO: Your team will move to a designated location. You can opt to use your crosshairs as a pointer, by positioning the crosshairs over the area that you want your team to move to, then issuing the 'MOVE TO… CROSSHAIRS' command. Selecting 'MOVE TO… MY TARGET' will have the same effect. Alternatively, you can use Nav Points: these are coordinates that mark certain key points in your field of operations, with names such as Charlie, Delta, Echo and Foxtrot. They will be listed in the submenu after you select 'MOVE TO'. Available Nav Points will be highlighted in green, unavailable ones will be highlighted in white.

BREACH: Open a door, throw in a grenade and clear the area on entering. This option will only be available in a relevant location, ie, you will not be able to 'BREACH' in the middle of the desert!

OVERWATCH: Your teammates will cover any area that you point to with your crosshairs, and alert you to any visible enemies.

CLEAR AREA: Bravo will sweep the designated area for hostiles: use your crosshairs to show them where to search.

MOUNT: Your teammates will enter a vehicle or man a turret or machine gun post.

ACTION: Your teammates will perform the Special Action indicated by your crosshairs.

HOLD POSITION: Your teammates will remain in their current position, although Jester will follow you if you get too far away. Talk about clingy…

HOLD FIRE: Your teammates will cease firing until commanded to recommence, or until engaged by an enemy.

REGROUP: Your teammates will return to your side.

ESCORT: If your mission involves escorting a VIP, ally, or prisoner, use this command to instruct Bravo to lead the escortee and follow any other additional commands.

COVER TARGET: Place your crosshairs over a specific area that is currently visible to your fireteam, then issue the 'COVER TARGET' command and they will open fire on any enemies that enter the designated area.

GET DOWN: All teammates will immediately go prone.

DISMOUNT: Teammates will exit a vehicle or turret.

HEADSET

If you have the optional USB headset, you can use it to issue commands during single-player missions, as well as during multiplayer gaming (see pages 112 to 182 for more on Multiplayer Mode). When you issue voice commands you still use the TCM, but instead of pressing buttons, you simply need to hold down ◎ and speak into the microphone.

TEAM COMMAND ACTIONS

Occasionally during a mission you will notice a small blue icon that appears at the bottom of the screen, similar to the orange Special Action icon (learn more about Special Actions on pages 17-19). When this appears, it means that you can issue an instant Team Command to Able and Bravo by pressing L2. What command you issue will depend on the circumstances: if you see a Satchel icon for instance, it means that you can instruct your team to place a Satchel explosive. The Team Command icon will only appear when you point your crosshairs at the relevant area, ie, you will only be able to command your team to place a Satchel bomb on a bridge when you point your crosshairs at the bridge in question (Fig. 6). If there is no other command available, tap L2 to have your team move to the crosshairs, and hold L2 to issue the default command of 'FOLLOW'.

06

ACTIONS

Although you're in charge of a crack unit, as their commander it's ultimately up to you to take the lead when the going gets rough. Your team can only help you up to a point, the rest of the time it's down to you to take on the bad guys face to face, and that's when the fun really starts! The following pages contain detailed descriptions of all the actions that are available to you in SOCOM 3, and when and how you can use them.

MOVEMENT

WALKING / RUNNING	
Use the left analog stick to move your character: tilt the stick gently to creep along slowly (ideal for stealthy situations); press harder to walk quickly or run.	

CHANGE BODY POSITION	
△	*Press △ to cycle between standing, crouching, and going prone (press firmly to go prone).*

GAME BASICS

WALKTHROUGH

MULTIPLAYER

EXTRAS

INDEX

HOW TO PLAY

HOW TO WIN

EQUIPMENT

CONTROLS

ONSCREEN DISPLAY

OBJECTIVES

MENUS

COMMANDS

ACTIONS

LOOK

Use the right analog stick to look around.

JUMP

Press ⬛ to jump over small obstacles.

PEEK

Use the ✦ and ✦ directional buttons to peek left and right: very useful for looking round corners.

CHANGE VIEWPOINT

Use ✦ and ✦ on the directional buttons to toggle between first and third-person viewpoints.

SWIMMING

Use the left analog stick to swim, in the same way as you would to move on land. Note that when swimming, you are unable to use your weapons. Tap △ to submerge and to resurface. When submerged, you will see an air meter next to the character's name onscreen. When you run out of air, you will automatically resurface.

FIRE

Press R1 to fire, throw or deploy your weapon.

R1

AIM

R

Use the right analog stick to aim your weapon.

TOGGLE SIGHTS

Depending on the capabilities of the weapon and/or scope that you have equipped, you can press ✛ on the directional buttons to zoom in on your target and also to enter first-person view. The number of times you must press ✛ will depend on whether or not you have a scope attached. You can also activate night-vision sights by pressing ✛, if available. Press ✛ to zoom out and back to your normal viewpoint. Note that your shooting accuracy will be enhanced when you are prone or crouching; this is especially true when using a scope, where you will hear the disturbing sound of your heart beating loudly as you try to steady your hand.

STRAFE

When firing your weapon (by holding down R1), you can strafe your opponents by pressing left and right on the left analog stick. Be aware, however, that your shooting will always be more accurate when you are standing still, or—even better—crouching or lying down.

RAPID RELOAD

You will reload when you try to fire on an empty magazine (provided you have enough ammo left), but you should press R3 if you want to reload manually ahead of time and avoid being forced to reload in the middle of a firefight.

R3

WEAPON FIRE MODE

Different weapons have different rates of fire: single-shot, two-shot burst, three-shot burst and fully automatic. Press **L3** to switch between all available firing modes.

L3

SWITCHING WEAPONS

L1

Tap **L1** to 'Quickswap' between your primary and secondary weapons. Press and hold **R2** to access the Inventory. Use ✦ and ✦ on the directional buttons to scroll through the menu. Press ⊗ to select a weapon or item, and **L1** to assign the weapon or item to the Hotswap facility. Press △ to drop a weapon.

THROWING A GRENADE

If you have a grenade in your Inventory, equip it using the method stated above, then hold down **R1** to see the grenade's trajectory. Move the right analog stick to guide the line to where you want the grenade to land, then release **R1** to launch the grenade. The harder you press **R1**, the further the grenade will fly.

R1

PLANTING A CLAYMORE MINE

R1

First equip the Claymore, then press **R1** to place it. You will then see a remote control detonator in your weapon slot. Press **R1** again to detonate the Claymore, making sure that neither you nor any of your teammates are standing right on top of it, of course! Note that you can set multiple Claymores if you so wish, and detonate them simultaneously by pressing **R1**.

PLANTING A PMN PRESSURE MINE

Select the PMN from your inventory and press **R1** to place it. The mine will be detonated when somebody steps on it– preferably the enemy and not one of your teammates!

R1

VEHICLE CONTROLS

MOUNT VEHICLE

When you approach any allied vehicle (on land or sea) that you can mount, you will see a Special Action arrow icon. Press ⊗ when you see the icon, to mount the vehicle. You may see several 'Mount' icons, depending on how many mounting spots the vehicle has. Once inside, press ⊗ again to dismount.

CHANGE SEATS

You know how it gets on a long journey–all those arguments about who wants to do the driving, and who wants to man the turret and take down the bad guys. Settle any such squabbles by pressing ⬍ and ⬌ on the directional buttons to change seats. Your teammates will automatically vacate any seat that you're in should you want to swap with them. When you enter a vehicle, a diagram will appear onscreen, showing the seating plan. Your team and any passengers will appear as blue dots, while you will be represented by an orange dot.

ACCELERATE

 When driving, press ⓡ1 to accelerate. Make sure that all your teammates are on board before you leave, and be careful not to run any of them down as they come toward the vehicle!

REVERSE

 When driving, press Ⓛ1 to reverse.

BRAKE

 When driving, press △ to brake.

STEER

When driving, use the left analog stick to steer the vehicle.

LOOK

 When driving, use the right analog stick to look around.

AIM WEAPON

 When manning a turret gun, use the right analog stick to aim your weapon.

GAME BASICS

FIRE WEAPON

R1   *When manning a turret gun, press R1 to fire.*

RESET CAMERA

R3   *Press R3 to reset the camera and return to the default 'Follow' view after looking around.*

SPECIAL ACTIONS

Throughout the game you will notice orange icons that appear at the bottom of the screen: sometimes they will have writing on them, sometimes not. These are the Special Action icons, and they appear when you have the opportunity to perform certain contextual actions that change according to the circumstances of your mission. Although the icons differ, the activation is always the same: press ⊗ to perform the Special Action. If you see arrows at either side of the icon, it means that you can perform more than one Special Action at this location. To scroll through the available actions and select one, hold down ⊗ and press the directional buttons either ✛ or ✛. Release ⊗ to carry out the selected action. Some Special Actions will soon become very familiar to you, such as 'Pickup Primary', but others that are mission sensitive will only appear once. Below you will see a list of the main Special Actions you can perform in the game.

PICKUP PRIMARY

This rifle icon appears when you find weapons dropped by the enemy. If you pick up an enemy weapon, you must leave your own weapon behind, so make sure the weapon you are acquiring is better than your current weapon. To pick up ammo for your currently equipped weapon, just walk over it.

PICKUP SECONDARY

This pistol icon appears when you find secondary weapons dropped by the enemy. As with a primary weapon, you must give up your current secondary weapon in order to acquire a new one.

CARRY/DROP BODY

Use this action to hide neutralized enemies and wounded teammates. Pick up the body and carry it to a more secluded area. Press ⊗ to drop the body after picking it up.

OPEN/CLOSE DOOR

This command lets you open and close any unlocked door.

PICKUP ITEMS

You will see this icon when you point your crosshairs at certain items that you can pick up. Be sure not to leave anything behind that might be useful later on.

CLOSE QUARTERS COMBAT

Sneak up behind the enemy and perform a Close Quarters Combat move when you see this icon. You may see a Rifle Butt or Knife icon, depending on circumstances.

CLIMB

This icon will appear when you find an obstacle that is too tall to be jumped over by pressing ⊙.

PLACE EXPLOSIVES

Every time you see the Place Satchel or C4 Charge icon, it means that you can lay some explosives. When you place C4, a timer will appear on your HUD to show how much time you have to clear the vicinity before the explosion.

CLIMB LADDER/LADDER SLIDE

The Climb icon appears when you approach a ladder: press ⊗ to climb the ladder. Once you are on the ladder, you will see the Ladder Slide icon: press ⊗ to slide quickly down the ladder.

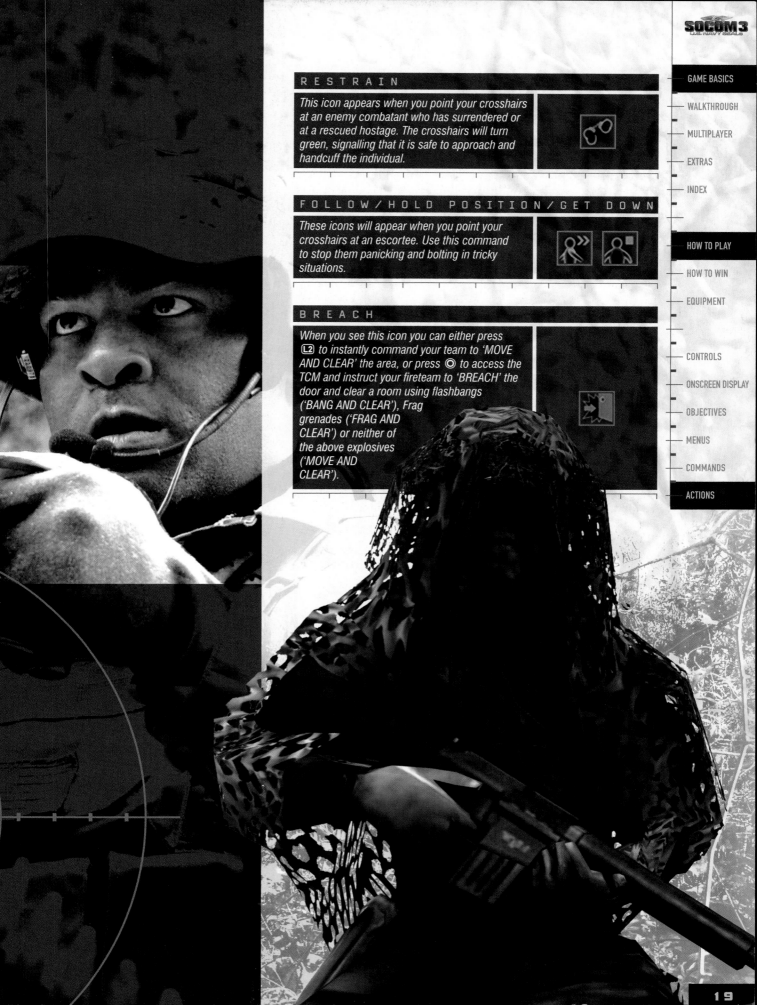

RESTRAIN

This icon appears when you point your crosshairs at an enemy combatant who has surrendered or at a rescued hostage. The crosshairs will turn green, signalling that it is safe to approach and handcuff the individual.

FOLLOW/HOLD POSITION/GET DOWN

These icons will appear when you point your crosshairs at an escortee. Use this command to stop them panicking and bolting in tricky situations.

BREACH

When you see this icon you can either press L2 to instantly command your team to 'MOVE AND CLEAR' the area, or press ◎ to access the TCM and instruct your fireteam to 'BREACH' the door and clear a room using flashbangs ('BANG AND CLEAR'), Frag grenades ('FRAG AND CLEAR') or neither of the above explosives ('MOVE AND CLEAR').

HOW TO WIN

Whether you're an experienced SOCOM veteran or a newcomer to the series, there's still a lot that you can learn to optimize your gaming experience, especially if you want to beat the game on all difficulty levels and unlock all possible 'extras'. Over the following pages you'll discover tips and tricks of the trade provided by our team of dedicated SOCOM experts. Follow their guidance and it will be only a matter of time before you ace every mission and achieve that much-prized 'A' ranking.

 ## SILENT BUT DEADLY

- Move slowly but surely through each mission. Plunging noisily ahead will ensure that you are overwhelmed and out-gunned. The slower you move, the quieter you will be, and the more likely you are to surprise the enemy. Cap 'em before they even know you're there to gain the upper hand. Sneaky, but effective.

- Take note of where you are walking: metal and wooden floors will tend to make more noise, so go extra slow when crossing these.

- Keep a low profile: unless you're running away (maybe after laying an explosive), it makes sense to remain crouched during most of the missions. Not only will you move more quietly and be harder to spot, your shooting will also be more accurate.

- When trying to avoid the prying eyes of patrolling enemies, be sure to hide the bodies of any guards that you take down. If their colleagues spot the bodies, they will become suspicious and raise the alarm (Fig. 1).

- When in doubt, wait it out. Watch patiently until patrolling enemies leave your immediate area. You'll save ammo and avoid unnecessary strife.

- Whenever possible, use silencers on your weapons to avoid alerting the enemy to your position. Close quarters knife and rifle-butt kills are a good way to silently take out the enemy without using up any ammo (Fig. 2).

- Use the cover provided by your environment whenever possible. If you're out in the open, use trees, bushes, rocks, and shadows to your advantage. In more built-up areas, you can hide behind doors and walls (Fig. 3).

GAME BASICS

UP CLOSE AND PERSONAL

- Sniping is an art in itself. It is a risk-free form of killing at a distance that ensures your enemies are completely unaware of your presence right up until the moment you take them down. Don't try sniping at close quarters, though, or you'll be a sitting duck, felled before you can say 'quack'.

- Sniping is more accurate from a prone position; aiming when crouching or standing is often more difficult. To put it plainly: the lower the stance, the more accurate the shot. In any case, try and keep as still as possible: you'll find that the crosshairs stop trembling and your heart will not beat quite so fast if you wait for a few moments before shooting (Fig. 1).

- Sniping multiple enemies can be devastatingly effective. Start with those farthest away to maximize your chances.

- Head shots are the most difficult of all, but also the most efficient, instantly downing the enemy and preserving precious ammo at the same time (Fig. 2).

- Some sniper rifles allow you to move when you are looking through the scope: use this facility to aim more accurately or to observe remote places when walking along.

- Be sure to use any available cover to remain hidden when sniping. You're at your most vulnerable when prone, with all your attention focused on the end of your scope. The last thing you want is for an enemy soldier to sneak up behind you when your sights are trained on his faraway buddy.

- In the lower corner of your scope is a distance meter. If the distance meter shows dashes, your target, even though you can see him, is beyond the effective range of your weapon. You will need to move closer to achieve the shot with the weapon you are using.

x4.0   11.1m   01

x4.0   11.2m   02

- SOCOM 3 is a team game, even in single-player mode. You're not operating all alone out there, you have the advantage of a crack team of U.S. Navy SEALs ready to do your bidding and back you up at every opportunity, so be sure to use them as wisely as possible. And don't forget, your teamwork rating counts toward your final grade.

- Your teammates can carry out many mission objectives for you, provided that you issue your instructions in plenty of time. For example, if you have to blow up a bridge, you can command them to lay the charges for you, but don't leave it until the last minute if it's a time-sensitive objective.

- Make sure your team isn't just following along behind you all the time. Synchronize your actions so that you all storm a particular location from different entry points and take the enemy by surprise (Fig. 1). They won't know who to shoot at first, and you'll be able to sweep up in the confusion.

- When you issue the 'FOLLOW' command to your teammates, they mimic your current stance, so watch out when standing up: you might be safely behind cover, but check that your teammates won't be exposed if *they* stand up. Similarly, take care that they don't get trapped in a hole or behind an obstacle and are unable to discharge their weapon if they follow your lead and lie down.

- Use all your teammates when escorting hostages: place one team in front and have the second team watch the rear (Fig. 2).

- Always provide cover for anyone defusing a bomb.

- Deploy your teammates on vehicles to blast your way through enemy lines (Fig. 3).

- Don't always send your teammates ahead of you into a dangerous area. They may take a bullet for you, but it's generally a good idea to protect them and keep them as active members of the team for as long as possible.

01

02

03

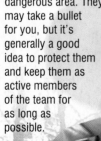

BATTLE TACTICS

- Strafing and running from side-to-side is a great way to avoid enemy fire.

- Whenever possible, reload before engaging the enemy. This will ensure that you don't waste precious seconds reloading in the middle of a raging battle.

- Use grenades efficiently: don't waste a grenade on one individual, save them for groups. Also, practice your throwing technique to increase your accuracy (Fig. 1).

- Scavenge weapons from the bodies of downed enemies to replenish your ammo and maybe even get your hands on a more effective weapon than the one that you have currently equipped. Note that you can only carry a certain number of weapons.

- Third-person view affords a wider angle of vision and the ability to peek around corners (Fig. 2). However, shooting from first-person view is more accurate, particularly with close-in combat.

- When aiming, wait for the crosshairs to turn red before you shoot, or you'll risk missing the enemy altogether and alerting them to your presence.

- Use the thermal scope to easily spot enemies during night missions, in dark areas, or when they're hiding in undergrowth (Fig. 3).

- Turn away from flashbangs to avoid being blinded (Fig. 4).

- Listen carefully: the background music will often change when an enemy has become aware of your presence. Act quickly when you hear the change in tone and you might be able to down them before they have time to alert anyone else. Enemies also occasionally chatter and make noise, making it easy to locate them even if they are well-hidden.

- Take care not to accidentally shoot your teammates, or any other allies, especially when you're using thermal or night vision, which can make it difficult to determine friend from foe without the differentiation provided by the colored crosshairs. Shooting an ally means instant mission failure, so look and think before you fire.

01

02

03

04

- Your teammate accuracy on turrets is better than yours in most cases. It is almost always better to let your teammates man the turrets.

- Take full advantage of vehicles: they often have powerful ordnance that you can commandeer and turn on the enemy. You can also run enemies down. If you have teammates with you, they will usually take control of any available turrets and shoot at the enemy while you drive. However, this can be a double-edged sword: sometimes it's best to take control of the turret yourself, as your shooting is usually more accurate than theirs (Fig. 5).

- Even the sturdiest of armored cars can be penetrated by enemy bullets, so be aware that you can still be hit while driving or while manning a vehicle's turret. You can also get blown up if caught in, or close to, an exploding vehicle, so if you notice clouds of smoke emanating from the engine, dismount and run away as far as possible!

- If you have a mission that involves taking down enemies in moving vehicles, don't waste time trying to hit the driver. Shooting at the vehicle and blowing it up is quicker and easier, as the vehicle provides a much bigger target (Fig. 6). The exception to this is if you're on a turret yourself, in which case, strafing across the passenger compartment will almost always bring the vehicle to a halt, making it easier to blow up.

05

06

ACTING SMART

- Perform only necessary actions: visiting a remote area or taking out a guard who poses no threat to your mission can cause you to be spotted.

- Be careful when killing enemies above you: if they're close to a gap, they may fall and be seen by other guards.

- Attack enemies from the rear rather than the front to avoid being seen (Fig. 1).

- You don't have to take down every single enemy: what matters most is that you fulfill your mission objectives, not that you neutralize every living terrorist in the vicinity (although it's fun to try)!

- Be sure to explore, when it's safe to do so: there are often a variety of ways to access a specific area, some easier than others.

- Adapt your arsenal to the requirements of the situation: avoid using sniper rifles indoors and opt for silenced weapons when you are close to heavily guarded enemy bases.

01

SOCOM3
U.S. NAVY SEALS

GAME BASICS

WALKTHROUGH

MULTIPLAYER

EXTRAS

INDEX

HOW TO PLAY

HOW TO WIN

EQUIPMENT

WEAPONS

VEHICLES

EQUIPMENT

U.S. Navy SEALs are part of one of the toughest fighting forces in the world, and they demand and expect the best equipment when in the field. Their weapons and explosives are designed to withstand the harshest punishment, and to survive the most extreme and brutal of conditions. Some items have even been specially developed by the SEALs themselves to fulfill their own unique needs. In SOCOM 3, weapons are more customizable than ever before, with over 30 weapons facilitating nearly 1000 different combinations.

WEAPONS

The Weapons list is divided into sections that correspond to the different types of weapon. Newcomers to the SOCOM series may not be aware of the meaning of some of the stats, so here is a brief description of each:

Load: This refers to the weight of the weapon, an important consideration as you may exceed your maximum equipment load if the weapon is too heavy.

Accuracy: How likely you are to hit your target.

Fire Modes: Weapons have four possible fire modes – single-shot (1), two-shot burst (2), three-shot burst (3) and fully automatic (4).

Volume: How much noise the weapon makes when you discharge it. Vital if you're on a stealth mission: there's no better way of alerting the enemy to your presence than firing off a few HK5 rounds!

Fire Rate: How quickly the weapon fires.

Fire Range: How far away you can accurately hit your target from.

To sum up, there is no perfect weapon: each mission requires a different approach, so be sure to read the mission briefing carefully to understand the combat environment into which you'll be deployed. Since you only have one primary weapon slot, the choice you make could determine the success or failure of the whole mission. For example, if the mission is to hunt down terrorists in a built-up urban area where you can expect to engage the enemy at close quarters, short-range, rapid fire weapons would be the ideal choice, rather than a single-shot sniper rifle.

ASSAULT RIFLES

AG-94

AMMO CAPACITY: 30

LOAD:

FIRE MODES: 1 2 3 4

FIRE RATE:

ACCURACY:

VOLUME:

FIRE RANGE:

Designed to ultimately replace the ubiquitous AK-47, the AG-94 boasts very little recoil, and an increased rate of fire, making it superior in every way to its older brother.

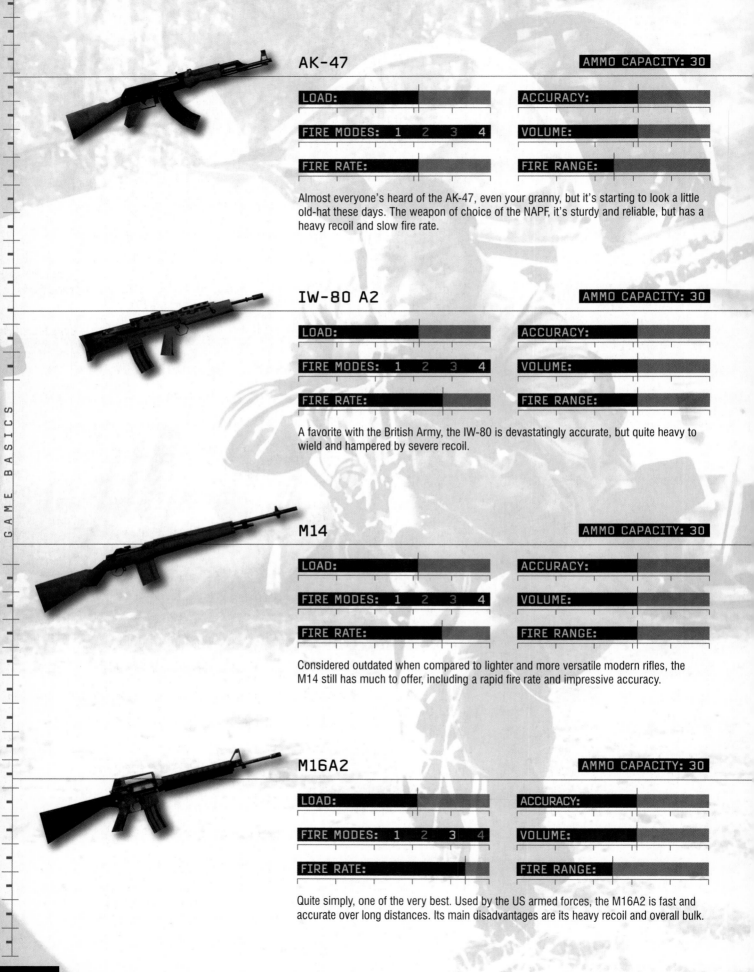

AK-47

AMMO CAPACITY: 30

LOAD:

FIRE MODES: 1 2 3 4

FIRE RATE:

ACCURACY:

VOLUME:

FIRE RANGE:

Almost everyone's heard of the AK-47, even your granny, but it's starting to look a little old-hat these days. The weapon of choice of the NAPF, it's sturdy and reliable, but has a heavy recoil and slow fire rate.

IW-80 A2

AMMO CAPACITY: 30

LOAD:

FIRE MODES: 1 2 3 4

FIRE RATE:

ACCURACY:

VOLUME:

FIRE RANGE:

A favorite with the British Army, the IW-80 is devastatingly accurate, but quite heavy to wield and hampered by severe recoil.

M14

AMMO CAPACITY: 30

LOAD:

FIRE MODES: 1 2 3 4

FIRE RATE:

ACCURACY:

VOLUME:

FIRE RANGE:

Considered outdated when compared to lighter and more versatile modern rifles, the M14 still has much to offer, including a rapid fire rate and impressive accuracy.

M16A2

AMMO CAPACITY: 30

LOAD:

FIRE MODES: 1 2 3 4

FIRE RATE:

ACCURACY:

VOLUME:

FIRE RANGE:

Quite simply, one of the very best. Used by the US armed forces, the M16A2 is fast and accurate over long distances. Its main disadvantages are its heavy recoil and overall bulk.

SOCOM3
U.S. NAVY SEALS

GAME BASICS

WALKTHROUGH

MULTIPLAYER

EXTRAS

INDEX

HOW TO PLAY

HOW TO WIN

EQUIPMENT

WEAPONS

VEHICLES

M4A1

AMMO CAPACITY: 30

LOAD:

FIRE MODES: 1 2 3 4

FIRE RATE:

ACCURACY:

VOLUME:

FIRE RANGE:

Despite its impressive accuracy and power, the M4A1 is disadvantaged by a tendency to overheat, and a disappointingly short range.

M8

AMMO CAPACITY: 30

LOAD:

FIRE MODES: 1 2 3 4

FIRE RATE:

ACCURACY:

VOLUME:

FIRE RANGE:

A standard issue state-of-the art piece of kit for the US Military. Its rapid fire rate and relative accuracy marks it down as one of the most deadly weapons in the world today. The M8's main drawback is the surprisingly heavy recoil.

MK .48

AMMO CAPACITY: 100

LOAD:

FIRE MODES: 1 2 3 4

FIRE RATE:

ACCURACY:

VOLUME:

FIRE RANGE:

Developed for US Special Forces, this powerful rifle with negligible recoil is hampered only by its relatively short range when compared to the likes of the M60E3 and RTK-74. Solve that problem by fixing it with a scope, and you've got almost the perfect assault weapon. Highly recommended.

STG 77

AMMO CAPACITY: 30

LOAD:

FIRE MODES: 1 2 3 4

FIRE RATE:

ACCURACY:

VOLUME:

FIRE RANGE:

A small, neat rifle that was originally developed for the Austrian Army. Accurate and easy to use.

RA-14

AMMO CAPACITY: 30

LOAD:		ACCURACY:	
FIRE MODES:	1 2 3 4	VOLUME:	
FIRE RATE:		FIRE RANGE:	

Developed for the Russian Spetsnaz, this sociable little weapon is the only rifle to share ammunition with the AK-47. Fully customizable, with lots of useful attachments.

SNIPER RIFLES

SNIPER RIFLES

M40A1

AMMO CAPACITY: 5

LOAD:		ACCURACY:	
FIRE MODES:	1 2 3 4	VOLUME:	
FIRE RATE:		FIRE RANGE:	

A bolt-action sniper rifle, hand made by the Marine Corps Marksmanship Training Unit at Quantico, Virginia, to their own demanding specifications.

M82A1A

AMMO CAPACITY: 10

LOAD:		ACCURACY:	
FIRE MODES:	1 2 3 4	VOLUME:	
FIRE RATE:		FIRE RANGE:	

An anti-material, heavy sniper rifle, the M82A1A uses devastating .50 BMG bullets, making it the perfect choice for penetrating light armor or breaking through cover.

M87ELR

AMMO CAPACITY: 10

LOAD:		ACCURACY:	
FIRE MODES:	1 2 3 4	VOLUME:	
FIRE RATE:		FIRE RANGE:	

A bolt-action, anti-material rifle that just has to be one of the best around, being both powerful and accurate, capable of shearing through light armor at considerable distance.

SOCOM3
U.S. NAVY SEALS

GAME BASICS

WALKTHROUGH

MULTIPLAYER

EXTRAS

INDEX

HOW TO PLAY

HOW TO WIN

EQUIPMENT

WEAPONS

VEHICLES

L96AW

AMMO CAPACITY: 10

LOAD:

ACCURACY:

FIRE MODES: 1 2 3 4

VOLUME:

FIRE RATE:

FIRE RANGE:

Developed for the British Army, this is an unparalleled sniper rifle. Deadly accurate, especially if fired when lying down.

SASR

AMMO CAPACITY: 10

LOAD:

ACCURACY:

FIRE MODES: 1 2 3 4

VOLUME:

FIRE RATE:

FIRE RANGE:

The initials stand for Special Application Scoped Rifle. Based on the Kalashnikov, this is an accurate sniper rifle with an impressively long range.

SR-25

AMMO CAPACITY: 10

LOAD:

ACCURACY:

FIRE MODES: 1 2 3 4

VOLUME:

FIRE RATE:

FIRE RANGE:

Originally developed for the U.S. Navy SEALs, the SR-25 has a faster fire rate than most sniper rifles, possibly reflecting the SEALs' need for accuracy and speed in the field.

MACHINE GUNS

552

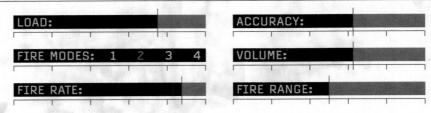

AMMO CAPACITY: 30

LOAD:		ACCURACY:	
FIRE MODES:	1 2 3 4	VOLUME:	
FIRE RATE:		FIRE RANGE:	

In the same class as the HK36, but heavier and not as compact. A very rapid rate of fire makes the 552 ideal for tackling multiple enemies, but be warned, its heavy recoil impairs accuracy.

9mm Sub

AMMO CAPACITY: 30

LOAD:		ACCURACY:	
FIRE MODES:	1 2 3 4	VOLUME:	
FIRE RATE:		FIRE RANGE:	

One of the most popular machine guns in the world, the 9mm is renowned for its lighting fast rate of fire and instantly recognizable looks. It's small, light, and very reliable, with negligible recoil.

F90

AMMO CAPACITY: 50

LOAD:		ACCURACY:	
FIRE MODES:	1 2 3 4	VOLUME:	
FIRE RATE:		FIRE RANGE:	

Inferior only to the HK7 in terms of rate of fire and stopping power, the F90 has superior ammo capacity, which considerably reduces reloading time. Comes complete with night vision and red dot. Expect to find this one in the hands of NSO terrorists during your missions in Poland.

HK5

AMMO CAPACITY: 30

LOAD:		ACCURACY:	
FIRE MODES:	1 2 3 4	VOLUME:	
FIRE RATE:		FIRE RANGE:	

A firm favorite with police forces and armies in over 50 countries around the world, not to mention Hollywood and Hong Kong film and television producers. It's lightweight, but loud, so not recommended for stealth-based missions.

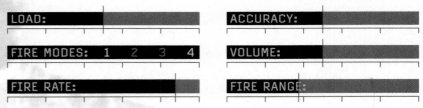

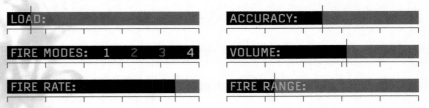

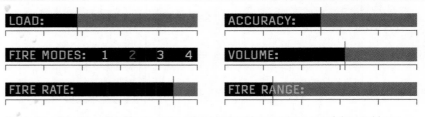

GAME BASICS

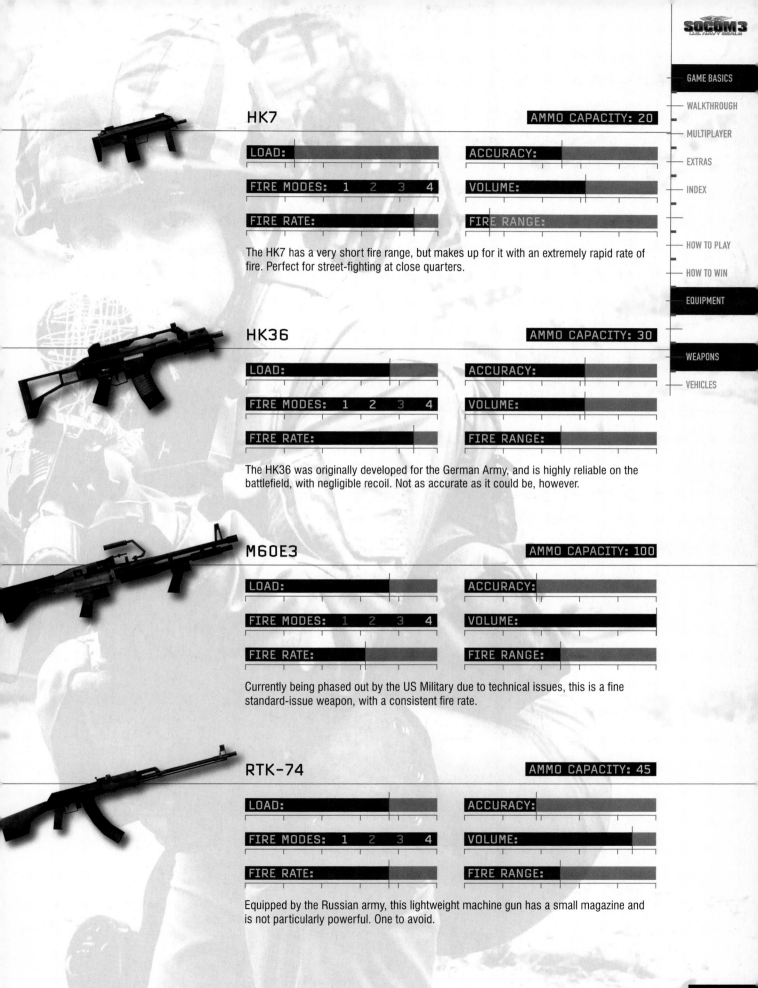

SOCOM3
U.S. NAVY SEALS

GAME BASICS
WALKTHROUGH
MULTIPLAYER
EXTRAS
INDEX

HOW TO PLAY
HOW TO WIN

EQUIPMENT

WEAPONS
VEHICLES

HK7

AMMO CAPACITY: 20

LOAD:

ACCURACY:

FIRE MODES: 1   2   3   4

VOLUME:

FIRE RATE:

FIRE RANGE:

The HK7 has a very short fire range, but makes up for it with an extremely rapid rate of fire. Perfect for street-fighting at close quarters.

HK36

AMMO CAPACITY: 30

LOAD:

ACCURACY:

FIRE MODES: 1   2   3   4

VOLUME:

FIRE RATE:

FIRE RANGE:

The HK36 was originally developed for the German Army, and is highly reliable on the battlefield, with negligible recoil. Not as accurate as it could be, however.

M60E3

AMMO CAPACITY: 100

LOAD:

ACCURACY:

FIRE MODES: 1   2   3   4

VOLUME:

FIRE RATE:

FIRE RANGE:

Currently being phased out by the US Military due to technical issues, this is a fine standard-issue weapon, with a consistent fire rate.

RTK-74

AMMO CAPACITY: 45

LOAD:

ACCURACY:

FIRE MODES: 1   2   3   4

VOLUME:

FIRE RATE:

FIRE RANGE:

Equipped by the Russian army, this lightweight machine gun has a small magazine and is not particularly powerful. One to avoid.

12 Gauge Pump

AMMO CAPACITY: 12

LOAD:		ACCURACY:
FIRE MODES: 1 2 3 4		VOLUME:
FIRE RATE:		FIRE RANGE:

A pump-action shotgun that could stop a charging elephant in its tracks. Not much use when facing multiple enemies, but ideal when clearing buildings or built up areas.

M4-90

AMMO CAPACITY: 8

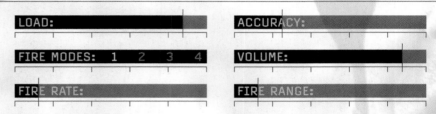

LOAD:		ACCURACY:
FIRE MODES: 1 2 3 4		VOLUME:
FIRE RATE:		FIRE RANGE:

One of the most modern tactical shotguns, the M4-90 is currently used by the US Military. On the plus side, it's magazine-fed and semi-automatic; on the minus side, its small clip size means that it requires frequent reloading.

TA 12 Gauge

AMMO CAPACITY: 12

LOAD:		ACCURACY:
FIRE MODES: 1 2 3 4		VOLUME:
FIRE RATE:		FIRE RANGE:

Available as either semi-automatic or pump-action, this shotgun is favored by Special Forces units due to its weighty firepower. Can be heavy and unwieldy in battle.

PISTOLS

SOCOM3
U.S. NAVY SEALS

GAME BASICS

WALKTHROUGH

MULTIPLAYER

EXTRAS

INDEX

HOW TO PLAY

HOW TO WIN

EQUIPMENT

WEAPONS

VEHICLES

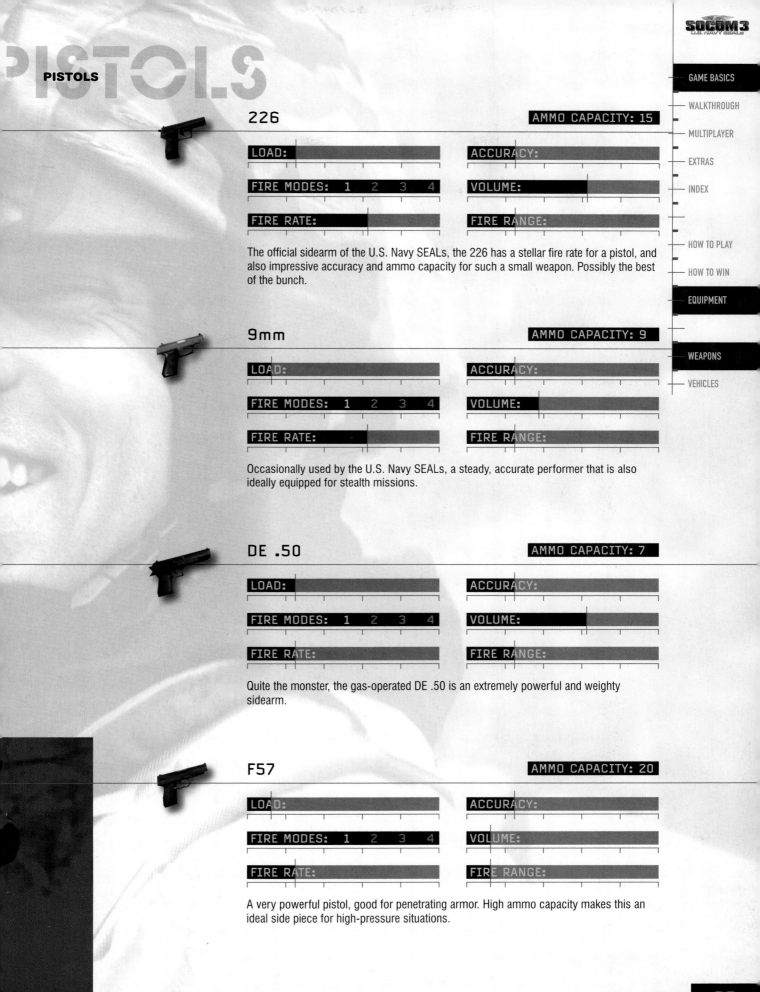

226

AMMO CAPACITY: 15

LOAD:

ACCURACY:

FIRE MODES: 1   2   3   4

VOLUME:

FIRE RATE:

FIRE RANGE:

The official sidearm of the U.S. Navy SEALs, the 226 has a stellar fire rate for a pistol, and also impressive accuracy and ammo capacity for such a small weapon. Possibly the best of the bunch.

9mm

AMMO CAPACITY: 9

LOAD:

ACCURACY:

FIRE MODES: 1   2   3   4

VOLUME:

FIRE RATE:

FIRE RANGE:

Occasionally used by the U.S. Navy SEALs, a steady, accurate performer that is also ideally equipped for stealth missions.

DE .50

AMMO CAPACITY: 7

LOAD:

ACCURACY:

FIRE MODES: 1   2   3   4

VOLUME:

FIRE RATE:

FIRE RANGE:

Quite the monster, the gas-operated DE .50 is an extremely powerful and weighty sidearm.

F57

AMMO CAPACITY: 20

LOAD:

ACCURACY:

FIRE MODES: 1   2   3   4

VOLUME:

FIRE RATE:

FIRE RANGE:

A very powerful pistol, good for penetrating armor. High ammo capacity makes this an ideal side piece for high-pressure situations.

Mark 23

`AMMO CAPACITY: 12`

LOAD:			ACCURACY:		
FIRE MODES:	1 2 3 4		VOLUME:		
FIRE RATE:			FIRE RANGE:		

Developed on behalf of the US Special Operations Command, the Mark 23 is powerful, with good range, and accuracy. If you run out of bullets for your primary weapon, the Mark 23 is a reliable standby.

Model 18

`AMMO CAPACITY: 17`

LOAD:			ACCURACY:		
FIRE MODES:	1 2 3 4		VOLUME:		
FIRE RATE:			FIRE RANGE:		

A very useful little sidearm, blessed with full automatic mode.

LAUNCHERS

LAUNCHERS

AT-4

`AMMO CAPACITY: 1`

LOAD:			ACCURACY:		
FIRE MODES:	1 2 3 4		VOLUME:		
FIRE RATE:			FIRE RANGE:		

A surprisingly lightweight shoulder-fired, single-shot, recoilless rocket launcher. Hard to say, but easy to use. Delivers 84mm High-Explosive Anti-Armor missiles. Perfect for stopping tanks and other armored vehicles.

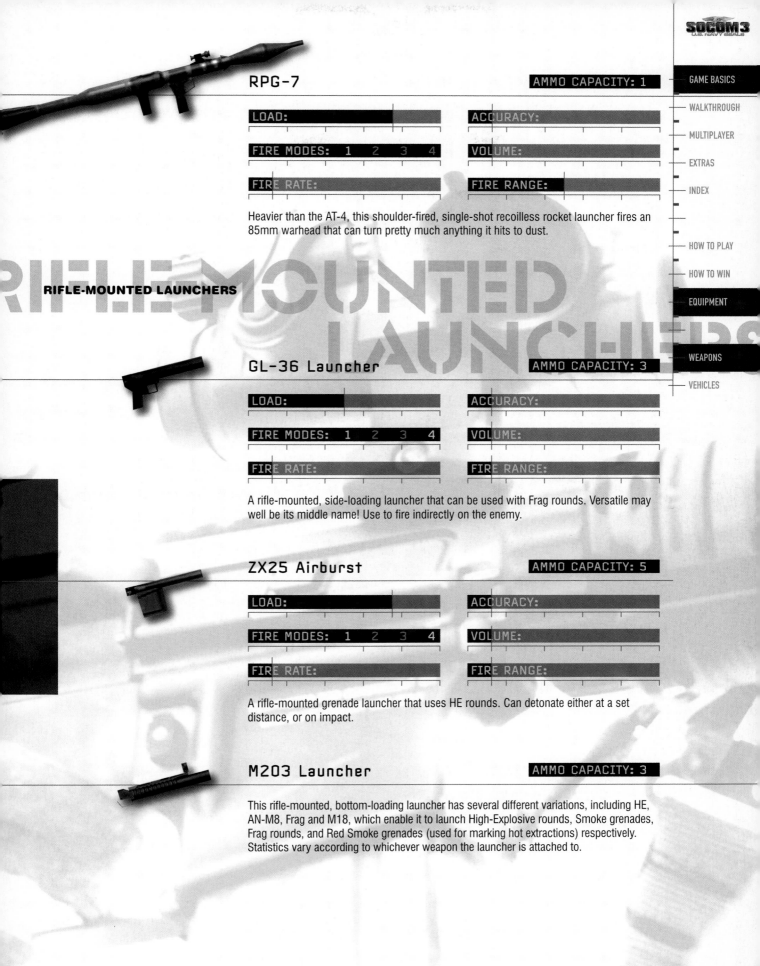

SOCOM 3
U.S. NAVY SEALS

GAME BASICS

WALKTHROUGH

MULTIPLAYER

EXTRAS

INDEX

HOW TO PLAY

HOW TO WIN

EQUIPMENT

WEAPONS

VEHICLES

RIFLE-MOUNTED LAUNCHERS

RPG-7

AMMO CAPACITY: 1

LOAD:

ACCURACY:

FIRE MODES: 1   2   3   4

VOLUME:

FIRE RATE:

FIRE RANGE:

Heavier than the AT-4, this shoulder-fired, single-shot recoilless rocket launcher fires an 85mm warhead that can turn pretty much anything it hits to dust.

GL-36 Launcher

AMMO CAPACITY: 3

LOAD:

ACCURACY:

FIRE MODES: 1   2   3   4

VOLUME:

FIRE RATE:

FIRE RANGE:

A rifle-mounted, side-loading launcher that can be used with Frag rounds. Versatile may well be its middle name! Use to fire indirectly on the enemy.

ZX25 Airburst

AMMO CAPACITY: 5

LOAD:

ACCURACY:

FIRE MODES: 1   2   3   4

VOLUME:

FIRE RATE:

FIRE RANGE:

A rifle-mounted grenade launcher that uses HE rounds. Can detonate either at a set distance, or on impact.

M203 Launcher

AMMO CAPACITY: 3

This rifle-mounted, bottom-loading launcher has several different variations, including HE, AN-M8, Frag and M18, which enable it to launch High-Explosive rounds, Smoke grenades, Frag rounds, and Red Smoke grenades (used for marking hot extractions) respectively. Statistics vary according to whichever weapon the launcher is attached to.

AMMUNITION

Slug Ammo

One-ounce slugs used instead of regular shotgun ammo to blast doors open during 'breach and clear'.

Double Ammo

Enables a SEAL to carry twice the usual amount of ammo for a primary weapon.

SCOPES

12X Scope

An ideal sniper attachment, providing 12.0x magnification and extreme clarity, even in darkness.

High Scope

Offers 6.0x, 10.0x and 16.0x magnification. In other words, a sniper's dream.

4x Scope

Provides 4.0x magnification, carried as standard on the M4A1 rifle.

Medium Scope

Provides 3.0x and 8.0x magnification, and can be used on the majority of assault rifles.

Red Dot

This brilliant little scope simulates a red dot in your viewfinder, without casting the telltale red shadow on your would-be victim.

Low Scope

A small scope with 1.5x and 3x magnification. Most suitable for short-range weapons.

Thermal Scope

An essential piece of kit that you should equip whenever possible. Uses state of the art heat-imaging technology to highlight body heat, making enemies clearly visible even in total darkness.

ACCESSORIES

Binoculars/Microphone

Not only does this piece of kit magnify your vision by 12x, it also enables you to eavesdrop on enemy conversations via the directional microphone.

Bipods 1, 2 and 3

Supports weapons when firing from a prone stance, therefore increasing accuracy.

Designator

Used to 'paint' targets in order to summon air strikes. Point at the target, as you would a weapon, then hold down R1 until the timer on the right of the screen counts down and the air strike is triggered.

ATTACHMENTS

Pistol Grip

Attach to the bottom of an assault rifle or machine gun to enhance accuracy when standing or crouching.

Pistol/Rifle Laser

Increases accuracy by casting a red dot onto the target. However, is clearly visible to the target.

SUPPRESSORS

Suppressor 1

Partially muffles the sound of the rifle discharging, while maintaining range of fire.

Suppressor/ Suppressor 2

Muffles pistol/rifle noise and muzzle flash, but also has a detrimental effect on range of fire.

GAME BASICS

SOCOM 3
U.S. NAVY SEALS

GAME BASICS

WALKTHROUGH

MULTIPLAYER

EXTRAS

INDEX

HOW TO PLAY

HOW TO WIN

EQUIPMENT

WEAPONS

VEHICLES

WEAPON LOADOUTS

As there are so many different possible combinations of weapons and accessories in SOCOM 3, the following table enables you to tell at glance which accessories and attachments go with which weapons. Where an item is able to be equipped, you will see 'Yes' entered in the column. Two separate tables are presented for SEAL and Terrorists weapons, as not all weapons are available to each party. Furthermore not all weapons are available in each mission and not all attachments can be fitted in each mission.

SEAL WEAPON LOADOUTS

WEAPON	TYPE	THERMAL SCOPE	SUPPRES-SOR	GRENADE LAUNCHER	SCOPE	RED DOT	4X SCOPE	LASER	GRIP	BIPOD
IW-80 A2	Assault	Yes	1, 2	-	L, M, H	Yes	Yes	Yes	Yes	-
M14	Assault	Yes	1, 2	-	L, M, H	-	Yes	-	-	3
M16A2	Assault	Yes	1, 2	M203 Frag, M203 HE	L, M, H	Yes	Yes	Yes	Yes	-
M4A1	Assault	Yes	1, 2	M203 Frag, M203 HE	L, M, H	Yes	Yes	Yes	Yes	-
M8	Assault	Yes	1, 2	GL- 36, M25 Airburst	L, M	Yes	Yes	Yes	-	1
MK .48	Assault	Yes	-	-	L, M	Yes	Yes	Yes	Yes	1
M40A1	Sniper	Yes	-	-	L, M	-	Yes	-	-	3
M87ELR	Sniper	Yes	-	-	L, M, H	-	Yes	-	-	3
L96AW	Sniper	Yes	-	-	L, M, H	-	Yes	-	-	3
SR-25	Sniper	Yes	1	-	L, M	-	Yes	-	-	3
HK5	SMG	-	2	-	-	Yes	Yes	Yes	Yes	-
HK7	SMG	-	2	-	-	Yes	Yes	Yes	Yes	-
HK 36	SMG	Yes	1, 2	GL- 36	L, M, H	Yes	Yes	Yes	Yes	-
M60E3	SMG	-	-	-	L, M	-	Yes	-	-	2
12 Gauge Pump	Shotgun							Yes		
M4-90	Shotgun	-	-	-	L	-	Yes	Yes	-	
226	Pistol	-	Yes					Yes		
9mm	Pistol	-	Yes	-	-	-	-	Yes	-	
Mark 23	Pistol	-	Yes					Yes		

TERRORIST WEAPON LOADOUTS

WEAPON	TYPE	THERMAL SCOPE	SUPPRES-SOR	GRENADE LAUNCHER	SCOPE	RED DOT	4X SCOPE	LASER	GRIP	BIPOD
AG-94	Assault	Yes	-	-	L, M, H	Yes	Yes	Yes	-	-
AK-47	Assault	-	-	GL-36	L, M	Yes	Yes	Yes	-	-
M16A2	Assault	Yes	1, 2	M203 Frag, M203 HE	L, M, H	Yes	Yes	Yes	Yes	-
STG 77	Assault	-	1	M203 Frag, M203 HE	L, M	-	Yes	-	Yes	-
RA-14	Assault	Yes	1	GL-36	L, M, H	Yes	Yes	-	Yes	-
M40A1	Sniper	Yes	-	-	L, M, H	-	Yes	-	-	3
M82A1A	Sniper	Yes	-	-	L, M, H	-	Yes	-	-	2
SASR	Sniper	Yes	1	-	L	-	Yes	-	-	-
552	SMG	Yes	1	-	L, M, H	Yes	Yes	-	Yes	-
9mm Sub	SMG	-	1	-	-	-	-	Yes	-	-
F90	SMG	-	1	-	-	-	-	Yes	-	-
M60E3	SMG	-	-	-	L, M	-	Yes	-	-	2
RTK-74	SMG	Yes	-	-	L, M	-	Yes	-	-	1
12 Gauge Pump	Shotgun	-	-	-	-	-	-	Yes	-	-
TA 12 Gauge	Shotgun	-	-	-	-	-	-	-	Yes	-
DE .50	Pistol	-	-	-	-	-	-	Yes	-	-
F57	Pistol	-	Yes					Yes		
Model 18	Pistol	-	Yes	-	-	-	-	Yes	-	-

EXPLOSIVES

SMOKE

A grenade that creates a plume of white smoke to either hide your activities or signal to other units.

M67

A fragmentation grenade that unleashes a devastating shrapnel blast when detonated.

C4

Explosive material that can be fashioned into different shapes to control the direction of an explosion. Often used for demolition work.

FLASHBANG

A non-lethal stun grenade that temporarily blinds and deafens its victims.

Claymore

An anti-personnel mine packed with C4 that sprays 700 steel pellets across a 100 meter radius, and is lethal over a range of 15 meters.

PMN

A pressure-sensitive anti-personnel weapon that sends fragments flying up to 100 meters away, and is lethal over a range of five meters.

HE

A high-explosive grenade.

Satchel

A satchel charge consists of packets of C4 strung together to cause one huge explosion. Generally employed as a means of blowing up armored vehicles, breaching doors and demolishing buildings.

RED SMOKE

A red smoke grenade, used to mark hot extractions.

M2 Mine

A device that uses magnetic sensors to destroy vehicles. Also disperses fragments across a 200 meter spread. Lethal over a range of six meters.

SOCOM 3
U.S. NAVY SEALS

GAME BASICS

WALKTHROUGH

MULTIPLAYER

EXTRAS

INDEX

HOW TO PLAY

HOW TO WIN

EQUIPMENT

WEAPONS

VEHICLES

VEHICLES

The introduction of player-controlled vehicles is one of the exciting new aspects of SOCOM 3. Vehicles now play a very important part in the game, and it's generally up to you to use them well. You will occasionally be instructed specifically to commandeer a particular vehicle, but most of the time the choice is yours. See page 16 to learn more about controlling vehicles.

Eurovan

Civilian bus-like transport van common in Eastern Europe. A very ordinary-looking box-shaped vehicle with four seats. Has no fixed armaments of any kind, although the large doors open at the sides, which means that team members who are not driving can shoot their own weapons. Note that the Eurovan only appears in Single-Player Mode.

Technical Pickup

The battered old pickup is the terrorists' vehicle of choice, but once you've eliminated the occupants you can commandeer it for your own use. It may not be the sturdiest ride you've ever seen, but the mounted turret can cause considerable damage in the right hands, ie, *yours*.

Armored Assault Vehicle

This is one of the most recognizable military vehicles in use today. You get the chance to drive one on your very first training mission. Designed for all weathers, all terrain use, it is extremely versatile, with several different mission-specific configurations. The standard armored version has a 360-degree fully rotating turret gun with 20 clips of 300 rounds apiece. The M1054 Up-Armored w/TOW is equipped with the powerful M-220 tube-launched, optically-tracked, wire-guided, anti-tank missile system. It can penetrate more than 90 centimeters of armor. Only fire one of these babies if you're sure that no allies are in the vicinity. The multi-gun version has one roof-mounted gun, and three side-mounted guns.

SUV

A four-wheel drive sport utility vehicle designed for off-road travel, with the general shape of a station wagon. Looks a lot like a technical pickup, but is sturdier and can therefore withstand more punishment.

SOC-R

An extremely fast strike-boat with a shallow draft, the Special Operations Craft - Riverine (SOC-R) is particularly suited to rapidly deploying SEALs in marshy inland waterways. Unlike the majority of vehicles in the game, the SOC-R is driven from the center seat while the side seats offer full 360-degree fire support. The two front-mounted machine guns are very effective high-fire-rate weapons, boasting 20 350-round clips useful for clearing shores of enemies; the rear-mounted grenade launcher is effective in depriving pursuing watercraft of their crews.

GAME BASICS

WALKTHROUGH

MULTIPLAYER

EXTRAS

INDEX

HOW TO PLAY

HOW TO WIN

EQUIPMENT

WEAPONS

VEHICLES

Ural Troop Carrier/Cargo

Ural trucks are often used by the enemy to move their troops and equipment around. They're slow and unwieldy, and generally don't have any ordnance, but they can still be deadly if you use them to run down several opponents at a time.

ALSV

Perfect for desert and jungle warfare, the ALSV is lightweight and easy to maneuver. The only drawback to this vehicle is that it is lightly armored, so keep moving to prevent the enemy from scoring a hit. The mounted gun can mow down scores of enemies in seconds flat, with a strike power of 20 clips of 300 shots apiece.

CRRC

The initials stand for Combat Rapid Raiding Craft, but to the untrained eye the CRRC looks just like a rubber dinghy! However, it's actually much more sophisticated than that: this lightweight inflatable craft can be quickly and easily assembled for rapid deployment (from submarines, fixed-wing aircraft, helicopters and small vehicles) and extraction of troops. It can seat up to 12 people, and is powered by either twin or single-shaft outboard motors. The CRRC has no ordnance, as its primary purpose is troop transportation.

Speedboat

A lightweight single-motor six-seater speedboat with very little in terms of cover, but good ordnance in the shape of front and rear mounted machine guns. Generally favored by enemy forces, but you occasionally get the chance to commandeer one for SOCOM use. The driver's seat is the front right.

2 ND CHAPTER

Watch out soldier! 15 grueling missions lie ahead of you. In the vast campaign areas – up to six times larger than those in previous SOCOM games – not only will you risk losing your way, you will also face intense enemy opposition at virtually every turn. The hostile units operating in the three AOs (Areas of Operation) are highly trained and ruthless in the extreme, with access to state of the art weaponry; the slightest error in judgment could have lethal consequences for you and your unit, so preparation is essential.

ROUGH

HOW TO USE THE WALKTHROUGH

The following Walkthrough will guide you safely through all of the missions. The first double-page spread of each section provides an annotated map as well as full operational details at a glance: this includes an overview of all Mission Objectives, recommendations for Optimum Equipment, and a brief description of the local Terrain. Subsequently, you will find comprehensive step by step instructions, designed to lead you and your team through your assignment unscathed.

① MAPS AND SYMBOLS

A detailed map of the area is presented at the start of each mission; among other things, the map indicates buildings where you can collect important objects, and pinpoints danger hotspots.

Various symbols on the map refer to key mission data, such as where an enemy ambush is likely to occur; the whereabouts of prime sniper points; vehicle locations; and where to expect Primary, Secondary, Bonus and Crosstalk objectives. Look on the back cover foldout to decode the relevant symbols.

This information should generally suffice to help you successfully complete a mission without reading the rest of the Walkthrough. We recommend this approach particularly for experienced players, as it enables you to formulate your own tactics and strategies without constantly referring to the text. This naturally makes for a more challenging gaming experience as you will have no prior knowledge of the secrets and tasks that lie ahead in each assignment.

If you are unsure of your location, compare your current position with the numbers on the map. These refer directly to the Walkthrough text, which clarifies all you need to know about a particular section, including the solution to any problem that you may come across.

② MISSION OBJECTIVES

Here you will find an overview of all Mission Objectives divided into Primary, Secondary, Bonus and Crosstalk. This will ensure that you have all of the tasks in front of you throughout the mission and that you don't miss any hidden objectives.

③ OPTIMUM EQUIPMENT

Choosing the correct kit for each mission is vital; select your equipment very carefully. For operations in large open spaces we strongly recommend fitting your rifle with a sniper scope, as this will greatly enhance the accuracy of your long-range shooting. For house-to-house close quarters combat, you will need to equip a powerful weapon with a rapid rate of fire as well as grenades to bomb and clear buildings. For those missions where stealth is a priority, it's always a good idea to fit silencers to your primary and secondary weapons.

The optimum equipment suggested in the Walkthrough is just one of many possible combinations: SOCOM 3 features over 30 different weapons and 20 different attachments, making a total of over 1,000 possible customizations. Experiment to determine the best kit for each mission.

④ TERRAIN

The terrain should be a decisive factor in your choice of weapon. Naturally, the landscape features in each AO will significantly affect your tactics on the battlefield. The brief analysis of the terrain in every mission pinpoints specific danger zones and areas of interest. Possible alternative routes will also be suggested. For example, the shortest way to infiltrate an enemy camp may not be always be the best one: if the side entrance is less heavily guarded than the front, you will be advised to use it, even if it means taking the long way round. Other strategically vital points are also mentioned here, eg, sniper positions by bridges, or on hills or rooftops.

SOCOM3

GAME BASICS

WALKTHROUGH

MULTIPLAYER

EXTRAS

INDEX

HOW TO USE THE
WALKTHROUGH

NORTH AFRICA

SOUTH ASIA

POLAND

5 WALKTHROUGH

The Walkthrough will lead you safely through the game as you learn how to complete all available objectives. This will ensure that you have a good overview of your current position at every stage of the campaign, and that the extensive missions are broken down into easily manageable chunks. The numbered text refers directly to specific points on the map, so that you can determine your exact position in the level at a glance. A header indicates the current Mission Objective.

The Walkthrough is set for difficulty level Lieutenant. You can still use this text as a reference if you opt to play at a higher level, for the strategy remains basically the same. However, it is important to note that the hostile units will then be much more alert. Your agents will be spotted at a far greater distance and the enemy will react to the slightest sound. Bear in mind too that the higher the difficulty level, the more accurate the enemy fire!

6 SCREENSHOTS

The many screenshots featured in the Walkthrough will help you to establish your location and will indicate where you can find the items required to complete your objectives. Other screenshots show sniper positions, or highlight points that are particularly relevant to your strategic movements, such as alternative routes. The numbers under the screenshots refer to the corresponding Walkthrough text, and vice versa.

7 GAME TIPS

In each assignment, you have the opportunity to complete hidden Bonus and/or Crosstalk objectives that are not included in the mission description. These are explained in Tip boxes. Sometimes the Tip boxes also contain useful additional hints and advice on alternative routes.

AFRICA

AFRICA

SOCOM3

GAME BASICS

WALKTHROUGH

MULTIPLAYER

EXTRAS

INDEX

HOW TO USE THE WALKTHROUGH

NORTH AFRICA

SOUTH ASIA

POLAND

FLASHPOINT

DEEP STRIKE

ESCALATION

RIPOSTE'S PRIMER

IN THE BALANCE

DAY OF RECKONING

WAKE OF THE FALLEN

MISSION OBJECTIVES

PRIMARY	SECONDARY	BONUS	CROSSTALK
1. Rendezvous with Bravo	1 – 14. Visit all Nav Points	1. Board SOC-R	None
2. Enter Walled City and Move to Extract		2. Eliminate Village Opposition	

OPTIMUM EQUIPMENT

AGENT	PRIMARY WEAPON	ATTACHMENT 1	ATTACHMENT 2	SECONDARY WEAPON	ATTACHMENT	EXTRA 1	EXTRA 2
Specter	M4A1	4x Scope	Suppressor 2	Mark 23	Suppressor	C4	M67
Jester	M4A1	4x Scope	Suppressor 2	Mark 23	Suppressor	Ammo	Flashbang
Killjoy	M4A1	4x Scope	Suppressor 2	Mark 23	Suppressor	Ammo	Flashbang
Simple	M4A1	4x Scope	Suppressor 2	Mark 23	Suppressor	Ammo	Flashbang

TERRAIN

The abundant mountains, vegetation, trees and hills in this level provide a variety of safe hiding places. The hollows and craters that you will come across soon after the insertion point are good places to take cover. The enemy will find it much harder to hit you when all they have to aim at is your shiny gun barrel poking out of the sand.

Further on in the mission, you will encounter numerous sniper posts. Use the 4x Scope to play the lurking marksmen at their own game: press ✛ twice on the directional buttons to zoom in and surprise the hapless shooter with a well-aimed head shot. If you don't hit him first time he will immediately return fire, but don't worry: at this range, 99% of his shots will be off-target, so stay cool and take another crack at it.

In the latter stages of the mission you will arrive at a walled town where you must engage the NAPF forces face to face in narrow alleyways. Seek cover behind crates, walls or vehicles, and remain hidden until the patrolling guards pass by. To aim at an opponent from behind cover, press the ✛ or ✛ directional button to peek left or right. Only your head and gun barrel will be exposed, making it more difficult for the enemy to hit you.

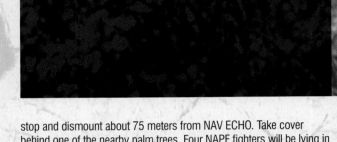

PRIMARY 1:
RENDEZVOUS WITH BRAVO ELEMENT
SECONDARY 1 – 14: VISIT ALL NAV POINTS

1 At the start of the mission you and your teammate Jester are nestled in a range of hills. As you will soon confront your first NAPF raiding party, make sure that your comrade is mentally prepared for battle. First, press ◎, to call up the Team Command Menu, then select FIRETEAM and choose the command FIRE AT WILL. Jester will now fire independently at anything that moves.

Now run northeast from the secure zone. When you reach NAV CHARLIE, proceed north and take up position at the front of the crater at NAV DELTA (Fig. 1), crouching down to avoid detection. The graphic on the bottom right of the screen indicates your current stance. Should you inadvertently stand up, quickly press ▲ to crouch back down.

2 Three enemies will approach from the north. First, concentrate on the crater just ahead of your position, where an NAPF soldier is taking cover. Press ✛ twice on the directional buttons to zoom in on his head as he peers over the crater's edge, trying to spot you. Once you have neutralized him, quickly head for the second rock, where another soldier is hiding. Again, aim for the head to save ammo by executing a one-shot takedown. After a while, the straggler will run west from the burning car towards the telephone pole. If you approach him he will then run to the crater where his comrade has just fallen, giving you a perfect opportunity to take him out. Now press ✛ twice on the directional buttons to switch back to third-person view.

After a short cutscene, Bravo team will arrive in an armored assault vehicle, but there's no time for 'high fives' as more NAPF fighters are bearing down on your position. Two soldiers will approach from the left, and crouch down. A third arrives from the north. Forget the other two for now and focus your attention on the third. He's harder to hit than his comrades as he's constantly on the move. Press (START) to access the Pause Menu and activate Aim Assist to help you lock onto your energetic (but not for long!) target. Once he's eliminated, turn left and assess the situation. Your teammates will probably have neutralized the other two enemies. If any remain, zoom in with your sniper scope and pick them off from a distance.

PRIMARY 2: ENTER WALLED CITY AND MOVE TO EXTRACT

3 Bravo Zulu! You have eliminated the first wave of NAPF fighters; the coast is clear! Now go board the armored assault vehicle (Fig. 2): you've got places to be and bad guys to neutralize!

You can swap positions in the vehicle with the ✛ and ✛ directional buttons. Get behind the wheel and head north. Follow the road, then stop and dismount about 75 meters from NAV ECHO. Take cover behind one of the nearby palm trees. Four NAPF fighters will be lying in wait behind the rocks to the right and left of the road. Issue the FIRE AT WILL command, then zoom in and pick them off one by one (Fig. 3).

4 Re-enter the armored assault vehicle and follow the route north. At NAV FOXTROT, turn right onto the unguarded road. As you proceed to NAV INDIA, six enemies will suddenly appear on the road. Waste no time and run them over! If you don't wipe them all out in one go, reverse and try again, or continue to NAV INDIA. When you get there, dismount and order your team to HOLD FIRE. Now run toward NAV JULIET and then continue to NAV KILO until a cutscene kicks in. Use your sniper scope to zoom in and neutralize the two NAPF men on the opposite side of the river. Swim to the other bank and board the SOC-R just ahead of NAV KILO (Fig. 4).

> **! TIP + TIP + TIP + TIP + TIP**
>
> **Bonus 1: Board SOC-R**
> To achieve the Bonus Objective, you simply have to board the SOC-R.

BONUS 2: ELIMINATE VILLAGE OPPOSITION

5 Issue the FIRE AT WILL command and take the boat to NAV LIMA. Go left, past the island situated about 100 meters from the Nav Point. Five enemies will be lying in wait on your right, but you'll have little chance against them from your position on the water, so disembark at the Nav Point and send Bravo team southeast. To do this, point your crosshairs to the southeast and order Bravo to MOVE TO CROSSHAIRS. The rocks here provide good protection against the approaching enemy. Proceed cautiously along the road. While the NAPF men are engaged by Bravo team, zoom in with the sniper scope to take them out one by one from behind the palm trees or the rocks.

01

02

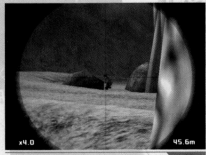

03

SOCOM3
U.S. NAVY SEALS

GAME BASICS

WALKTHROUGH

MULTIPLAYER

EXTRAS

INDEX

HOW TO USE THE
WALKTHROUGH

NORTH AFRICA

SOUTH ASIA

POLAND

FLASHPOINT

DEEP STRIKE

ESCALATION

RIPOSTE'S PRIMER

IN THE BALANCE

DAY OF RECKONING

WAKE OF THE
FALLEN

6 You will see a small cluster of houses in the direction of NAV PAPA. Assemble Bravo team by issuing the FOLLOW command and go prone so that they follow suit. Crawl along to the wall and snipe the two Tangos who are taking cover behind it. An M67 grenade works wonders here too, although it's not particularly stealthy – nothing announces your arrival quite like a huge explosion! When you have taken out these three Tangos, along with the five that you dealt with previously on the road, you will have achieved the second Bonus Objective. However, you still have some work to do before you move on, as there are two more enemies hiding up on the rooftops (Fig. 5). Climb the respective ladders to reach them. Fortunately, the Tangos will automatically surrender when they see you on the ladder. Restrain at least one of them to trigger the 'Trail' Nav Point.

7 Run to the 'Trail' Nav Point that has just appeared and continue down the trail. Press ⊗ to climb up the ledge. On your way to NAV ROMEO, eliminate the two guards patrolling the path. You will eventually arrive at the entrance to the walled town. Take down the two enemies by the pond and head for the main entrance. Just before you reach the steps, command your squad to HOLD POSITION and prepare to learn the true meaning of 'explosive'. When you approach the main gate a Special Action icon will appear at the bottom of the screen. Press ⊗ to place the C4 on the main entrance door. Now get clear! You only have four seconds to detonation!

The entrance to the walled town is now open. Order your team to FIRE AT WILL, as an enemy may be waiting for you behind the door you have just blasted.

Open the door on the left and continue straight ahead through the archways. Warning: a guard will be waiting on the left to ambush you. Run to NAV VICTOR and the path will shortly lead to a square. An enemy will be hiding behind a crate ahead of you, so take him out quickly. Two of his comrades will rush down the steps behind him. Neutralize them, then take cover behind the crates.

8 You now have a choice of two routes: either run up the steps, or head left. Both will eventually lead to NAV WHISKEY! We opt to sprint left. You can relax for a few precious moments as you are in no immediate danger. Run through the streets until you come to another square. Four NAPF fighters will be patrolling here, some of whom will head for the nearest Nav Point when they detect you. Pursue them, but be aware that two more will be waiting in ambush to the left, just behind the next house. Order one of your team members to throw a grenade to eliminate them. The remaining Tangos will then appear in front of you. Spring back to make your presence known, and keep moving to avoid enemy fire. Meanwhile, your fellow combatants can take care of the other soldiers. Move to NAV XRAY then begin proceeding towards NAV YANKEE. Exit through the gateway and run left. Continue along the route to the target destination. Warning: a fighter will run directly at you: take him out with a well-aimed shot before he gets close. Further on, the route leads under the walls to a large, open square.

9 Run across the square and head for cover behind the crates. Order your squad to get behind the crates with the MOVE TO command.

You must stop the guards from reaching the guns mounted on the wall. Peek out at them from behind cover and pick them off (Fig. 6).

Once you have dispatched the two guards, run to the mounted gun. More fighters will rush down from the wall opposite. Neutralize them with the mounted gun and run to the second gun just above it. A tank will blast through the gateway in front of you and a sizeable phalanx of NAPF fighters will storm the square. Continue to take out Tangos until support arrives to help with the tank, then head to the Extraction Point at NAV YANKEE and hold position there until a chopper arrives to transport you from the battle zone..

AFRICA

SOCOM3

GAME BASICS

WALKTHROUGH

MULTIPLAYER

EXTRAS

INDEX

HOW TO USE THE
WALKTHROUGH

NORTH AFRICA

SOUTH ASIA

POLAND

FLASHPOINT

DEEP STRIKE

ESCALATION

RIPOSTE'S PRIMER

IN THE BALANCE

DAY OF RECKONING

WAKE OF THE
FALLEN

MISSION OBJECTIVES

PRIMARY	SECONDARY	BONUS	CROSSTALK
1. Meet Resistance Forces	1. Defeat Enemy Vehicles	1. Stop Runaway Vehicle	1. Destroy Transmitter
2. Ambush Convoy	2. Silence Well Radio		
3. Secure Fortified Well			
4. Destroy Radio Tower			
5. Meet Resistance Leader			

OPTIMUM EQUIPMENT

AGENT	PRIMARY WEAPON	ATTACHMENT 1	ATTACHMENT 2	SECONDARY WEAPON	ATTACHMENT	EXTRA 1	EXTRA 2
Specter	M4A1	4x Scope	Suppressor 2	Mark 23	Suppressor	Satchel	AT-4
Jester	M4A1	4x Scope	Suppressor 2	Mark 23	Suppressor	M67	AT-4
Killjoy	M4A1	4x Scope	Suppressor 2	Mark 23	Suppressor	M67	AT-4
Simple	M16A2	4x Scope	M203 Frag	Mark 23	Suppressor	M67	AT-4

TERRAIN

Barren, hilly desert landscapes are predominant in this mission, so with its lush vegetation, the tranquil pond beside the heavily fortified NAPF compound looks like an idyllic oasis! However, the SEALs aren't here to fun around: the lake provides excellent cover for infiltrating the compound from the rear. The patrolling guards can also be efficiently overpowered by rushing out of the undergrowth to attack them. Enter the compound via the hole in the rear wall, and then proceed to destroy the well radio.

For the second part of the mission, you have a choice of routes. To reach the radio tower, you could attempt to storm the compound with all guns blazing, via the heavily guarded main entrance, meeting the resultant hail of bullets head-on, and probably coming off second best and very, very 'neutralized'. The alternative route is much more civilized and effective. This takes you to the rear of the compound. Use the scope to cap the Tangos silently from a safe distance, before blowing up the tower.

PRIMARY 1: MEET RESISTANCE FORCES

1 On your way to meet the resistance fighters, you will come to an abrupt halt in the desert, as danger thunders towards you across the dunes. Mount the first ALSV, accompanied by Jester; Bravo unit will automatically take control of the second ALSV. Now drive north to the palm trees. Swap to the turret gun when you are behind the dune (Fig. 1).

SECONDARY 1: DEFEAT ENEMY VEHICLES

Shoot at the first Pickup, which will be straight ahead of you. Aim first at the guys with the guns, then fire at the hood of the vehicle. Your problem will be solved moments later by a huge explosion. If Bravo team has not yet destroyed the second Pickup, get on the case and do it yourself. Move in the direction of NAV CHARLIE to find it. Now that you have achieved the Secondary Objective, drive to NAV CHARLIE; Bravo will follow you in the second ALSV. Climb up the hill to meet the Resistance Fighters.

PRIMARY 2: AMBUSH CONVOY

2 In a short cutscene, your allies describe how a convoy of three empty trucks was seen passing through a nearby street about an hour earlier. The trucks were on their way to pick up supplies, and will probably return later via the same route. Re-enter the ALSV and follow the Resistance Fighters to NAV DELTA.

3 Stay in your ALSV (Fig. 2). Quickly command your team to FIRE AT WILL. A Pickup will appear, followed by two Ural trucks. Switch to the turret to take them out.

> **TIP + TIP + TIP + TIP + TIP**
>
> **Bonus 1: Stop Runaway Vehicle**
> *Once you have neutralized all of the enemies, stay on the road for a few seconds longer, as a third truck will soon approach your position. Eliminate it to complete the Bonus Objective.*

SECONDARY 2: SILENCE WELL RADIO

4 Drive to NAV ECHO. On arrival, command the team to HOLD FIRE and order Bravo to HOLD POSITION. You must now operate in total silence, leaving Bravo behind. Proceed to the lake and swim toward the walled compound. You will see two guards patrolling: one on the left side of the lake and the other on the wall. Sneak silently into the bushes next to the wall (Fig. 3).

5 Remaining under cover, dispatch the two guards with well-aimed head shots from your silenced weapon. Run to the rear of the compound and climb up on the debris to reach the hole in the wall. Now proceed with extreme caution. Use the sniper scope to pick off the three men directly in front of you (one on the left and two on the right), then jump down into the compound. Adopting a prone position, take out the guards ahead of you to the left, one by one. Finally, neutralize their comrade who is guarding the fortress wall to the right. Continue to sneak northward and enter the building, where you'll find the well radio (Fig. 4). Destroy it to accomplish the Secondary Objective. Note that if you alert the guards before you reach the well radio, and they have time to call in reinforcements, you will fail the Secondary Objective.

PRIMARY 3: SECURE FORTIFIED WELL

Having destroyed the communications network, command your team to FOLLOW and FIRE AT WILL. Advance eastward to the steps and eliminate the guard at the bottom. The next enemy will be lying in wait on the wall to the left, and two more will be stationed on the right, above the main entrance. Use the tree, or tent, in front of you as cover and take out the guards. The last fighter is to your right. Eliminate him to secure the compound and accomplish the Primary Objective. Exit the camp and command Bravo to mount the Pickup in front of the main gate.

01

02

03

04

GAME BASICS

WALKTHROUGH

MULTIPLAYER

EXTRAS

INDEX

HOW TO USE THE WALKTHROUGH

NORTH AFRICA

SOUTH ASIA

POLAND

FLASHPOINT

DEEP STRIKE

ESCALATION

RIPOSTE'S PRIMER

IN THE BALANCE

DAY OF RECKONING

WAKE OF THE FALLEN

PRIMARY 4: DESTROY RADIO TOWER

6 The time has come to destroy the radio tower and black out the entire enemy communications network. Return with Jester to the ALSV and drive to NAV INDIA. Just after the Nav Point, the road bends slightly to the left, then to the right. Reduce your speed, take control of the turret gun, and swiftly eliminate the three Tangos lurking over on the right. Two more fighters will be posted only a few meters away, on the left this time, so take them out in similar fashion. Proceed to NAV JULIET until you see a mountain on the left with a path leading to the summit. The route ahead, via NAV JULIET, is barred by a gate, so you must continue on foot. You will come to a fork in the path after a few meters (Fig. 5).

7 The left fork leads directly to the compound's main entrance. However, this is a heavily guarded area, so proceed via the dirt road on the right that leads up to the rear entrance. When you get near to the top, crawl along to avoid alerting the enemy to your presence. At the rear entrance, run south behind the first building and eliminate the lurking guard. Another Tango will be hiding in the long grass further west, at the opposite end of the compound. Use the sniper scope to pick him off. Advance cautiously along the side of the building and peek around the corner at the end. Neutralize the guards. Proceed west to the opposite end of the compound and look round the corner of the second building. Another enemy will be lurking here: take him out with a well-aimed shot. Now run to the radio tower and plant the Satchel charge (Fig. 6).

When you are a few meters clear, the whole lot will blow! HooYa! You have accomplished a Primary and Crosstalk Objective. Two more Bogies lie in wait at the main entrance.

> **!** TIP + TIP + TIP + TIP + TIP
>
> **Crosstalk 1: Destroy Transmitter**
> *The Crosstalk Objective is automatically achieved when you complete the Primary Objective of this mission.*

PRIMARY 5: MEET RESISTANCE LEADER

Sprint back to the ALSV; an enemy Pickup will arrive moments after you reach your ride. Commandeer the turret gun and destroy the Pickup before the raiders get a chance to dismount. Follow the road northeast, moving on through NAV ROMEO and NAV VICTOR to reach NAV WHISKEY.

8 Slow right down about 160 meters from NAV WHISKEY and take out the two Tangos that are lurking in the bushes to the right, before moving on. Approximately 80 meters from NAV WHISKEY a Ural truck will approach from the right, accompanied by two soldiers. More troops will jump out when it comes to a stop. Use your turret gun to dispatch them from a safe distance. A little further on the right you will see the Resistance Leader's tent. Dismount and approach him to complete the final Primary Objective and this mission (Fig. 7).

05

06

07

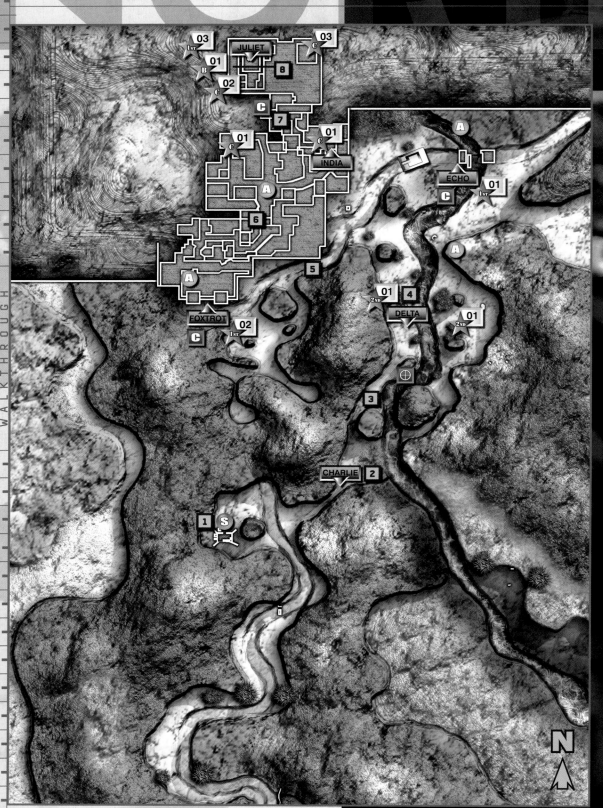

AFRICA

SOCOM3
U.S. NAVY SEALs

GAME BASICS

WALKTHROUGH

MULTIPLAYER

EXTRAS

INDEX

HOW TO USE THE
WALKTHROUGH

MISSION OBJECTIVES

PRIMARY	SECONDARY	BONUS	CROSSTALK
1. Destroy Bridge	1. Rescue Downed Pilot	1. Obtain Delivery Ledger 1	1. Rescue Allied Prisoners
2. Secure Main Gate			2. Obtain Troop Manifest
3. Demolish Supply Depot			3. Obtain Delivery Ledger 2

NORTH AFRICA

SOUTH ASIA

POLAND

FLASHPOINT

DEEP STRIKE

ESCALATION

RIPOSTE'S PRIMER

IN THE BALANCE

DAY OF RECKONING

WAKE OF THE
FALLEN

OPTIMUM EQUIPMENT

AGENT	PRIMARY WEAPON	ATTACHMENT 1	ATTACHMENT 2	SECONDARY WEAPON	ATTACHMENT	EXTRA 1	EXTRA 2
Specter	MK .48	4x Scope	Bipod 1	Mark 23	Suppressor	Designator	Satchel
Jester	MK .48	4x Scope	Bipod 1	Mark 23	Suppressor	M67	Satchel
Killjoy	MK .48	4x Scope	Bipod 1	Mark 23	Suppressor	M67	Flashbang
Simple	MK .48	4x Scope	Bipod 1	Mark 23	Suppressor	M67	Flashbang

TERRAIN

The landscape at the start of the mission consists of barren, hilly, desert. After a few hundred meters you will reach a fertile river valley. As your squad advances through the lush vegetation, they will encounter an abundance of trees, long grass and rocks that can be used as cover. However, this region is swarming with enemies who are equally adept at using the environment to their advantage, making them particularly difficult to detect and hit. Maintain vigilance, and monitor your surroundings very closely before sneaking toward the next tree, rock or bush: you never know what danger may be lurking.

The scenery at the bridge and in front of the main entrance to the walled town is typical of the region; here rocks provide your only refuge from NAPF attacks. Hide behind them when the tank is advancing toward you, or use them as cover if the two gun turrets on either side of the bridge start firing at you.

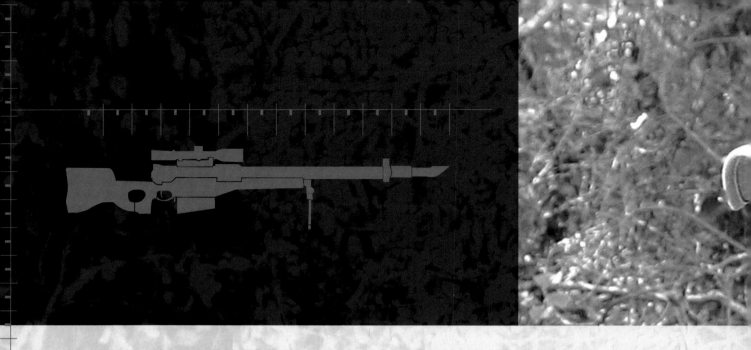

SECONDARY 1: RESCUE DOWNED PILOT

1 Your squad will be dropped in a small valley. Run east through the gorge where the Resistance Fighters are waiting for you. Command your team to FIRE AT WILL, as your first two enemies are just a few hundred meters away, perched up on the rocks like sitting ducks; a couple of decent shots will easily finish them off, even at this distance. Head north and go left, past the rock.

2 A cutscene will kick in, showing an NAPF anti-aircraft emplacement shooting down a US helicopter. Miraculously, the pilot survives the crash, so your immediate concern is to safely extract the stranded airman from the conflict zone. But the enemy has other ideas, and you'll soon see the Tangos crossing the river to the north of your position in order to get to him first and finish the job. Zoom in and snipe at them from a distance, then hold L2 to send Bravo team to where the fighters were just positioned. Continue northward and take cover behind the rock. The enemies to the north will engage with Bravo team, so help your buddies by zooming in with your sniper scope and taking out their attackers. You should now be able to see the burning helicopter wreckage and the pilot standing just to the left of it. Take care that he doesn't get injured in the crossfire!

3 Send Bravo team in the direction of the helicopter and advance across the river. You still have enemies to the north to deal with, two of whom will be hiding in the grass. Crouch down and eliminate them, then sneak toward the pilot (Fig. 1).

Now escort the pilot back to NAV DELTA (order Bravo team to follow you) to accomplish your Secondary Objective.

PRIMARY 1: DESTROY BRIDGE

Stay on the left bank of the river and crawl northward. A teammate will point out that there are enemy guns nearby: the first is on the mountain to the right. Use your sniper scope to pick off the two guys at the gun from a safe distance (Fig. 2).

4 A message will alert you to the presence of an NAPF tank in the vicinity. Proceed northward, and arrive just in time to see the lumbering behemoth crossing the bridge. Take cover behind the nearest rock and wait until the tank stops in front of you. Now select the Designator by pressing R2. Aim the crosshairs at the tank and hold R1 for four seconds. A countdown will indicate when you can release the button (Fig. 3).

01

02

GAME BASICS

WALKTHROUGH

MULTIPLAYER

EXTRAS

INDEX

HOW TO USE THE
WALKTHROUGH

NORTH AFRICA

SOUTH ASIA

POLAND

FLASHPOINT

DEEP STRIKE

ESCALATION

RIPOSTE'S PRIMER

IN THE BALANCE

DAY OF RECKONING

WAKE OF THE
FALLEN

With the tank now 'painted' as a target, a missile will descend from the skies like an avenging comet and annihilate its quarry. From your current position you should be able to see the second machine gun emplacement on the left of the bridge. Use your skill to pick off the two Tangos posted there at long range. There's one more enemy on the right of the bridge, so take him out as well.

Now run to the bridge and kill the opponent on your left. Suddenly two more enemies will appear from the south. Then go onto the bridge and crouch down in the middle. When the Satchel charge icon appears at the bottom of the screen, press ⊗ to place the bomb. Run back up toward the walled town, and watch as the explosion destroys the NAPF's key strategic supply route.

PRIMARY 2: SECURE MAIN GATE

Now run southwest to the walled town and sneak south along the wall. Here, a path on the right leads round to the main gate.

5 Run in the direction of NAV FOXTROT, where an intense battle rages. The Resistance Fighters are positioned to your left, and the NAPF forces are defending the main entrance to the right. Time for you to join the fray, taking care to avoid accidentally firing on your allies! Up ahead to the southwest several NAPF soldiers are dug in behind a wall of sandbags. Zoom in and pick them off one by one. Now sneak along the front of the fortress wall. At the corner, lean to the left and take out the enemy soldiers before they get a chance to fire back at you. Bingo! You have secured the main gate!

PRIMARY 3: DEMOLISH SUPPLY DEPOT

Enter the walled town and head for the left archway; neutralize the two soldiers who are lurking in the shadows (Fig. 4).

Advance cautiously under the archway. Find cover on the right and peek out to the left. A couple of accurate shots will eliminate the two soldiers in the square. Run toward the steps. A Tango will be standing guard at the other end of the street. After taking him out, move carefully along the side of the house on your right. The next enemy will be waiting at the end of the alleyway, and there's another at the foot of the steps. After dispatching both of them, run down the steps and follow the path left.

57

6 When you reach the next archway, order Bravo team to move over to the far side of the arch, while you remain just in front of it. Lean out to the left and pick off the guards in the square. Now sneak your way northward, keeping close to the walls on the left. An enemy will be hiding behind the crates to the left of the next intersection. Order Bravo to throw a hand grenade at this target by pointing your crosshairs at the crates, calling up the TCM with ◎, selecting Bravo, then DEPLOY and FRAG. The soldier will be blasted from his hiding place, and you can safely move on. Warning! Another enemy will run toward the intersection from the east.

! TIP + TIP + TIP + TIP + TIP

Crosstalk 1: Rescue Allied Prisoners
Proceed northward over the intersection, remembering to take Bravo team with you. Stop on the left and take cover behind the crates and barrels. You can safely neutralize the enemy at the end of the street from this position. Continue north, still sticking tight to the walls of the houses on the left. You will see some barrels on the left when you peek around the next corner. Use them as cover while you take out the two soldiers up ahead. This action will free the captured Resistance Fighters (Fig. 5). To complete the second part of this Crosstalk Objective, you will have to rescue more prisoners later on in the mission.

Run back to the square and follow the street east, staying close to the wall on the left. At the corner of the next house, peek cautiously into the alleyway on the left and take out the unsuspecting Tango. Proceed left along the side of the houses and stop at the left-hand bend in the street. You should spot your next target at the far end of the street. Shoot him, then advance toward the body and head down the steps. Taking out the approaching guards completes the first Crosstalk Objective.

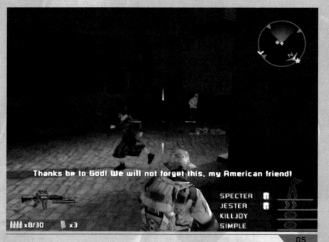

Thanks be to God! We will not forget this, my American friend!

x8/30   x3

SPECTER   R
JESTER   R
KILLJOY
SIMPLE

05

7 Run down the steps and surprise the Tango lurking to the right of the crates. Sprint in the direction of NAV JULIET until you reach a gate. A cutscene will inform you of the fierce resistance that lies ahead. Seven shooters with itchy trigger fingers will be staking out the large square beyond the gate, and, to make matters worse, a machine gun is mounted in the middle of the courtyard. Press **L2** to send Bravo team behind the crates to the north. You and Jester should sprint over to the other side of the courtyard and shoot your way along the right flank. Stay crouched behind the crates as much as possible, and pick your enemies off one by one.

8 Now run to the warehouse, avoiding the front entrance and instead heading around the side to the back door, taking Bravo team with you. Take out the enemy in front of the entrance and sneak inside the warehouse, where another Tango will be waiting for you. Now kill the opponent on the walkway above, then dodge left when another soldier comes through the door. Greet him with a well-aimed head shot. With the coast relatively clear, it's safe to continue.

TIP + TIP + TIP + TIP + TIP

Crosstalk 2: Obtain Troop Manifest
Crosstalk 3: Obtain Delivery Ledger 2
Bonus 1: Obtain Delivery Ledger 1
Once all the NAPF forces have been neutralized, run south to the small room that contains two large crates. Take the Troop Manifest from the front crate (Fig. 6).

Now climb the steps behind you. Turn left at the top and take Delivery Ledger 1 from the table (Fig. 7).

Go back outside and enter the garage, where you'll find Delivery Ledger 2 on the table (Fig. 8).

If you want to accomplish all Bonus and Crosstalk Objectives, please read the Tip boxes before performing the next action. At the foot of the steps you will see some crates. Place a Satchel charge in front of one of the small crates (Fig. 9) to complete the mission.

TROOP MANIFEST — SPECTER / JESTER / KILLJOY / SIMPLE — x25/30 — x4
06

DELIVERY LEDGER — SPECTER / JESTER / KILLJOY / SIMPLE — x25/30 — x4
07

DELIVERY LEDGER — SPECTER / JESTER / KILLJOY / SIMPLE — x11/30 — x5
08

SATCHEL CHARGE — SPECTER / JESTER / KILLJOY / SIMPLE — x49/100 — x3
09

SOCOM3
U.S. NAVY SEALS

GAME BASICS

WALKTHROUGH

MULTIPLAYER

EXTRAS

INDEX

HOW TO USE THE
WALKTHROUGH

NORTH AFRICA

SOUTH ASIA

POLAND

FLASHPOINT

DEEP STRIKE

ESCALATION

RIPOSTE'S PRIMER

IN THE BALANCE

DAY OF RECKONING

WAKE OF THE
FALLEN

MISSION OBJECTIVES

PRIMARY	SECONDARY	BONUS	CROSSTALK
1. Disable Launcher Site 1	1. Check Missile Warheads	1. Prevent Further Launches	1. Prevent Further Launches
2. Disable Launcher Site 2	2. Destroy ZSU		
3. Disable Launcher Site 3			
4. Disable Launcher Site 4			

OPTIMUM EQUIPMENT

AGENT	PRIMARY WEAPON	ATTACHMENT 1	ATTACHMENT 2	SECONDARY WEAPON	ATTACHMENT	EXTRA 1	EXTRA 2
Specter	M8	Thermal	Suppressor	Mark 23	Suppressor	AT-4	C4
Jester	M8	Thermal	Suppressor	Mark 23	Suppressor	M67	Flashbang
Killjoy	HK5	Suppressor	Rifle Laser	Mark 23	Suppressor	M67	Flashbang
Simple	HK5	Suppressor	Rifle Laser	Mark 23	Suppressor	M67	Flashbang

TERRAIN

The terrain is similar to that which you've experienced on your previous missions: sparsely covered by vegetation and dotted with gentle hills. Other than from inside the launcher sites, most of your cover in this mission will be provided by trees or rocks. And don't think that your safety will be guaranteed by the comforting cloak of darkness: the enemy soldiers are equipped with the same night vision and thermal imaging apparatus as your own squad, therefore canceling out any advantage you might have had.

In the latter stages of the mission, the route will lead you to a disused mine. Here the cave entrances and tunnels are swarming with enemy soldiers! The battle conditions are claustrophobic, similar in nature to those of previous urban skirmishes, so the same rules of engagement apply: hug the walls, and proceed very carefully when you reach any forks in the path, as you could suddenly find yourself surrounded.

PRIMARY 1: DISABLE LAUNCHER SITE 1

1 Order Bravo to hold position and run northward with Jester, up the path on the right. Don't venture on to the road! 80 meters from NAV CHARLIE hide behind the rock and switch to thermal vision by pressing the ✛ directional button three times. You should soon spot two guards a little way to the northwest, but you won't immediately be able to see the other soldier who is lurking behind the nearby building. You must eliminate him first, as he will raise the alarm the moment he sees you. Continue a few meters to the right, then take cover behind the large rock in front of the buildings. Meanwhile, the soldiers will have walked over to the shacks and started smoking cigarettes. Wait for the third guy to appear and take him out with a single bullet to the head. Now shoot the other two. See, smoking really *does* damage your health! Note: if, after all your efforts, someone raises the alarm, you will be pursued by NAPF forces in two Pickups later in the mission.

2 Run on toward NAV DELTA and veer off to the left along the rocks. You should see the first missile launcher site up ahead. You will also see a guard in front of you. It's too dangerous to pick him off from your current position, as you might miss and raise the alarm. You must get a little closer before you can deal with him, so press Ⓐ to go prone, and crawl behind the small rock located 67 meters away from NAV DELTA. A few seconds later three guards will walk in your direction: take them out when they reach the road. Now eliminate the two opponents at the entrance. Creep past the building until you see the small gate on your right. Sneak into the complex and take out the guard standing next to the launcher. Then kill the sniper on the storage tank. Immediately take out the guard patroling to your right, preventing him from setting off the alarm. Enter the building to your right to destroy the radio transmitter. Order Bravo team to follow you and issue the FIRE AT WILL command. Now neutralize all the guards in the immediate vicinity, from the safety of the building. Your teammates may take care of them, but if not, it's up to you to take them all down. Proceed to the mobile missile launcher and set the C4 explosives (Fig. 1).

> ⚠ **TIP + TIP + TIP + TIP + TIP**
>
> **Bonus and Crosstalk Objectives**
> Don't wait too long to destroy the missile after entering the site: if alerted, the enemy will try to trigger the missile launch sequence shortly after you enter the compound, and you will have failed your Bonus and Crosstalk Objectives.

SECONDARY 1: CHECK MISSILE WARHEADS

Go over to the long crate next to the missile launcher and press ⓧ when you see the Special Action icon. Bingo: you have just checked the missile warheads and have therefore accomplished your Secondary objective.

SECONDARY 2: DESTROY THE ZSU

Run back to the road and continue north to NAV ECHO. A message will reveal your next mechanical adversary, a ZSU anti-aircraft tank. Keep advancing, but stay well away from the road. Proceed right from the road, keeping close to the hills. Zoom in with the Thermal Scope and, if possible, avoid switching back for the next few minutes, as it will be much easier to detect the enemy in thermal mode.

3 You will spot two guards on the road in front of you. Pick them off at a safe distance. You should also take out the Tango on the tower to the northeast from this relatively safe position. Now run left across the road, sticking close to the upturned platform in front of the compound. At the end of the platform, lean left and dispatch the guard. Run straight to the northeast. Two guards will be waiting to be neutralized just behind the rock. A little further on to the north you will find another radio transmitter hidden behind some crates (Fig. 2). Blow it to pieces!

To the north you can see the ZSU tank. Blow it away with a missile to complete the Secondary Objective. Move to NAV FOXTROT and kill the remaining guards.

PRIMARY 2: DISABLE LAUNCHER SITE 2

4 When you reach the second launcher site proceed exactly as before. Keep to the left, and sneak up to kill the guards in front of the compound, before infiltrating the site. Take out the opponent located to the north. Eliminate the guards in front of the building on the right, destroy the radio transmitter inside, then neutralize the rest of the soldiers. The sniper spot on the rock to the left of the launcher is an ideal vantage point from which to safely eliminate the guards at the back of the camp. (If you previously raised the alarm you can also kill the enemies parked in their Pickup trucks to the northeast of this position.) Go back down and place the C4 charge on the missile launcher as quickly as possible. Piece of cake! Or, if you're feeling a little reckless, you could try another slightly more risky method. Drive the Ural truck left by the NAPF at the first launcher site full-pelt into the middle of Site 2 without stopping. Leap out and quickly place the C4. This will stop the NAPF launching the missile before you can get to it, should they be alerted to your presence when you try to sneak your way in.

Now continue northward and kill all the guards who appear. Infiltrate the building on your left and destroy the radio transmitter (Fig. 3).

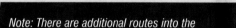

TIP + TIP + TIP + TIP + TIP

Note: Instead of moving through the gap in the fence, you can head back to the centre of the camp and drive the Pickup to NAV KILO. You will find it next to the building where you destroyed the second radio. On your way to the third launcher site your teammate will use the turret gun to take out any nearby Tangos. When you arrive at the site you can also use this powerful weapon to kill the next batch of enemies.

PRIMARY 3: DISABLE LAUNCHER SITE 3

5 Stick to the left side of the road and take out the four guards that you meet on your way to NAV KILO. Keep left and take the small path up to the mountains in front of the entrance to the launch site (Fig. 4).

From here, it's easier to zoom in and use your thermal scope to pick your enemies off from a safe distance. Warning! Two NAPF soldiers will also be patrolling this route. Take them out silently. Follow the path down and enter the site. Sneak through the entrance and destroy both the radio transmitter in the building next to the entrance and, of course, the missile launcher. Now proceed to NAV PAPA.

TIP + TIP + TIP + TIP + TIP

Note: There are additional routes into the compound. On the right of the main entrance you'll find a gap in the fence. A short distance further to the right you'll find another path that leads to a ledge, an ideal position from which to show off your sniper skills.

PRIMARY 4: DISABLE LAUNCHER SITE 4

6 Follow the path into the mountains that leads to NAV PAPA and enter the warren-like mine complex (Fig. 5).

Just a few meters into the mine you'll get the opportunity to take down an NAPF soldier using a close quarters combat move, such as a stealth kill. You will then arrive in a large cave where the path leads off to the left. Shoot the three patrolling guards, then run toward NAV VICTOR and kill the guard in the passageway to your right. Head up the slope. A short way toward NAV WHISKEY you can pick off another Tango. Now go left up the slope, still heading for NAV WHISKEY. Here, a guard will be trying to escape up ahead of you: take aim and stop him in his tracks. A further enemy will attack you seconds later from a tunnel on the right. Deal with him. Another will appear behind the crates up ahead in the direction of NAV WHISKEY. Shoot him! Follow the path to NAV XRAY. Warning! A guard will suddenly appear behind you at the turn that leads into the next tunnel. Take him out! On arrival at the Nav Point, eliminate the two guards on your left. Another guy will now appear from the north. Eliminate him too! Now run across the three planks and head west. This brings you to a tunnel system that will lead to NAV YANKEE and the last missile launcher site.

7 Kill the guard up on the rock directly in front of you then use this excellent vantage point and take out as many of the other guards that are patrolling below as you can. Now destroy the radio transmitter in the building to the northeast of your position, before disabling the fourth and final missile launcher. Bravo Zulu! If you disabled all the launchers before the enemy launched the missile, you will also have accomplished the Bonus and Crosstalk objectives.

SOCOM 3
U.S. NAVY SEALS

GAME BASICS

WALKTHROUGH

MULTIPLAYER

EXTRAS

INDEX

HOW TO USE THE
WALKTHROUGH

NORTH AFRICA

SOUTH ASIA

POLAND

FLASHPOINT

DEEP STRIKE

ESCALATION

RIPOSTE'S PRIMER

IN THE BALANCE

DAY OF RECKONING

WAKE OF THE
FALLEN

AFRICA

MISSION OBJECTIVES

PRIMARY	SECONDARY	BONUS	CROSSTALK
1. Defend CHA Positions	1. Defend North Position	1. No CHA Points Overrun	1. No CHA Points Overrun
2. Rendezvous with CHA Force	2. Defend Center Position		
3. Assist Counter-Attack	3. Defend South Position		
4. Move to Extract			

OPTIMUM EQUIPMENT

AGENT	PRIMARY WEAPON	ATTACHMENT 1	ATTACHMENT 2	SECONDARY WEAPON	ATTACHMENT	EXTRA 1	EXTRA 2
Specter	M8	4x Scope	ZX25 Airburst	Mark 23	Suppressor	Smoke	Designator
Jester	M16A2	High Scope	-	Mark 23	-	AT-4	Ammo
Killjoy	MK .48	-	Bipod 1	Mark 23	-	Smoke	Ammo
Simple	M16A2	-	High Scope	Mark 23	-	AT-4	Ammo

TERRAIN

A sandstorm has blown up in the desert, and your fireteam is caught slap bang in the middle! Burning hot sand swirls around like a gritty tornado, making it hard to see further than a few feet in front of your face. Not that there is actually anything to look at should the sandstorm ever abate, however! A vast, desolate landscape of nothingness stretches as far as the eye can see; endless sand dunes drift on into infinity, peppered with the odd isolated rock. The few palm trees and CHA sandbag defenses scattered around provide your only cover, as there's precious little else for you to hide behind, not even a stray camel.

Your first task is to defend three CHA outposts as waves of enemy fighters roll in from all directions. Deploy your units at key strategic points and make sure that your comrades find adequate cover. Also, regularly check the position of each team member, to prevent anyone becoming inadvertently isolated in the heat of battle.

Use any objects in your immediate surroundings for cover; palm trees, sandbags and rocks all offer some degree of protection.

Cover is more vital than ever when Pickups or tanks are advancing toward you. Be warned! If you are caught unprotected and in the open, you will not only increase your risk of being fired on, you will also be in serious danger of getting run over by enemy vehicles.

Feel free to use the CHA mounted machine-guns to fire on the advancing NAPF forces, but be aware that their effective range is limited, so sometimes you'll have to dismount and switch back to your own weapon. If you run out of ammo, just take a gun from one of the downed enemies! Some will even be considerate enough to leave behind the correct ammo for your firearm. How thoughtful!

The scenery becomes more varied toward the end of the mission, when you enter the ruins of a town that has been razed to the ground by the NAPF. Take care of the snipers in the ruins!

PRIMARY 1: DEFEND CHA POSITIONS
SECONDARY 1: DEFEND NORTH POSITION

1 Order your team to FIRE AT WILL and run to the northern outpost at NAV CHARLIE. The instant that you arrive, you'll see the first wave of elite enemy troops advancing from the north toward your position. Order Bravo to move to the small rocks on the left while you use the right machine gun to fend off the interlopers. You will probably have to leave the mounted gun from time to time to attack Tangos that are out of its range. Zoom in with your scope and pick them off. It is crucial that you avoid accidentally killing any team members or allies, or the mission will be over.

Once you have defeated all the enemies, the second onslaught will arrive from the north, this time accompanied by a technical truck. Remain at the same position and repel the enemy contingent. Neutralize the driver and the turret gunner to put the vehicle out of action. It will then turn white on your compass, and you can safely commandeer it and drive it behind allied lines for safekeeping. You'll soon have defeated the second wave of enemies, but there's no time to stop and pat yourself on the back, as the sound of approaching artillery fire announces that there's a third assault on the way!

The NAPF will approach from the valley to the east this time, so immediately switch to the gun on the right and command your comrades to FOLLOW. Next, order them over to your right, where they can watch over the path that leads to your current position (Fig. 1). Bravo will deal with the fighters attacking from the east, while you aim the mounted machine-gun at the troops advancing from the northeast, with Jester watching your back as usual. You can also use the Pickup turret gun to eliminate the enemies.

The enemy will approach again from the north for the fourth assault. Return to the left gun and order your teammates to move next to the small rocks to your left. You will now face another NAPF technical.

The fifth and final wave will approach from the north. Remain where you are and watch and wait until a tank trundles into view. Switch to the designator, then aim it at the tank and hold down **R1** to call up an air strike. Be sure to stay well behind the sandbags (Fig. 2)!

Moments later the tank will be scrap metal. Shoot the remaining Tangos and drive the Pickup to NAV DELTA.

PRIMARY 1: DEFEND CHA POSITIONS
SECONDARY 2: DEFEND CENTER POSITION

2 When you reach NAV DELTA use the mounted machine-gun to stave off the first attack wave. Bravo should stay in the technical and use the turret.

Second and third fighter units will attempt to storm your position from the east, with two technicals accompanying the third onslaught. Use the mounted gun to mow them down.

A cutscene will then kick in, a dramatic interlude before you're hurled back into the fray.

PRIMARY 1: DEFEND CHA POSITIONS
SECONDARY 2: DEFEND SOUTH POSITION

3 Now mount the technical and travel toward NAV ECHO to reach the southern outpost. Shortly afterward, an enemy unit will approach from the north. Order Bravo to mount the technical. Grab the mounted gun on the left and neutralize any Tangos that attempt to penetrate your defenses.

The second attack will come from the southeast. Use the gun on the right to eliminate the attackers and destroy the two technicals.

The final brigade will emerge from the east. Hold your position and select the designator, as another tank is approaching. From behind cover, aim the designator at the tank the moment you spot it (Fig. 3) to call down the strike.

! TIP + TIP + TIP + TIP + TIP

Bonus 1: No CHA Points Overrun
Crosstalk 1: No CHA Points Overrun
Note: If you moved quickly enough and reached all of the outposts before the enemy could commandeer them, you will have fulfilled the Bonus and Crosstalk Objectives.

03

04

PRIMARY 2: RENDEZVOUS WITH CHA FORCE

4 Proceed to NAV INDIA to rendezvous with the CHA troops and achieve another Primary Objective. An allied tank will be waiting for you here.

PRIMARY 3: ASSIST COUNTER-ATTACK

5 Head toward NAV JULIET, following the tank into the ruins. Kill the enemy on the bridge ahead of you (Fig. 4) then take out the two Tangos to the left and right of his position. Move carefully to NAV JULIET as there are several enemies lurking in the ruins: take them all out from a safe distance. At NAV JULIET you will be attacked by a couple of enemies approaching from the north; they will also be accompanied by a tank. Take cover behind the rocks and use the designator to destroy it. Take out all remaining enemies to secure the position and complete the mission.

SOCOM3
U.S. NAVY SEALs

GAME BASICS

WALKTHROUGH

MULTIPLAYER

EXTRAS

INDEX

HOW TO USE THE
WALKTHROUGH

NORTH AFRICA

SOUTH ASIA

POLAND

FLASHPOINT

DEEP STRIKE

ESCALATION

RIPOSTE'S PRIMER

IN THE BALANCE

DAY OF RECKONING

WAKE OF THE
FALLEN

AFRICA

MISSION OBJECTIVES

PRIMARY	SECONDARY	BONUS	CROSSTALK
1. Rescue Civilian	1. Find Marcy in the Madersa	1. Obtain Intel	1. Obtain Intel
2. Capture Colonel Sarwat	2. Escort Marcy to Safety		

OPTIMUM EQUIPMENT

AGENT	PRIMARY WEAPON	ATTACHMENT 1	ATTACHMENT 2	SECONDARY WEAPON	ATTACHMENT	EXTRA 1	EXTRA 2
Specter	HK36	Thermal	-	Mark 23	-	Flashbang	Designator
Jester	HK36	GL-36 Frag	-	Mark 23	-	M67	Flashbang
Killjoy	HK36	GL-36 Frag	-	Mark 23	-	M67	Ammo
Simple	HK36	GL-36 Frag	-	Mark 23	-	M67	Flashbang

TERRAIN

This entire mission takes place in the narrow streets of the same walled town that you first visited in the training mission, back when you were a raw recruit; my how time flies! You start in front of the gate of the walled town, where you can swim across the pond and approach the fort unseen.

The usual rules of house-to-house combat apply here: monitor the intersections very carefully, clear houses with Frag or Flashbang grenades, and above all use every barrel, market stall and crate as cover when fighting in open squares. The walls are of varying heights, and certain places will serve as ideal makeshift sniping posts.

You get the chance to employ some teamwork strategy in the narrow streets. While you send Bravo to attack an enemy position, Able can run quickly around the block to take out the fighters that are still engaged with Bravo from behind their cover.

Be careful not to neutralize all enemies at the end of the mission: you might find it difficult to distinguish Colonel Sarwat from his NAPF fighters and he must be taken alive at all cost. If you accidentally shoot him, the mission will end and you will have to start again from the previous Checkpoint.

PRIMARY 1: RESCUE CIVILIAN
SECONDARY 1: FIND MARCY IN THE MADERSA
SECONDARY 2: ESCORT MARCY TO SAFETY

1 Your team will be dropped at the front gate of the walled town. A guard is patrolling by the main entrance, and another Tango will be standing just behind the gate. Order your team to HOLD POSTION. Now swim across the pond and creep along the wall to get close enough to the guard to silently eliminate him. Sneak through the gate and kill the second guard, who will be standing inside, to your right. Use the wall for cover and take him out with a well-aimed head shot to save ammo. The next fighter will be conveniently waiting to be neutralized on the left, behind the small archway. Re-group, switch to the HK36, issue the FIRE AT WILL command and run through the vaulted passage until you reach a small gate. Open it and go through.

2 When you enter the square, two soldiers will storm toward you from the alley to the south. Take them out, then sneak a few steps left toward NAV ECHO. Assume a prone position to help you hold your weapon steady as you aim. Switch to the Thermal Scope and you will see two more soldiers that can be picked off from a safe distance with two accurate head shots. Continue following the street toward NAV ECHO.

3 Proceed a few meters into the narrow alley on the left just past the crate. Make sure you don't rush through the archway, as another enemy will be waiting to ambush you. Switch to thermal view and go prone, then neutralize the guard. Proceed along the alley through the arch.

4 A few meters ahead you will come to a square, just before NAV ECHO. Marcy Raines is hiding to the left in the ornate Madersa. Approach her, making sure that all your teammates follow you. Restrain her to complete the Secondary Objective. Now things will really start to heat up! First, order Marcy to stay where she is: do so by standing directly in front of her and pressing ⊗ when the relevant icon appears on screen. This ensures that she stays safely inside the Madersa while you lead your team back toward the square. Take up a position in the archway and look for cover behind the walls. A half dozen or so enemies will storm toward you. Pick them off from your position of safety (Fig. 1).

So, the coast is clear… or is it? Appearances can be deceptive. In the street leading south, another soldier could be standing at the right of the entrance to the first building. Eliminate him.

Return to Marcy and order her to follow you in the same way in which you just ordered her to stay put. Head into the square and use the TCM to order Bravo to MOVE TO…NAV FOXTROT so that they will clear the path ahead for you and your precious charge. Follow your two comrades at a distance to ensure that Marcy does not inadvertently get ventilated in any crossfire!

5 You will encounter armed resistance just beyond the first archway. One soldier is on the steps up ahead, and another is hiding behind a crate to your right. Bravo will take care of them while you hang back, although you may have to help your buddies out from time to time – don't tell them we said so, but you're still the best sharpshooter out there! Once your pursuers are neutralized, follow the street in the direction of NAV FOXTROT, but don't venture too close to the square at the end, as two Tangos will be lying in wait for you there. Bravo should have already eliminated them, but make sure that the coast is completely clear before you advance. When you get to the square, Marcy will automatically run to freedom through the gate on the right and you will have fulfilled your first Primary Objective and another Secondary Objective. Now proceed cautiously toward NAV INDIA, making sure that you command Bravo to FOLLOW, otherwise they'll stay at NAV FOXTROT, and they're not much good to anyone there!

PRIMARY 2: CAPTURE COLONEL SARWAT

6 Get rid of the two Tangos approaching you from the left. Run through the archway and follow the alley round until you see some steps ahead. An enemy is lying in wait in the building above the steps. Advance slowly to the corner of the house, keeping to the right. Monitor the situation above the steps. Another enemy will appear. Peek along the street to the right, where one more will be lurking. Sneak over and take him out. Now creep up the steps and monitor the entrances to the two houses. As no one immediately rushes out, position yourself at the entrance to the left building and cautiously peer inside and shoot the guard. Repeat this action at the opposite entrance. The situation will change should the two Tangos detect your presence and storm out of their respective buildings, so remain vigilant!

7 Run down the steps and back toward NAV JULIET until you pass through two smaller arches. The road forks just beyond here and things will start to get really tricky! First, sneak left – you will see a marketplace up ahead swarming with enemy fighters. A well-coordinated attack can make light work of this potential problem. Order Bravo to go behind the market stall just in front of you (Fig 2). Now run back with Jester and take the right fork that leads to the rear of the square. While Bravo engages the enemy at close quarters, you can pick the rest off from a safe distance. Approximately eight men will be standing directly in front of you: first shoot the soldiers to your right, before taking care of the men coming down the steps to the left, and finally neutralizing the ones shooting at you from the balcony above!

Once you have eliminated all opposition, issue the FOLLOW command. You now have two possibilities: either proceed southeast through the arch, or go up the steps. It doesn't matter which route you take, as both lead to the same point. We opt to take the steps. Go to the top and kill the two guards on your left (if you haven't already done so), then turn right and go through the arch, toward NAV KILO. Two archways later, a couple of enemies will dash out from the left. Neutralize them.

8 Continue through the vaulted passage until you reach a wooden door. Press ⊗ to open it when the relevant icon appears at the bottom of the screen (Fig. 3). Go through the door to trigger another cutscene.

9 General Mahmood has escaped, so now your attention focuses on his second-in-command, Colonel Sarwat. Run right out of the room to the outside, where you'll see Mahmood's helicopter taking off. There is a T-72 tank in the courtyard below; don't be fooled by the fact that it's outlined in white on the Compass Map, this big dumb hunk o' steel is anything but neutral! Aim your Designator at it to call down an air strike. Now it really is neutral. After the fireworks, run down the steps. Dispatch the guards in the square, using your Thermal Scope for maximum efficiency. One has barricaded himself behind some crates and another is in the archway to the right. Watch out for the Tango running down the steps on your left and proceed up those same steps once you've got rid of him. At the top, sneak forward through the archway and take out the two guards in the next two rooms. Advancing north, you will soon come to another square. Eliminate all the guards in the vicinity, including those in the courtyard below.

TIP + TIP + TIP + TIP + TIP

You will return to this spot later in the mission, when the situation will be much easier to handle thanks to your current actions!

Run back through the two rooms to the steps. Climb the steps on your right. Sneak across the square to the archway and neutralize the guard on your right. Run to the balcony and shoot the guard below. Go back through the door on your right. Continue through the room and then proceed northwest until you reach NAV PAPA and a small bridge. Open the red door in front of you (if shut) to come face to face with three Tangos. Advance with extreme caution, as you are now deep in the heart of the enemy HQ. Pay special attention to the guards who rush toward you from the passage on the right, and deal with them swiftly.

10 Now proceed to the large central room. Here, Sarwat will be waiting for you. Sarwat immediately runs out; you must avoid killing him at all costs.

TIP + TIP + TIP + TIP + TIP

Bonus 1: Gather Intel
Search the room and take the two documents that you find on the tables (Fig. 4). Bravo Zulu! You have achieved a Bonus Objective!

Now pursue Sarwat: go through the door that he used to escape and kill the guard on the left. Run to the right. Kill the guard lurking at the next corner and follow the path left where you will find Sarwat lying in wait for you. Hide behind the crates to dodge his fire until he flees, then follow him through the next rooms. Suddenly he will stop again: wait a few seconds until he flees and head after him. Run through the square that you cleared a short while earlier. Sarwat will finally surrender at the courtyard steps, although he may give himself up before that, depending on how quickly you catch up with him. Restrain him to complete the mission.

02 / 03

04

WAKE OF THE FALLEN

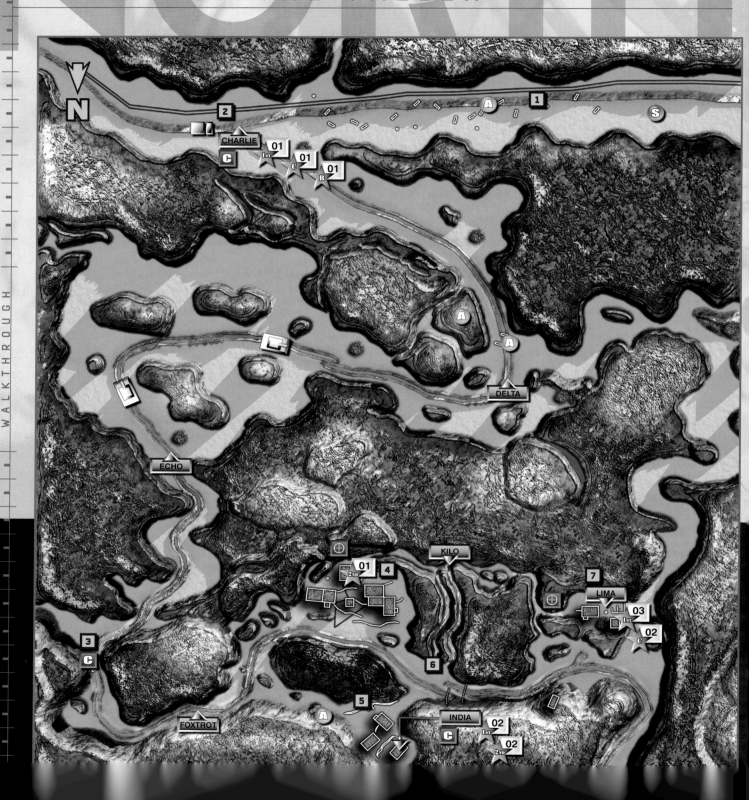

AFRICA

MISSION OBJECTIVES

PRIMARY	SECONDARY	BONUS	CROSSTALK
1. Search Road for Mahmood	1. Search North Village	1. Capture Surrendering NAPF Troops	1. Capture Surrendering NAPF Troops
2. Search Village	2. Search South Village		2. Complete Mission
3. Capture General Mahmood			

OPTIMUM EQUIPMENT

AGENT	PRIMARY WEAPON	ATTACHMENT 1	ATTACHMENT 2	SECONDARY WEAPON	ATTACHMENT	EXTRA 1	EXTRA 2
Specter	M16A2	High Scope	Rifle Laser	Mark 23	Suppressor	AT-4	Designator
Jester	MK .48	4x Scope	Rifle Laser	Mark 23	Suppressor	HE	AT-4
Killjoy	HK36	4x Scope	Suppressor 2	Mark 23	Suppressor	M67	AT-4
Simple	SR25	12x Scope	Bipod 3	Mark 23	Suppressor	M67	Smoke

TERRAIN

The varied scenery here provides new strategic opportunities at virtually every Nav Point. The most important ground rules for this mission are as follows: look for good sniper spots in the mountains, always stay behind cover, never leave yourself unprotected in the middle of the highway, scope the hills for hidden enemy soldiers, and check around every corner of the narrow alleyways in the villages.

Watch out for ambushes in the latter stages of the mission: burning cars blocking your path usually means a trap. Approach these situations with extreme caution and monitor your immediate surroundings very closely.

The usual street-fighting battle tactics apply in the villages. Have your teammates use grenades to clear out buildings, and be sure to thoroughly search all of the rooms in order to find important information about Mahmood's movements.

Bonus 1: Capture Surrendering NAPF Troops
Crosstalk 1: Capture Surrendering NAPF Troops

1 Once you reach the highway, immediately issue the HOLD POSITION command. Use the burning vehicles as cover and fight your way forward to NAV CHARLIE. As you push ahead, shoot all NAPF soldiers that are wearing red headscarves, ideally from a safe distance using the high-powered scope. Some of the other enemies (usually the ones wearing the black turbans) will start to surrender. You can tell that they want to turn themselves in when your crosshairs change from red to green. To capture them, approach from behind and press ⊗ when you see the 'Restrain' icon. Make sure that you have eliminated all nearby enemies before you attempt to shackle your captive, as their more militantly-inclined comrades will shoot them to prevent them from surrendering. You must capture four soldiers in total to accomplish the Bonus Objective (Fig. 1).

PRIMARY 1: SEARCH ROAD FOR MAHMOOD
Once you have achieved the Bonus Objective, re-group and order your team to FIRE AT WILL. Run to NAV CHARLIE and mount the TOW-launcher equipped Humvee.

PRIMARY 2 SEARCH VILLAGE
SECONDARY 1: SEARCH NORTH VILLAGE
2 Follow the dirt route north. Dismount approximately 120 meters from NAV DELTA and dispatch the Tango up on the hill to the right; note that another fighter will run down from the right side of the hill. The enemy has set up a roadblock a little further on: eliminate the troops at the burnt out cars. The best way to do this is to go up the hill to the left and assume a prone position (Fig. 2), then zoom in and pick off the enemies one by one. Try not to waste your TOW missiles as you only have 20 and you'll need at least two to handle an upcoming armored threat. Mount the armored assault vehicle and drive through the wrecked cars to NAV DELTA, then onward in the direction of NAV ECHO. 170 meters from the Nav Point you will spot the first tank, which is guarded by the enemy. Take control of the TOW launcher and destroy the metal giant from a safe distance. Be very careful that your vehicle is far away from the

tank. If your ammo runs out, dismount and use your AT-4 launcher, or aim the designator to call down an air strike. Either way, be careful when on foot, as the tank can move surprisingly fast, and will mow you down before you have time to blink if you give it half a chance. A second tank will be lying in wait just a short distance around the next bend.

3 A few meters past NAV ECHO you will find Mahmood's abandoned Ural truck. A burnt out vehicle blocks the road, so you must proceed on foot from this point. When you reach NAV FOXTROT, you will see a village to the southwest. Run left along the hills toward the lightly guarded rear entrance. There is also a path leading up the hill here, where an excellent sniper point (Fig. 3) enables you to safely pick off the soldiers who are patrolling in the village below. When you have neutralized the threat in the village, head back down to the building directly in front of you (Fig. 4). An enemy that you couldn't see from your sniper position will be waiting for you in the house.

4 Storm the dwelling using a flashbang grenade. Your teammates can take care of the guard in the house. Go inside and climb the stairs. Take the document on the table next to the window and exit the house.

PRIMARY 2: SEARCH VILLAGE
SECONDARY 2: SEARCH SOUTH VILLAGE
5 Run toward NAV INDIA, using the palm trees and rocks for cover as you advance. Zoom in and eliminate the guard at the entrance to the village, as well as his comrades a little further on. Watch out for the soldiers on the plateau to the east. Now run along the range of hills to the building at NAV INDIA. Another enemy will be hiding behind the house. Enter the building and take the document from the table (Fig. 5).

01

02

PRIMARY 3: CAPTURE GENERAL MAHMOOD
CROSSTALK 2: COMPLETE MISSION

6 The documents taken from the two houses reveal the location of Mahmood's hideout. It's time to flush him from his hole! Head southwest along the range of hills and take the mountain pass. Proceed in the direction of NAV KILO. An enemy will be waiting for you 100 meters from NAV LIMA. Eliminate him and continue along the path. Keep going straight ahead, past the trail that leads off to the right. A few meters further you will come to a plateau, which just happens to be a perfect spot for sniping at soldiers in the village below. When you have eliminated all visible enemies, follow the path left that takes you down to the rear of the village. If you missed any stragglers, you'll now have to take them out at close quarters, so be vigilant.

7 Run to the village square and neutralize the remaining enemies. More Tangos will emerge from a truck that draws up in front of the village. (Alternatively, you can take out the truck with your AT-4 if you haven't used it.)Hide behind palm trees, buildings and rocks and eliminate them from safe cover. Head to the central ruin (indicated by a gold star on your Compass Map) and approach the wooden floor-hatch, which is the entrance to Mahmood's underground lair (Fig. 6). Good work, Sailor! You have successfully completed your North African assignment!

03

04

05

06

NAUTICAL SALVAGE

ZULU
04
1ST
03
C
6
02
B
01
C
A
7
C
WHISKEY
YANKEE
02
1ST
03
1ST
03
B
02
C
VICTOR
XRAY
5
A
ROMEO
A
A
A
A
4
LIMA

KILO
2
3
A
LIMA
A
01
B
INDIA
A
JULIET
01
FOXTROT
C
1ST
A
DELTA
A
A
ECHO
S
1
A
CHARLIE
A

N

ASIA

SOCOM3
U.S. NAVY SEALS

GAME BASICS

WALKTHROUGH

MULTIPLAYER

EXTRAS

INDEX

HOW TO USE THE
WALKTHROUGH

NORTH AFRICA

SOUTH ASIA

POLAND

NAUTICAL SALVAGE

FRIEND OR FOE

HEART OF THE FIST

MISSION OBJECTIVES

PRIMARY	SECONDARY	BONUS	CROSSTALK
1. Secure Outpost		1. Obtain Intel	1. Overhear Arms Shipment
2. Secure Breakneck and Cargo		2. Overhear Arms Shipment	2. Recon Warehouse
3. Recon Warehouse		3. Obtain Shipping Manifest	3. Complete Mission
4. Meet Magpie and Extract			

OPTIMUM EQUIPMENT

AGENT	PRIMARY WEAPON	ATTACHMENT 1	ATTACHMENT 2	SECONDARY WEAPON	ATTACHMENT	EXTRA 1	EXTRA 2
Specter	M4A1	Suppressor 2	High Scope	Mark 23	Suppressor	Ammo	C4
Jester	M4A1	Suppressor 2	4x Scope	Mark 23	Suppressor	Ammo	Flashbang
Chopper	HK5	Suppressor 2	Red Dot	Mark 23	Suppressor	M67	Ammo
Flash	HK5	Suppressor 2	Red Dot	Mark 23	Suppressor	Ammo	M67

TERRAIN

The numerous palm trees and rocks dotted along the river bank provide protection against the raiders' attacks. Conditions in the shipyard call for street fighting tactics, with abandoned steel containers creating a maze of narrow alleyways. You will also have the opportunity to explore some of the derelict ships: the steel hulks are a labyrinth of claustrophobic chambers and sunken corridors.

When in the boat, always proceed slowly, monitoring your surroundings very closely. The moment you detect an enemy presence, order your team to FIRE AT WILL to eliminate the threat.

In the shipyard, keep a constant lookout for cover, and remain crouched or prone at all times as the place is riddled with raiders. Keep an eye out for good sniper positions, as these will provide a vital strategic advantage over your opponents.

In the area surrounding the warehouse near the end of the mission you must operate in total silence and only use a weapon with a suppressor to eliminate enemies. This is your sole means of obtaining vital extra information!

PRIMARY 1: SECURE OUTPOST

1 Mount the SOC-R at the insertion point and proceed to NAV CHARLIE, then on to NAV DELTA. You'll notice that you've been joined by an extra hand, a Brit called Bullfrog. He will man the on-board guns alongside your teammates, giving you some much-needed extra firepower. When you disembark Bullfrog will stay in the boat.

The first enemy will appear on the left, with another a little further up on the right bank. Order your team to FIRE AT WILL. Continue down river, where you'll soon spot another soldier lying in wait in the bushes on your left, around 100 meters from NAV DELTA. A second will immediately rush forward from the right: eliminate them both. Another raider is positioned on the platform on the right bank and two more enemies are waiting for you on the right bank at the Nav Point. Meanwhile your comrades will probably have neutralized the other enemies on the shore. If you look toward NAV ECHO you will see a bridge: a soldier is hiding in the undergrowth just left of it. Advance with extreme caution along the bank toward the bridge and eliminate the enemy. Proceed to NAV ECHO, then on to NAV FOXTROT where more fighters will be lying in wait on both banks. You will engage in a fierce battle at the bridge at NAV INDIA where approximately six raiders are holed up. Dismount, go prone, and zoom in with your scope to pick them off. You will see an enemy speedboat in the distance. Sneak on to the bridge, take aim and shoot the on-board gunners and pilot. Next, proceed to NAV JULIET. When you arrive, stop the boat close to the right bank, a few meters from the bridge. You have reached a raider outpost.

2 Creep north and issue the HOLD FIRE command. Before you reach the bridge, eliminate the two raiders on the right. Go prone at the other end of the bridge and use your scope to observe the outpost entrance. Pick off the two guards patrolling nearby at long range. Keep monitoring the watchtower where a sniper is laying in wait. He can't see you, but you can definitely see him: eliminate him with a good head shot. Now creep east to the right side of the camp. Take out the Tango in the watchtower. Guards will be patrolling around the entrance (Fig. 1): pick them off from a safe distance and continue to monitor the outpost interior. Shoot any other raiders that wander across your viewpoint. Stay down, creep northeast to the rear of the camp and sneak inside. When you have neutralized all the raiders in the outpost you will be cleared by HQ. You can then safely explore the vicinity.

TIP + TIP + TIP + TIP + TIP

Bonus 1: Obtain Intel
Ignore the radio instruction to return to the boat. Instead enter the outpost and take the map from the table (Fig. 2). Good work! You have achieved a Bonus Objective!

PRIMARY 2: SECURE BREAKNECK AND CARGO

3 Mount the SOC-R and proceed through NAV KILO in the direction of NAV LIMA. Stop the boat and dismount when you see a burning barrel on the right bank up ahead (don't worry about Bullfrog: he'll stay behind, minding the boat as always). Two more Tangos will be waiting to be wiped out here. Now continue toward NAV LIMA. Another raider will be lurking on the left bank some 100 meters from the Nav Point, so take him down. You will find that 40 meters from NAV LIMA the river is blocked by debris, so walk around the barrier to reach the other side (Fig. 3). Swim around the left flank to the shipyard entrance and order your team to HOLD FIRE. Assume a prone position and monitor the area closely. One guard is patrolling here, and another is positioned on the hull. Conserve your ammo and eliminate them both with a head shot. Run westward to the hulk and enter the steel colossus through the hole in the side. Follow the corridor to the stern. Once up on deck, shoot the raider to your left in the head, commandeer his mounted machine gun (Fig. 4) and mop up the raiders that are guarding the area below; this will handily conserve your ammo. If you have problems locating your quarry, zoom in and neutralize them with your M4A1.

01

02

03

SOCOM3

GAME BASICS

WALKTHROUGH

MULTIPLAYER

EXTRAS

INDEX

HOW TO USE THE
WALKTHROUGH

NORTH AFRICA

SOUTH ASIA

POLAND

NAUTICAL SALVAGE

FRIEND OR FOE

HEART OF THE FIST

Bonus 2: Overhear Arms Shipment
Crosstalk 1: Overhear Arms Shipment
A short cutscene will play just before you reach the warehouse, provided that you have remained undetected until this point. You overhear the enemies discussing plans and have therefore achieved another Bonus Objective and the first Crosstalk Objective. Completing this task unlocks the Destroy Arms Shipment Bonus and Crosstalk Objectives in the next mission.

PRIMARY 3: RECON WAREHOUSE
CROSSTALK 2: RECON WAREHOUSE

6 If your team is still holding their position back in the shipyard, order them to FOLLOW. You're going to need their support from now on, and stealth is no longer a priority. Shoot the guard that is standing directly in front of the warehouse to the east. Two raiders will be lurking in a small hut to your right. Aim through the window and shoot them both in the head. Now enter the warehouse and take the steps up to NAV YANKEE. A cutscene kicks in. Your mission: Stop the truck!

TIP + TIP + TIP + TIP + TIP

Bonus 3: Obtain Shipping Manifest
Take the Shipping Manifest from the table in the warehouse to accomplish another Bonus Objective.

PRIMARY 4: INTERCEPT TRUCK
PRIMARY 5: MEET MAGPIE AND EXTRACT
CROSSTALK 3: COMPLETE MISSION

7 Step onto the iron walkway at the back of the warehouse. Two enemies are waiting for you in the warehouse below. Eliminate them by firing through the iron grating from above (or snipe the enemies through the second floor window), then head down the steps. Another raider will cross your path as you exit the building: take him out, then proceed through the gap in the fence to your left. Look left along the building and neutralize the enemy on the wooden balcony up above. Run towards NAV ZULU and eliminate the Tango across the pond to the north. Meanwhile, the truck has escaped with the dangerous shipment on board. Proceed to NAV ZULU to rendezvous with Magpie and finish the mission.

4 Go back through the hulk to the yard and turn right, skirting along the sides of the containers on your way to NAV ROMEO. If you haven't wiped out all the raiders, deal quickly with those still hiding among the containers. Creep south, monitoring the upper deck of the hulk on the left, as another two Tangos are patrolling here: pick them off with a head shot each. You will see the next two enemies a little further south and you can also take them out from here. Now proceed southwest. Run across the yard to the open container and sneak along to the end. Use the yellow crane as cover and neutralize the three enemies that are standing to the south. Continue to NAV VICTOR. Run to the end of the yard and go through the hole in the ship's hull. Two enemies will be lurking just around the next corner. Sneak along silently, lean out and take them down from safe cover. Proceed to NAV WHISKEY and set a C4 charge to blow open the door that leads to the cargo deck (Fig. 5). Cross the empty deck and go through the doorway on the left. Congratulations, you have just completed a Primary Objective, but you still have a lot of work to do. An enemy will be lying in wait to the right, just beyond the next doorway. Eliminate him! Advance through the hull until you reach the exit.

5 Order your team to HOLD POSITION and HOLD FIRE. Go prone and crawl through the exit. Monitor your right flank and look north. Two guards will be patrolling near the open container. Wait until they walk into view then zoom in and pick them off. Now advance carefully northeast. Look up to see a manned machine gun on a watchtower to the right. Zoom in and pick off the gunner. Climb up the crates on the left of the watchtower (Fig. 6). Assume a prone position on top of the crates and silently take out the raider patrolling here. Now climb down the ladder and sneak north along the path. Take out the guy who is standing to the far north.

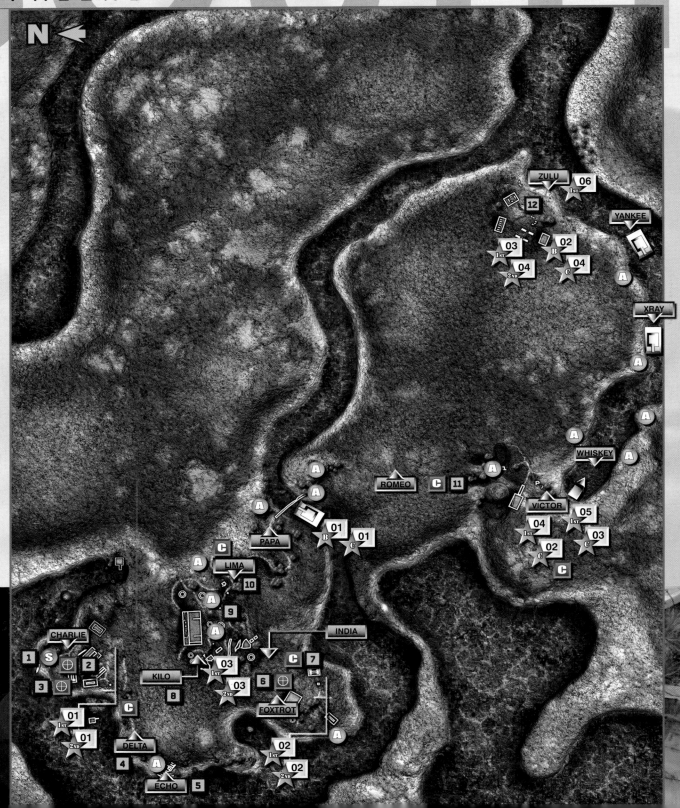

N

ZULU 06 1ST

12

YANKEE

03 1ST
02 B
04

04 2ND
04 C

XRAY

A

A

A

WHISKEY A

ROMEO C 11

A

A

A

VICTOR 05 1ST

04 1ST
02 C
03 C

C

PAPA

B 01
01 C

C

LIMA

10

A

9

A

CHARLIE

1 S
2
3

C

01 1ST
01 2ND

DELTA

4
A

ECHO 5

KILO

8

03 1ST
03 2ND

INDIA

C 7

6

FOXTROT

A

02 1ST
02 2ND

ASIA

SOCOM3
U.S. NAVY SEALS

GAME BASICS

WALKTHROUGH

MULTIPLAYER

EXTRAS

INDEX

HOW TO USE THE
WALKTHROUGH

NORTH AFRICA

SOUTH ASIA

POLAND

NAUTICAL SALVAGE

FRIEND OR FOE

HEART OF THE FIST

MISSION OBJECTIVES

PRIMARY	SECONDARY	BONUS	CROSSTALK
1. Gather Intel at First Village	1. Uncover the Mole (in first village)	1. Destroy Arms Shipment	1. Destroy Arms Shipment
2. Gather Intel at Second Village	2. Uncover the Mole (in second village)	2. Obtain Intel	2. No Non-Combatants killed
3. Disrupt Raider Operations	3. Cut Communications		3. Liberate Village
4. Liberate Magpie's Village	4. Demo Cache		4. Obtain Intel
5. Keep Magpie Alive			
6. Move to Extract			

OPTIMUM EQUIPMENT

AGENT	PRIMARY WEAPON	ATTACHMENT 1	ATTACHMENT 2	SECONDARY WEAPON	ATTACHMENT	EXTRA 1	EXTRA 2
Specter	M16A2	High Scope	Rifle Laser	9mm pistol	Suppressor	Flashbang	Satchel
Jester	M4A1	Suppressor 2	High Scope	Mark 23	Suppressor	Flashbang	Satchel
Chopper	L96AW	-	High Scope	9mm Pistol	Suppressor	Flashbang	Satchel
Flash	M4A1	Suppressor 2	4x Scope	9mm Pistol	Suppressor	M67	Satchel

TERRAIN

This mission takes you to a hot, humid, jungle region. During the long campaign, you will pass stunning beaches and cross the picturesque Karnaphuli River. Plumes of mist rising from the tropical waters may seem tranquil, but the situation you're about to confront will demand focus and concentration!

You will have ample opportunity to stalk and ambush your foe in the lush jungle vegetation. Proceed with caution however: the Fist and Fire raiders have intimate knowledge of the area, and can turn the tables on you with little notice. Advance very cautiously, constantly monitor your surroundings, and make good use of the ample cover the jungle affords. Choose your targets carefully and do not compromise your stealth until you absolutely have to. The key to jungle warfare is patience and steady reduction of opposing forces; full-on assault is not advised. When you reach your strategic objective, there will be plenty of opportunities to confront your enemies in the open as they fiercely defend their communication lines and supplies, and patience in the beginning will significantly reduce the resistance you will encounter at your final mission objective.

Wherever possible, avoid walking unprotected in the middle of a path. Instead, look for unguarded routes on either side, off the beaten track. The enemy can easily spot you from distance as you advance across open sections of beach: your camouflage is designed to mimic jungle vegetation, not sand, so keep well clear of these areas.

Enemies are constantly hiding in the mists swirling over the Karnaphuli River and the huge risk here is that you spot the marauding raiders or speedboats too late.

SECONDARY 1: UNCOVER THE MOLE (IN FIRST VILLAGE)

1 Command your team members to HOLD FIRE and HOLD POSITION. You should also initially command Magpie to HOLD POSITION (to do so, first select 'Friendly' in the TCM). Run down the path leading south. Crouch down at the third rock as a guard will appear in front of you. Scope in on your enemy and eliminate the threat. Continue sneaking south until you come to a rock on your left. Now sneak along the left side of the rock (Fig. 1), using the bushes as cover. A guard will be patrolling nearby. He must not detect your presence, so shoot him!

2 Use Binoculars or your scope to watch the village below very closely from your safe position. You will see two villagers in the immediate vicinity and can monitor one of them from your position: he's working the field to the south. When you aim your binoculars at him (or zoom in with your scope), a cutscene will reveal whether or not he's the mole. If he is the traitor, your Secondary Objective will be completed and you don't have to spy on the second villager. However, if you don't get a 'heads-up' that the mole has been revealed, you will have to check up on the second villager. Sneak west, then proceed northwest and go behind the house. Watch out for guards patrolling the routes.

3 Peek around the corner at the end of the hut. A guard could be patrolling or may appear directly in front of you. When the coast is clear, use the binoculars to check the beach area where the second villager is working. Once you have exposed the mole, you will have achieved your Secondary Objective.

PRIMARY 1: GATHER INTEL AT FIRST VILLAGE

Systematically neutralize the five guards that are patrolling around the village, keeping well under cover. One raider will be patrolling just ahead of you and another will be stationed in the hut in the center of the village. A third will be watching the area to your left, close to the first villager you were observing earlier. The fourth raider will be guarding the beach, and the last will be patrolling the rear of the village next to the beach. Note how the enemies change positions: they will immediately move to another location the moment they detect your presence. Issue the FOLLOW command to get the rest of the team to re-join you, especially Magpie.

Now approach your friendly villager, ie, the one who isn't the mole! He will tell Magpie some important information.

SOCOM3
U.S. NAVY SEALS

GAME BASICS

WALKTHROUGH

MULTIPLAYER

EXTRAS

INDEX

HOW TO USE THE
WALKTHROUGH

NORTH AFRICA

SOUTH ASIA

POLAND

NAUTICAL SALVAGE

FRIEND OR FOE

HEART OF THE FIST

SECONDARY 2: UNCOVER THE MOLE (IN SECOND VILLAGE)

4 Run to NAV DELTA. When you get there you will spot two raiders patrolling up ahead. They are coming straight for you! Assume a prone position to the left of the path, zoom in and take them both out. Now advance cautiously to the ruins. The next three enemies will also be lying in wait for you here. Stay on the right and creep along behind the large rocks on the beach. One raider will be standing on the right by the ruins and another will be patrolling nearby to the left. Aim for their heads and shoot them from a safe distance. Continue crawling toward NAV ECHO. An enemy will materialize from the mist so take him out. Now your route is clear! Again, note how the enemies change positions: they will immediately move to another location the moment they detect your presence.

5 Order the team to HOLD FIRE. Follow the path northeast along the beach. At the shore, run left along the rocks and through the water to the village. Sneak to the village entrance in the direction of NAV FOXTROT and make sure you stay on the right side of the path. At the end of the hill, command your team to GET DOWN. Go prone and use the binoculars or scope to monitor the village (Fig. 2).

6 Two more villagers will be working here: watch them through the binoculars from your position. The first villager is busy in front of the house to the east. The other villager is by the well to the southeast. If the villagers don't appear at their positions immediately, just wait a few moments. However, under no circumstances should you break cover. You have now found the second mole and completed another Secondary Objective.

PRIMARY 2: GATHER INTEL AT SECOND VILLAGE

Command your team to FOLLOW. After eliminating the two guards in your immediate vicinity, turn your attention to the remaining enemies. One of them will be near the well in the center of the village. Another will be patrolling further away toward the beach. The last raider will be standing near the house that rests on stilts by the beach. Attack him from two flanks. While Bravo diverts his attention to the left, you can pick him off from the right.

Now lead Magpie to the friendly villager to learn the exact location of the raider base.

SECONDARY 3: DESTROY RAIDER COMMUNICATIONS

7 Run toward NAV INDIA, then in the direction of NAV JULIET until you reach a large rock with a path leading either side. Two raiders will be standing just beyond it. Creep silently from the left or right and have Bravo attack from the other flank to eliminate your quarry. Advance to NAV JULIET. You will see a small stone column next to a large rock (Fig. 3), approximately 30 meters from the Nav Point. Climb up the ledges to the left of the rock. Now the situation will really start to heat up: you are approaching one of the raiders' central communications installations. Remember to check your left flank for enemies as you climb up. A Tango will be patrolling on the raised walkway ahead. Take him out! Another will be standing to his left: deal with him in the same way. Sneak westward and take cover behind the columns. Now pick off the enemy patrolling to your right. Proceed cautiously to NAV KILO, keeping behind the wall at all times!

8 You can take out several enemies with the scope through the gap in the wall a few meters south (Fig. 4). Proceed a little further left and climb over the wall. If you haven't already done so, eliminate the raiders that are stationed on the large stone bridge opposite you. Drop down onto the path below and advance toward the Nav Point. The enemy's communications equipment is located in the ruins. Wipe out any raiders guarding the position and destroy the equipment (Fig. 5).

PRIMARY 4: LIBERATE MAGPIE'S VILLAGE
PRIMARY 5: KEEP MAGPIE ALIVE
BONUS 1: DESTROY ARMS SHIPMENT
CROSSTALK 1: DESTROY ARMS SHIPMENT
CROSSTALK 3: LIBERATE VILLAGE

9 Now enter the ruins to the southeast via the tunnel and climb up the ladder. If you did not already kill the two guards patrolling just beyond the hut, take them out now. Pick off the raider who is running north along the walls. Exit the hut cautiously and sneak left under the path, then straight along the wall. The next raider will appear in front of you shortly after: eliminate him! Another of his comrades will be lurking a little distance away in the ruins, next to the statue.

10 Now advance to NAV LIMA. Stealthily take out the first raider, and then his two companions around 60 meters from NAV PAPA.

04

05

! TIP + TIP + TIP + TIP + TIP

Bonus 1: Destroy Arms Shipment
Crosstalk 1: Destroy Arms Shipment
Walk toward NAV PAPA and stay on the right side next to the hill. When you've reached the end of the hill go right, towards the water's edge. Three speedboats will approach. Your best strategy now is to kill the driver to stop the boats, then take out the other passengers. Note: the boats will only appear if you have completed the objective Overhear Arms Shipment in the previous mission.

At the bridge, take out the enemy on top (Fig. 6) and then another manning a machine gun turret at the opposite end. Head west, go prone next to the bridge, and switch to your scope. Shoot all the Tangos on the opposite bank, then cross the bridge. You will run straight into an ambush just beyond the bridge, with four enemies lurking to your left. As soon as you approach their position, these guys will run away. Try to eliminate them all, otherwise they will be waiting for you further on toward NAV ROMEO.

11 On your way to NAV VICTOR you will meet an old friend of Magpie's. He describes how the raiders destroyed his village. Now run to the village and kill all the enemies at the entrance. Three raiders are a little further on toward the beach: neutralize them!

Three enemy boats will be moored by the side of the river; a dozen raiders storm in from two flanks. Eliminate all the enemies from safe cover. Look for protection behind the burning huts near the beach or find some rocks or palm trees. Be warned, this is a very tough battle. You will need to take it slow and sure, and keep

06

Magpie well away from the action. If you succeed in routing the raiders and saving the villagers you will automatically complete two more objectives.

TIP + TIP + TIP + TIP + TIP

Crosstalk 2: No Non-Combatants killed
Crosstalk 3: Liberate Village
Take out all enemies in Magpie's village to complete Crosstalk Objective 3. If all civilians remain alive you will have completed this second Crosstalk Objective.

PRIMARY 3: DISRUPT RAIDER OPERATIONS
SECONDARY 4: DEMO CACHE
PRIMARY 7: MOVE TO EXTRACT

Hey, look, it's Bullfrog waiting for you in the boat! Boy is he relentless! Mount the SOC-R and proceed to NAV WHISKEY, then move on to NAV X-RAY. Two enemies will appear on the left bank: use the on-board guns to wipe them out. A raider speedboat will appear some 60 meters from the Nav Point and another Tango will attack you from the right bank. Again, use the on-board gun to eliminate them and destroy their boat! Now advance to NAV YANKEE. The next enemy speedboat will emerge from of the mist from the right. Destroy it! Another raider is lying in wait nearby on the right bank. Once you get rid of him, proceed to NAV YANKEE and then on to NAV ZULU.

12 A total of seven enemies will be waiting for you as you arrive at the base. Three will storm out of the building on the right, one will be in the trench near the supplies, two Tangos will be in the left sector of the base and the seventh one will be located in front of the left building. Look for cover behind crates or behind the building on the right. Neutralize all the enemies and enter the building on the right, then move and clear the building on your left. Make sure you obtain the intel from the table (see below), then place the satchel charge in the trench when you see the Special Action icon. Run to the Extraction Zone to finish the mission.

TIP + TIP + TIP + TIP + TIP

Bonus 2: Obtain Intel
Crosstalk 4: Obtain Intel
You will find an important document on the table behind the door in the building to the left (Fig. 7). Take it to accomplish another Bonus and Crosstalk Objective.

SPECTER
JESTER
CHOPPER
FLASH

x5/30   x5

07

HEART OF THE FIST

N

01
2ND

A
INDIA

C
JULIET

KILO

04
1ST

C

06
C

A

02
2ND

6

C

02
C

02
1ST

02
B

02

03

A

05
1ST

07
C

4

5

LIMA

7

PAPA

09

05
C

A

B

03
C

04

3

A

FOXTROT

01
B

01
C

03
1ST

C

03
2ND

8

ROMEO

ECHO

2

01
1ST

A
DELTA

CHARLIE

S   1

ASIA

SOCOM3
U.S. NAVY SEALS

GAME BASICS

WALKTHROUGH

MULTIPLAYER

EXTRAS

INDEX

HOW TO USE THE
WALKTHROUGH

NORTH AFRICA

SOUTH ASIA

POLAND

NAUTICAL SALVAGE

FRIEND OR FOE

HEART OF THE FIST

MISSION OBJECTIVES

PRIMARY	SECONDARY	BONUS	CROSSTALK
1. Secure Beach	1. Locate First Crate	1. Capture Ibrahim Abbas	1. Capture Ibrahim Abbas
2. Capture Hari Raman	2. Locate Second Crate	2. Find Terrorist Contact List	2. Capture Hari Raman
3. Locate the Breakneck Cargo	3. Locate Third Crate	3. Destroy Speedboat	3. Find Terrorist Contact List
4. Secure Breakneck Captain			4. Destroy Speedboat
5. Secure Breakneck First Mate			5. Locate the Breakneck Cargo
			6. Secure Breakneck Captain
			7. Secure Breakneck First Mate

OPTIMUM EQUIPMENT

AGENT	PRIMARY WEAPON	ATTACHMENT 1	ATTACHMENT 2	SECONDARY WEAPON	ATTACHMENT	EXTRA 1	EXTRA 2
Specter	M16A2	High Scope	Rifle Laser	226	Suppressor	Flashbang	C4
Jester	M4A1	Suppressor 2	Low Scope	Mark 23	Suppressor	Flashbang	Flashbang
Chopper	L96AW	-	High Scope	9mm Pistol	Suppressor	Flashbang	Flashbang
Flash	M4A1	Suppressor 2	4x Scope	9mm Pistol	Suppressor	Flashbang	Flashbang

TERRAIN

The beach area is very flat, affording you a clear line of sight, but the same holds true for your enemy, so be careful! The shoreline is very heavily guarded; the enemy has dug three trenches and set up machine gun posts to defend them. A large number of soldiers also patrol this sector armed to the teeth, so proceed with extreme caution. Always stay out of sight when close to the barricades, and fire at the enemy from under cover. You will find plenty of wooden pallets and corrugated iron sheets lining the barbed-wire fence. Should you stray to the wrong side of the barricades, crawl back to safety and hope no one noticed.

The overall strategy for navigating the tunnel system is the same as for fighting in narrow city streets. Use the many wooden pallets, crates and boxes for cover; sneak silently to the corners and peek ahead; open all doors with extreme caution, and breach rooms or areas by deploying flashbang grenades.

PRIMARY 1: SECURE BEACH

1 From the beach, proceed slowly west on the narrow strip of land next to the water. Use your scope to zoom in through the barricade and take out the first two soldiers at the mounted guns just a few meters away. Another enemy will be standing slightly to the left, by a palm tree: neutralize him with a well-aimed head shot. Keep close to the barricade and sneak along to NAV CHARLIE. The water is deep in places, so expect to have to swim some of the way, and be sure to stay submerged to maximize your cover. Look to the right when you're approximately 20 meters away from the Nav Point. Move in tight to the barricade and peek through one of the gaps (Fig. 1). Stand up and scope in on the second bunker, using your sharpshooting skills to pick off the guards stationed behind the guns.

Crouch back down and advance cautiously along the barricade. Peek around the next corner; an enemy will be lurking just a few meters to your left! Quickly neutralize him. You should now get a message saying that the beach is clear and you have fulfilled your Primary Objective. However, you should still take the time to clear the beach of enemies to ease your passage through the rest of the mission. Proceed toward NAV DELTA, sticking to the right side of the barricade.

2 The next enemy will be just to the left of the second bunker. When you have eliminated him, advance cautiously toward the Nav Point. Two more raiders will appear approximately 30 meters from NAV DELTA. Assume a prone position, then zoom in and pick them off. At NAV DELTA keep left and sneak to the third bunker. From cover, pick off the three enemies whose heads are visible above the bunker. Another raider will run toward you from the direction of NAV ECHO: take him out immediately. Proceed along the path to NAV ECHO.

PRIMARY 3: LOCATE THE BREAKNECK CARGO
CROSSTALK 5: LOCATE THE BREAKNECK CARGO
SECONDARY 1: LOCATE FIRST CRATE

3 The path bends sharply to the right just after you come to a large rock 50 meters to NAV FOXTROT. Creep to the right corner and lean out, then zoom in and scope the two guards, starting with the one manning the mounted gun. Follow the path toward NAV FOXTROT. Go left at the turret to discover a path leading to a small camp. Go prone 40 meters from NAV INDIA and crawl forward until you see the first hut. Stay on the right side, next to the hill. From time to time you will see an enemy emerge from the hut: kill him. Now continue in the direction of NAV INDIA, keeping to the right side of the path. You should see three enemies to the north: two of them just a few meters in front of you; the third Tango will be manning the turret. After killing them all, move on to NAV INDIA. Take out the enemy who is patrolling to your left. Just behind his position you will find the first cargo crate (Fig. 3). Use the turret gun to kill the enemies who are patrolling near NAV JULIET.

Bonus 1: Capture Ibrahim Abbas
Crosstalk 1: Capture Ibrahim Abbas

You must avoid killing the man wearing the red bandana: he is Ibrahim Abbas, the Fist and Fire's second-in-command. Abbas will lay down his weapon and surrender after the flashbang grenade explodes. When he does this, rush in and restrain him (Fig. 2).

IBRAHIM ABBAS

SPECTER
JESTER
CHOPPER
FLASH

RESTRAIN

02

Then go back to NAV INDIA and follow the path that leads east. 25 meters from NAV FOXTROT two enemies will attack: take them out. A few meters ahead on the left side you'll see a cave entrance. Order Bravo to BANG AND CLEAR the cave. Shoot the Tango who runs out. Once Abbas is secured, proceed toward NAV INDIA.

PRIMARY 3: LOCATE THE BREAKNECK CARGO
CROSSTALK 5: LOCATE THE BREAKNECK CARGO
SECONDARY 2: LOCATE SECOND CRATE

4 Run to NAV JULIET: enter the stone building and disable the generator. This will turn out the lights in the tunnel system. Run into the hut opposite and go through the large hole in the wall on your right (Fig. 4). Take the wooden steps down into the tunnel. At the bottom, sneak toward NAV KILO. Two enemies will be standing in the barracks. Eliminate them and take cover behind the wall. Advance to NAV LIMA, but watch out: a raider will be waiting for you up ahead at the entrance to the lower room. Seek cover behind a crate and sneak along. The next guard will be lurking to the rear of the lower room. After you have taken him out, you will find the Breakneck's second cargo crate (Fig. 5) right in front of you.

SPECTER
JESTER
CHOPPER
FLASH

01

SPECTER
JESTER
CHOPPER
FLASH

03

SPECTER
JESTER
CHOPPER
FLASH

04

GAME BASICS

WALKTHROUGH

MULTIPLAYER

EXTRAS

INDEX

HOW TO USE THE
WALKTHROUGH

NORTH AFRICA

SOUTH ASIA

POLAND

NAUTICAL SALVAGE

FRIEND OR FOE

HEART OF THE FIST

PRIMARY 4: SECURE BREAKNECK CAPTAIN
CROSSTALK 6: SECURE BREAKNECK CAPTAIN

5 Go down the passage at the back of the room and advance to NAV LIMA. Two enemies will be lurking there. One is standing directly ahead, the other is hidden behind the crates on the right: shoot them both, then continue straight on. You will see a door on the right. Go past it and sneak down the steps at the end of the corridor. Kill the Tango to the south. Another raider will be guarding the captain of the Breakneck just around the corner to the right. Shoot the guard in the head and restrain the hostage. Another enemy will now approach from the south: take him out.

PRIMARY 2: CAPTURE HARI RAMAN
CROSSTALK 2: CAPTURE HARI RAMAN

6 Run back to the door, which is actually the entrance to Hari Raman's private quarters. Open the door and toss a flashbang grenade into the room. The villain will surrender without a struggle, so waste no time in handcuffing him (Fig. 6).

> **TIP + TIP + TIP + TIP + TIP**
>
> *Bonus 2: Find Terrorist Contact List*
> *Crosstalk 3: Find Terrorist Contact List*
> You will find the Contact List on a table in the room.

PRIMARY 3: LOCATE THE BREAKNECK CARGO
CROSSTALK 5: LOCATE THE BREAKNECK CARGO
SECONDARY 3: LOCATE THIRD CRATE

7 Now follow the path toward NAV PAPA. Command your team to FIRE AT WILL. Two guards will be patrolling in the next room. Use the walls, pallets and crates as cover as you attempt to take them down. This room also contains the Breakneck's third and final cargo crate.

PRIMARY 5: SECURE BREAKNECK FIRST MATE
CROSSTALK 7: SECURE BREAKNECK FIRST MATE

Follow the maze of passages to NAV PAPA and eliminate the two enemies that you run into on the way. Afterwards, proceed to NAV ROMEO.

8 Two guards will be waiting just beyond the tunnel exit. Advance slowly and use the crates in front of you as cover. A third enemy may approach you from the northeast: shoot all three!

> **TIP + TIP + TIP + TIP + TIP**
>
> *Bonus 3: Destroy Speedboat*
> *Crosstalk 4: Destroy Speedboat*
> **9** You will see a raider speedboat in the water ahead (Fig. 7). Use the turret gun at the hut to shoot the boat until it bursts into flames, completing another Bonus and Crosstalk Objective.

In the hut to your left you will see another guard and the Breakneck's First Mate. Deploy a flashbang grenade to clear the hut without harming the civilian. Shoot the enemy if he doesn't surrender, and restrain the hostage. Bravo Zulu! You have crushed the Fist and Fire, intercepted the deadly Breakneck cargo, and removed a serious threat that was menacing the global community: all in a day's work for the U.S. Navy SEALs!

SOCOM3
U.S. NAVY SEALS

GAME BASICS

WALKTHROUGH

MULTIPLAYER

EXTRAS

INDEX

MISSION OBJECTIVES

PRIMARY	SECONDARY	BONUS	CROSSTALK
1. Maintain Stealth Profile	1. Create a Diversion	1. Keep Guards Unsuspicious	1. Create a Diversion
2. Recon the Windmill	2. Bravo Overwatch		2. Bug the House
3. Recon the House	3. Bug the Computer		
4. Bug the House	4. Bug the Phone		
5. Move to Extraction			

OPTIMUM EQUIPMENT

AGENT	PRIMARY WEAPON	ATTACHMENT 1	ATTACHMENT 2	SECONDARY WEAPON	ATTACHMENT	EXTRA 1	EXTRA 2
Specter	SR-25	Suppressor 1	Thermal	226	Suppressor	Satchel	-
Jester	SR-25	Suppressor 1	Thermal	Mark 23	Suppressor	Smoke	Smoke
Deadpan	SR-25	Suppressor 1	Thermal	9mm Pistol	Suppressor	Smoke	Smoke
Coldkill	SR-25	Suppressor 1	Thermal	9mm Pistol	Suppressor	Smoke	Smoke

TERRAIN

This scenery in this location offers every opportunity for your unit to complete their assignment undetected. It is night, so the guards' vision will be greatly reduced. The derelict buildings, long grass and plentiful trees and rocks all provide numerous opportunities for cover. Never venture out on to the open road; always stay on the grassy verge. Ideally (with Bravo keeping watch), you should cause a distraction to lure the guards away from Bogdan Kurasz's house and out of the immediate vicinity.

The choice of lookout position is of great strategic importance: can your comrades monitor the whole area from their location and do they run the risk of being exposed and discovered?

Finally, you must avoid detection at all costs when making your escape to the Extraction Point.

PRIMARY 2: RECON THE WINDMILL

1 A truck will appear ahead of you at your insertion point. A terrorist will dismount and walk left along the road to the bridge. Another Tango will head toward the ruins opposite your current position. Start by issuing the HOLD FIRE command. Sneak

a little way toward the road, then creep a few meters to the west. Assume a prone position and shoot the terrorist to the left of the bridge in the head. His buddy will be patrolling in front of the ruins. You can easily pick him off from where you are (Fig. 1).

2 Another terrorist will be patrolling the hills to the north. Advance cautiously toward him. Ideally, crawl through the long grass nearby. Shoot him and head toward NAV CHARLIE, then on to NAV DELTA. Be careful, as there will still be guards patrolling in the area, despite your previous handiwork. When you reach a small pond bisected by a road, head to the west until you reach a rock: go right then drop to a prone position and wait for a hostile to wander directly toward you. Now follow the path to reach the windmill. A cutscene will kick in, and a terrorist will appear up ahead in front of the windmill. Move toward it, then turn east and walk to the corner. Peak round the edge and take out the enemy hiding there. Now crawl north behind the windmill and approach the entrance to automatically achieve the first Primary Objective. Another Tango will be patrolling to the east but you probably won't be able to see him at the moment: wait a few seconds and take him out when he arrives. Move to the hill with the tree on it which is located to the southeast. Over on the far side of the next hill you will see another guard lying in wait.

SECONDARY 1: CREATE A DIVERSION
CROSSTALK 1: CREATE A DIVERSION

3 Enter the windmill. Place a Satchel charge to blow the structure up and attract the terrorists' attention with the almighty explosion.

SECONDARY 2: BRAVO OVERWATCH
PRIMARY 3: RECON THE HOUSE

Now you must act quickly. Before the short cutscene plays, run straight to NAV ECHO, keeping to the left as much as possible. Take great care not to be detected, as the explosion will bring more terrorists running over to investigate the commotion. Don't waste your good work by running into the Tangos as they investigate the distraction. When you see the house up ahead, around 50 meters from the Nav Point, creep up the left path to the hill that leads to the Overwatch spot. Once you reach it tell Bravo to stay at this position and Coldkill will announce that she and Deadpan intend to watch the farmhouse.

4 Order Bravo to HOLD POSITION (Fig. 2), then approach the house to complete another Primary Objective. Infiltrate the house through the front door as soon as the two terrorists inside have headed for the windmill.

PRIMARY 4: BUG THE HOUSE
CROSSTALK 2: BUG THE HOUSE
SECONDARY 3: BUG THE COMPUTER
SECONDARY 4: BUG THE PHONE

A laptop will be on the table in the room to the right of the front door. Place the first bug there (Fig. 3). Now run into the adjoining room and place the second bug on the telephone (Fig. 4).

TIP + TIP + TIP + TIP + TIP

Be quick! One of the terrorists is on his way back to the farmhouse, and will discover you if you dawdle too much.

PRIMARY 5: MOVE TO EXTRACTION

5 Escape through the back door and go prone the instant you exit the house. Take aim at the enemy who is patrolling by the barn opposite and shoot him in the head. You can now choose how to complete the mission:

Route 1: Issue the FOLLOW command. Sneak back to NAV FOXTROT. You will come to a large open area around 50 meters from the Nav Point. Two enemies will be waiting there: one to the north and another to the northwest. Use the Thermal Scope to zoom in and neutralize them both, then proceed carefully toward the next Nav Point. If you turn left, monitor the left area particularly closely: a terrorist will be lurking in the grass by the crag! A second enemy will also be hiding approximately 50 meters away on the left. You may not have to kill this one, just sneak west through the long grass to the next Nav Point.

You will reach a road approximately 160 meters from NAV INDIA. Do not venture into the middle of the highway unprotected, as two more enemies will be lurking to the south. Instead, proceed along the right side of the road to stay under cover. When you reach the Extraction Point (at NAV INDIA), you will have completed the mission.

Route 2: You could also exit the combat zone in a Eurovan. The vehicle is on the road in front of the farm building opposite (Fig. 5).

Mount the van and drive directly to the Extraction Zone at NAV INDIA. You will pass two terrorists on the way. Keep as far away from them as possible to avoid detection.

In both these solutions, and of course during the entire mission, it is crucial to avoid attracting the guards' attention, otherwise, you will fail the Bonus Objective, and the mission as a whole.

03

04

05

SOCOM3
U.S. NAVY SEALS

GAME BASICS

WALKTHROUGH

MULTIPLAYER

EXTRAS

INDEX

HOW TO USE THE
WALKTHROUGH

NORTH AFRICA

SOUTH ASIA

POLAND

NIGHTCRAWLER

STATE SECURITY

RETRIBUTION

WATERLOGGED

BREWED CHAOS

PRIMARY	SECONDARY	BONUS	CROSSTALK
1. Find and Secure First Lady	None	None	1. First Lady Uninjured
2. Neutralize Enemy Boat Crew			2. Mission Success
3. Evacuate First Lady			
4. Prevent Terrorist Escape			

OPTIMUM EQUIPMENT

AGENT	PRIMARY WEAPON	ATTACHMENT 1	ATTACHMENT 2	SECONDARY WEAPON	ATTACHMENT	EXTRA 1	EXTRA 2
Specter	M4A1	Suppressor 2	4x Scope	Mark 23	Suppressor	Flashbang	HE
Jester	HK5	Suppressor 2	Red Dot	Mark 23	Suppressor	M67	Flashbang
Deadpan	HK5	Suppressor 2	Red Dot	Mark 23	Suppressor	M67	Flashbang
Coldkill	M4A1	Suppressor 2	4x Scope	Mark 23	Suppressor	M67	Flashbang

TERRAIN

The mission starts in a vast dockside area in the port of Gdansk, where containers, wooden pallets and barrels provide excellent cover. In the second part of the mission, you travel around the city's canals. Since you are vulnerable to attacks from the land when on the water, try and get to your destination as quickly as possible and don't hang around waiting to be shot at like a sitting duck. A short tunnel system takes you to the bombed-out inner city. You will find ample cover here behind vehicles, barrels, walls or among the ruins. You can also enter many of the buildings; the windows in the upper floors offer some superb sniper positions.

The success of this mission will depend on a quick trigger finger, accurate marksmanship and efficient teamwork. During the land-locked section of the operation, locate the enemy positions from a safe distance; let Bravo pin the enemy down with suppressing fire so that you can approach from the flank and attack the surprised enemy from behind their cover. Oh, and by the way, make sure you leave Poland's First Lady in a safe place at all times… but don't forget to go and collect her when it's safe!

PRIMARY 1: FIND AND SECURE FIRST LADY

1 Command the team to FIRE AT WILL, and advance cautiously southwest along the side of the container. You will see four terrorists and the First Lady by the loading crane. Always attack the enemy from two flanks to disorientate them: while Bravo is firing at the enemy from the right side of a container, run left and pick off the distracted terrorists from the opposite position.

PRIMARY 2: NEUTRALIZE ENEMY BOAT CREW

Once you have eliminated the first wave of Tangos, approach the First Lady. Turn your attention to the four enemies coming from the east. Use the same tactics as before to neutralize them, then order the First Lady to FOLLOW and have her join you in the terrorists' speedboat which is anchored to the east (Fig. 1).

2 On your way to NAV DELTA you will be confronted by two enemy assault boats. Concentrate on driving while your teammates get busy firing on the Tangos until their boats explode. Make sure you are far enough away from the vessel or the blast could injure both your team and the First Lady. Turn right into the tunnels at the Nav Point and follow the covered waterway. When you emerge, enemies will appear to the left and right on the street above the canal on your way to NAV ECHO. You are more vulnerable on the water, so it makes sense to avoid trying to shoot them until you reach dry land. A third enemy assault boat will be waiting some 90 meters from the Nav Point. Switch to the gun again and take out the terrorists. Don't worry about the guards on the street here: your teammate will use the second gun to deal with them. The danger will soon be eliminated, as there are relatively few opponents left in the area.

PRIMARY 3: EVACUATE FIRST LADY
CROSSTALK 1: FIRST LADY UNINJURED

3 Disembark at NAV ECHO and swim to the small entrance to the sewer system (Fig. 2). Turn right, left, then right again. Danger is lurking beyond the next tunnel. Order the First Lady to Hold Position and proceed cautiously. Proceed to NAV FOXTROT, killing the two terrorists that you meet on your way. Order the First Lady to FOLLOW, then climb the ladder, take the steps up and open the door at the end of the corridor.

4 You can see into the street from the window, so zoom in and shoot the four soldiers that are running toward your position. Advance toward NAV FOXTROT, but leave the First Lady behind. Sneak to the bend in the road. Dive for cover behind the trash container as three enemies will storm you from the left. Turn right when you have eliminated them. Run left along the wall and peek into the street that leads east. Two terrorists will be patrolling straight ahead of you and

two others are positioned a little further behind. Eliminate them at a safe distance. Take cover behind the white Eurovan parked on the right side of the street. The enemies you failed to eliminate just now will also take cover. One is to your right behind the next corner. A grenade will flush him out. Now advance cautiously east. Look for cover behind the trash container on the left and take out the next wave of terrorists. Three will be standing in the street on the left and two more lurking behind the open door of the bar directly in front of you. Order Bravo to go behind the car on the right to confuse the enemy!

5 The moment that you enter the bar, another terrorist may rush through the door on the other side of the building. Stay alert! If he doesn't come inside, you can pick him off from the window. Exit via the door on your right and sneak right along the wall. An enemy will be waiting just around the next corner: eliminate him. Take cover behind the trash container and neutralize the three terrorists that are standing in front of the bridge. Run back to the First Lady and order her to FOLLOW. Now return to the bridge, and ask her to wait when she joins you there. Cross the bridge toward NAV INDIA. Leave the street and advance through the ruins up ahead. Look for cover behind the walls; four enemies will ambush you! Take them all down. While Bravo engages the terrorists in the ruins, run around the outside of the derelict buildings and eliminate the remaining fighters from the rear. Now go back, collect the First Lady and leave her at the ruins.

6 Proceed through the red door at NAV INDIA and follow the stairway up. Advance all the way along to the end of the corridor and enter the room on the right. You can eliminate the two enemies that are lurking in the square from the window here. Fetch the First Lady again and escort her across the main square to NAV JULIET to complete a Primary and Crosstalk Objective.

PRIMARY 4: PREVENT TERRORIST ESCAPE
CROSSTALK 2: MISSION SUCCESS

7 Shortly afterward, a radio message will announce that two enemy vehicles are approaching from the north. Mount the Eurovan to the south and turn into the street leading south. There are three cars parked on the street: park the Eurovan between them to create a makeshift roadblock (Fig. 3).

The terrorists will stop their vehicle in the middle of the square and get out. Scope in and pick them off one-by-one, using nearby vehicles and barriers as cover. You will have successfully completed the last two objectives once you have defeated all of the enemies.

SPECTER
JESTER
DEADPAN
COLDKILL

x30/30   x5

03

RETRIBUTION

ECHO

DELTA
C
01
1ST
02
2ND

3
A

4 CHARLIE
A

2
01
2ND

6
5 FOXTROT
C
02
1ST

A

7

8

S 1

A

INDIA
03
1ST

A
A

04
1ST
9
C
8

N

WHISKEY
A
A

A

C 13
VICTOR
b

14
A

A

A
YANKEE

C
A
A
A
A
A
A
A
07
1ST

N

SOCOM3
U.S. NAVY SEALS

GAME BASICS

WALKTHROUGH

MULTIPLAYER

EXTRAS

INDEX

HOW TO USE THE
WALKTHROUGH

NORTH AFRICA

SOUTH ASIA

POLAND

NIGHTCRAWLER

STATE SECURITY

RETRIBUTION

WATERLOGGED

BREWED CHAOS

MISSION OBJECTIVES

PRIMARY	SECONDARY	BONUS	CROSSTALK
1. Neutralize Outer Patrols	1. Neutralize Road Patrols	1. Restrain Arms Dealer	1. Disable Generators
2. Clear Ruins Area	2. Neutralize House Patrols		2. Restrain Arms Dealer
3. Clear the House	3. Obtain Intel		
4. Infiltrate the Barn			
5. Infiltrate Salt Mine			
6. Secure Salt Mine			
7. Secure FATCAT			

OPTIMUM EQUIPMENT

AGENT	PRIMARY WEAPON	ATTACHMENT 1	ATTACHMENT 2	SECONDARY WEAPON	ATTACHMENT	EXTRA 1	EXTRA 2
Specter	M16A2	4x Scope	Rifle Laser	226	Suppressor	Ammo	Flashbang
Jester	M16A2	Thermal Scope	Rifle Laser	226	Suppressor	M67	M67
Deadpan	HK36	4x Scope	Suppressor	226	Suppressor	M67	M67
Coldkill	HK36	Thermal Scope	Suppressor	226	Suppressor	M67	M67

TERRAIN

The terrain you will traverse in this extensive mission is extremely varied. At the start you are dropped in the same area of operation that you infiltrated in the mission before last. Ruins, long grass, trees and rocks offer many hiding places and opportunities for cover. Lakes and rivers enable you to sneak unnoticed deep behind enemy lines. Even so, you should avoid venturing into the middle of roads unless specifically instructed to do so.

The second part of the mission takes you through a claustrophobic maze of tunnels in an old salt mine, where you will discover plenty of perfect hiding places along the way. If you disable the generators and black out the lights, the resulting cloak of darkness will enable you to move through the passages in relative safety. However, you should still check around every corner and monitor your immediate surroundings very carefully.

In the latter stages of the mission your enemies will be harder to spot as they hide in the long grass and lurk behind tall trees, barrels, wooden fences and hills. Use the rocks as cover to appreciably reduce your exposure to enemy fire.

PRIMARY 1: NEUTRALIZE OUTER PATROLS
SECONDARY 1: NEUTRALIZE ROAD PATROLS

1 Mount the armored assault vehicle and drive across the bridge in the direction of NAV CHARLIE. The first two enemies will be guarding the road to your left: shoot them in the head. Continue to the leaning tree on the hill. Eliminate the two enemies to the southwest, then drive along the right side of the hill. By taking out the two Tangos waiting here, you will complete the first Secondary Objective in the mission.

PRIMARY 1: NEUTRALIZE OUTER PATROLS
SECONDARY 2: NEUTRALIZE HOUSE PATROLS

2 Now drive to NAV CHARLIE, when you reach the Nav Point your gunner will automatically kill the two enemies to the south. Dismount the vehicle, then swim across to the far bank of the river to reach the hideout.

3 When you reach the other side, creep up the right side of the hill toward NAV DELTA. Shoot the two terrorists that are standing on the slope. Enter the house and kill the enemy lurking inside to accomplish one Primary and one Secondary Objective.

PRIMARY 2: CLEAR RUINS AREA

4 Go back to the armored assault vehicle and drive to NAV ECHO. You will spot two enemies to the southeast, roughly 100 meters from the Nav Point. One is standing next to a tree, the other just to the left. Shoot them both in the head, then dismount and run 20 meters to the right and head through the gap in the rock just before NAV ECHO. Continue along the river bank in the direction of NAV FOXTROT. Swim left when you are approximately 115 meters east of the Nav Point and crawl up the slope on the opposite bank toward NAV FOXTROT.

5 You will now see the familiar ruins up ahead: get ready for a fierce skirmish. While lying in the grass (Fig. 1) or on the road you can, from a safe distance, eliminate the terrorists that are patrolling the area. Creep north from behind the bombed-out building and neutralize them.

PRIMARY 3: CLEAR THE HOUSE

! TIP + TIP + TIP + TIP + TIP

Things start to get complicated. You can choose to run straight over the hill to NAV INDIA, but we strongly advise against this and would recommend that you take the route explained in points 6 and 7. The moment you set foot on the road you will find yourself in the middle of an enemy ambush: a platoon of soldiers and two technicals will be lying in wait for you here. Your situation could not be more dire, as you will find little cover along the highway and the technical drivers will try their very best to run you over!

6 Our suggested route is circuitous, but much safer. Advance along the road in front of the ruins. Follow the path north and, around 180 meters from NAV INDIA, go prone and crawl toward the Nav Point. Be warned, two enemies will spring up on the plateau ahead of you, so stay frosty and eliminate them! Leave the road and turn left (west) to reach the lake. Run left along the path leading to the windmill that you reduced to rubble in the mission before last. Survey your demolition work in the harsh light of day. The large sails, once the powerhouse behind the millstone, lie in pieces in the rubble.

7 Run under the sail to the rear of the mill. Now proceed to NAV INDIA, which should be roughly 100 meters away (Fig. 2). Sneak toward the large rock just ahead of you. An enemy will be patrolling the path to the right (east) of your position. Advance to the left side of the rock and kill the enemy to the northeast. Proceed toward the hill with the tree just in front of the house. An enemy will appear from the left (north) approximately 60 meters from NAV INDIA, so neutralize him.

Scramble to the tree and sprint to the house entrance. Open the door and dispatch the enemy who is lurking behind it. Shoot the next guy who storms toward you from the right. Meanwhile an enemy technical will draw up outside. You will be protected from hostile fire when in the house, so run to the back door to complete a Primary Objective.

GAME BASICS

WALKTHROUGH

MULTIPLAYER

EXTRAS

INDEX

HOW TO USE THE
WALKTHROUGH

NORTH AFRICA

SOUTH ASIA

POLAND

NIGHTCRAWLER

STATE SECURITY

RETRIBUTION

WATERLOGGED

BREWED CHAOS

PRIMARY 4: RECON THE BARN

8 Proceed to the back door, open it and drop to a prone position, but under no circumstances leave the house. To the north you will see a technical with two passengers and one soldier a little way behind. Two additional technicals will be circling the house. (Note that if you took out any technicals earlier in the mission they will not appear here). Keep under cover in the house and take out all the enemies: fire through the windows or doors and use the wall in front of the hideout for cover. Once you have eliminated all the terrorists, look to the barn. A Tango is standing just in front of the farm building, so take him out from distance and creep toward the barn. Look out for his buddy who may approach you from the south. From here, leave Bravo behind and command them to FIRE AT WILL. Go to the right entrance of the barn and peek inside. An NSO guard will be crouched in front of the straw bales (Fig. 3), and another hiding just behind. Order Bravo to storm the front entrance to distract the Tangos, and then run left, all the way round to the side entrance, and shoot them from behind. Now run through the two doors on the right to achieve another Primary Objective. Jump down through the trapdoor in the back room to enter the salt mine.

PRIMARY 5: INFILTRATE SALT MINE
SECONDARY 3: OBTAIN INTEL

9 Issue the HOLD FIRE command and follow the tunnel down. A terrorist will be patrolling at the bottom of the long spiral walkway in the huge vaulted cavern: eliminate him. Follow the passageway until it forks, approximately 17 meters from NAV LIMA. Sneak into the area on the left where you can hear a generator running. This will achieve the Primary Objective Infiltrate Salt Mine. Look to the right, around the next corner. Take aim and pick off the guard with a single shot.

TIP + TIP + TIP + TIP + TIP

Crosstalk 1: Disable Generators (First Generator)
Disable the generator in front of you (Fig. 4). As you proceed through the mines, listen for the sounds of running generators. There are a total of four you must disable to complete the Crosstalk Objective.

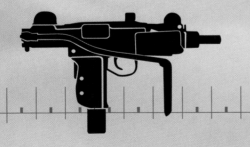

10 Follow the tunnel south. Two terrorists will be lurking in the briefing room on the right. Eliminate them, then collect the intel from the laptop on the table to accomplish the Secondary Objective (Fig. 5). Return to the tunnel and head south.

**Crosstalk 1: Disable Generators
(Second Generator)**
*You will find the second generator in the room where
you eliminated the two enemies and found the intel: disable it.*

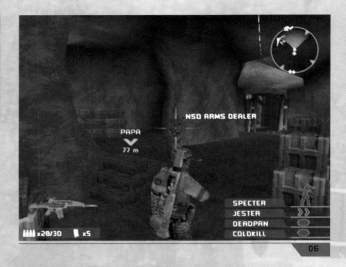

06

BONUS 1: RESTRAIN ARMS DEALER
CROSSTALK 2: RESTRAIN ARMS DEALER

Now you must avoid attracting the guards' attention at all times, otherwise you will fail your next Bonus Objective. Peek right at the next junction into the area up ahead, but don't venture up there. If the coast is clear, advance a little further forward to the next bend. Issue the HOLD POSITION command.

11 Refrain from opening fire in the armory until you've captured your quarry. The terrorist in this room just happens to be the very arms dealer that you are looking for. He will surrender when you approach him. Restrain him to complete a Bonus and Crosstalk Objective (Fig. 6). Two enemies may now storm the room if the guards in the surrounding area have been alerted to your presence. If so, eliminate them.

07

**Crosstalk 1: Disable Generators
(Third Generator)**
*The third generator is located to the right of the
walkway in the room where you captured the arms dealer
(Fig. 7).*

PRIMARY 6: SECURE SALT MINE

Now order your teammates to FOLLOW and FIRE AT WILL. Sneak down the passage to the southeast and eliminate the two enemies. Return to the room where you secured the arms dealer and proceed to the passage that leads east. Shoot another terrorist. Return to the third generator and follow the walkway on the left of the generator. Run north along the path. Go right at the next fork and take out the terrorist lurking around the corner. Re-enter the tunnel and continue north.

08

**Crosstalk 1: Disable Generators
(Fourth Generator)**
*Disable the fourth and final generator 55 meters
from NAV PAPA (Fig. 8) to complete the Crosstalk
Objective.*

PRIMARY 7: SECURE FATCAT

12 Go in the direction of NAV PAPA and turn left at the next fork, kill the guard in this room and go back where you just came from. Now move forward to NAV PAPA, turn left at the next fork and go prone. Crawl forward to the platform to the left of the scaffolding. From here, look left past the planks and pick off the guard opposite. Now climb up onto the scaffolding. Run forward a few meters and kill the enemies below to secure the salt mine and to accomplish Primary Objective 6. Head down to NAV PAPA. Follow the path that leads to NAV ROMEO (Fig. 9). Three enemies will appear a few meters ahead, from the direction of NAV VICTOR. Use the walls for cover or crouch to minimize your exposed target area. When these guys have breathed their last, follow the tunnel to the next bend. Another enemy will be lying in wait just beyond–take him out, then emerge blinking into the welcome daylight.

13 The next two enemies are waiting to your right. Use trees, barrels and planks as cover to evade their fire, then run south and follow the path east toward the abandoned train wagons. Advance cautiously, avoiding the path. The first enemy will appear from the north when you reach the first wagon. Stay under cover and take him out with some well-aimed shots. Keep to the left of the second wagon and sneak through the ferns. The next terrorist will emerge from the east. After him, more enemies will head toward you from behind the second wagon and also from the south. Pick them off from a prone position. Once you have neutralized them all, continue creeping toward the third wagon. A further enemy will jump out at you from the northeast. Kill him and advance right along the path from which the terrorist approached. Another enemy will spring out from behind the wrecked vehicle to the southeast: eliminate the threat. Run north in the direction of NAV XRAY where you will see a corroded barrel to your left. Head down to the river.

09

14 At the other side of the bank, climb up the series of ledges. Be warned, at the top, two terrorists will be standing over to your right. Climb the upper-left ledge and peak out from behind the rock to safely eliminate them. Now proceed northeast on your perilous journey. Three enemies will appear from the path below from the northwest, 60 meters from NAV YANKEE. Eliminate them from a safe distance as they will throw grenades if you get too close to them. When you reach the wagon, kill the two terrorists lurking to the northeast, then proceed toward NAV ZULU. Stay on the right until you come to a barbed-wire fence, and continue in the direction of NAV ZULU. Between five and seven enemies will storm the field in front of you. Take them out from a safe distance. Meanwhile, your teammates can deploy grenades and/or lay down suppressing fire to help contain the Tangos. Go prone and sneak forward in the direction of NAV ZULU, paying close attention to the surroundings. Continue to crawl through the long grass and remove the danger with two good head shots. You will sight two guards to the west, around 25 meters from the Nav Point. Once you have cleared the route to the shack, storm the dilapidated hideout and restrain FATCAT to achieve the final mission objective and complete your assignment (Fig. 10).

TIP + TIP + TIP + TIP + TIP

If you had followed the main path, you would have crossed the bridge on the left, but this route would have exposed you to more enemy attacks.

10

N

XRAY
04
03 1ST
01 01
C
B

WHISKEY
7
VICTOR
02 1ST

ROMEO

PAPA
LIMA

C 6

KILO

5

JULIET C

INDIA
4
FOXTROT

01
2 1ST
3
S
CHARLIE
DELTA
1

MISSION OBJECTIVES

PRIMARY	SECONDARY	BONUS	CROSSTALK
1. Locate Dr. Mironova		1. No Terrorists Engaged	1. No Terrorists Engaged
2. Locate Krzystof Gryc			
3. Move to Extract			
4. Maintain Stealth			

OPTIMUM EQUIPMENT

AGENT	PRIMARY WEAPON	ATTACHMENT 1	ATTACHMENT 2	SECONDARY WEAPON	ATTACHMENT	EXTRA 1	EXTRA 2
Specter	M4A1	Suppressor 2	Thermal	Mark 23	Suppressor	Smoke	Smoke
Jester	SR-25	Suppressor 1	4x Scope	Mark 23	Suppressor	Smoke	Smoke
Deadpan	552	Suppressor 1	Low Scope	226	Suppressor	Smoke	Smoke
Coldkill	552	Suppressor 1	Low Scope	226	Suppressor	Smoke	Smoke

TERRAIN

You are virtually invisible to the enemy under the comforting cloak of darkness and will be able to go about your business all but unseen in the flooded streets of the Polish city of Wroclaw. Bridges and rooftops provide plentiful sniper positions. So much for the positive aspects, now for the bad news! More enemies patrol this area than in any other assignment so far! The interiors of the two target buildings are crawling with Tangos, so infiltration will be difficult. Luckily, the two target individuals that you need to scope out can be located from outside.

01

02

PRIMARY 1: LOCATE DR. MIRONOVA

1 Order Bravo to HOLD POSITION. Run toward NAV CHARLIE. An enemy will be patrolling behind the two red trash containers. Wait until he is far enough to the south to enable you to sneak east unseen. Your objective is the brewery that you can see up ahead, easily identifiable by its distinctive chimney stack (Fig. 1). Make your way cautiously there. You will see terrorists to the north and east, but luckily they will ignore you as you wade across to the brewery. You will see a tree in front of the building, with a ladder to the right of it. Climb the ladder to the roof. Below you to the south you will see an enemy patrol. If the Tango is close to you, order Able to HOLD POSITON. Once the Tango has gone, command Jester to follow you. Proceed to the loft window (Fig. 2) and climb through. Advance to the railing and use your thermal scope to check out the area below. Dr. Mironova will be standing at the back of the room, to the right (Fig. 3). You may have to move a little further left along the platform to spot her, so be sure to remain out of sight. Zoom in on her to accomplish the first Primary Objective in this mission.

PRIMARY 2: LOCATE KRZYSTOF GRYC

2 Climb back down the ladder and head south until you come to a row of houses (Fig. 4). An enemy may be standing directly in front of you to the south. If so, wait until he looks west. Avoid getting to close to him and advance east. Stay on the right by the row of houses. At the end of the street, proceed north, sticking close to the houses on the right.

3 70 meters from NAV FOXTROT there are two more terrorists to the left. Proceed cautiously to the next house and monitor the nearby terrorists. After a short while the two guys will wander off westward. When they are out of sight, continue running north, still on the right. The sniper might see you if you move quickly, run into the open, or otherwise draw attention to yourself. Run past him toward NAV FOXTROT and stay on the right.

03

4 Turn west at the end of the street and sneak slowly forward. Keep to the left of the two vehicles, as an enemy is patrolling on the first floor to the right. Another terrorist is also on the bridge up ahead, but don't worry, he can't see you. At NAV INDIA, turn north, to the right of the bridge. Run up the steps to a much-needed checkpoint before climbing over the fence.

the south. Hold on until the enemy boat has gone past and then advance cautiously west past the guard. Keep to the right along the building. Another guard will be patrolling to the left near to NAV XRAY and will soon be joined by an enemy boat. Wait until they have disappeared and then run to the extraction point.

TIP + TIP + TIP + TIP + TIP

The route beyond the fence leads to a heavily guarded square. If you assume a prone position at the entrance, you will see the first guard directly ahead of you; lurking around the exit to the northwest. Neither can see you. To the west, a terrorist is watching the inner courtyard from the first floor. There is a fourth enemy opposite him, directly north. It is practically impossible to cross this courtyard without being seen, so avoid this route!

5 After scaling the fence, go through the door on your left. Run up the steps and open the door at the top. Observe the Tango patrolling to the left of your position. When he gets to the far end of his patrol route (to the north) (Fig. 5), quickly follow the path left, take the right bend and go through the next door on the left. Take the steps down and watch the patrolling guard through the windows. When he is some distance away from you (to the east of the square), sprint out of the back door and run to the exit on the left, through the alleyway between the apartment buildings. Climb over the fence to reach another checkpoint.

6 Follow the path and climb over the metal fence. Run to the right along the row of houses toward NAV PAPA. When you come to the end of the street, advance to NAV ROMEO. You will remain undetected by the boat crew and the enemies to the west provided you keep to the right in this area. When you reach the Nav Point, swim further north. Keep to the right as before. You will now pass the safe house where Kryzstof Gryc is hiding out (not very well, it has to be said) on a porch at the rear of the building (Fig. 6). Use your thermal scope at NAV VICTOR to locate him and achieve another Primary Objective.

PRIMARY 3: MOVE TO EXTRACT

7 Now wade toward NAV WHISKEY and, as before, keep to the right to avoid detection by the guards. When you get there, look for cover behind the red trash container roughly 50 meters from NAV WHISKEY. A terrorist will be patrolling the front part of the house, facing the next Nav Point. Wait a moment behind the container (Fig. 7); he will stop a few meters in front of you to

GAME BASICS

WALKTHROUGH

MULTIPLAYER

EXTRAS

INDEX

HOW TO USE THE
WALKTHROUGH

NORTH AFRICA

SOUTH ASIA

POLAND

NIGHTCRAWLER

STATE SECURITY

RETRIBUTION

WATERLOGGED

BREWED CHAOS

MISSION OBJECTIVES

PRIMARY	SECONDARY	BONUS	CROSSTALK
1. Clear Safehouse Area		1. Commandeer Enemy Boat	1. Neutralize Dr. Mironova
2. Clear the Courtyard			2. Clear the Brewery
3. Neutralize Dr. Mironova			3. Neutralize Krzysztof Gryc
4. Clear the Brewery			
5. Neutralize Krzysztof Gryc			
6. Defend Brewery			

OPTIMUM EQUIPMENT

AGENT	PRIMARY WEAPON	ATTACHMENT 1	ATTACHMENT 2	SECONDARY WEAPON	ATTACHMENT	EXTRA 1	EXTRA 2
Specter	M16A2	High Scope	Rifle Laser	Mark 23	Suppressor	Ammo	M67
Jester	HK5	Red Dot	Rifle Laser	Mark 23	Suppressor	Ammo	M67
Deadpan	M16A2	4x Scope	Rifle Laser	Mark 23	-	Ammo	M67
Coldkill	HK5	Red Dot	Rifle Laser	Mark 23	-	Ammo	M67

TERRAIN

The final assignment takes you back to Wroclaw, where the situation has escalated: you are now operating in daylight and are therefore more visible to the enemy. In this mission you should use bridges and rooftops to eliminate terrorists from a safe distance with your scope. Naturally the flooded streets of this Polish metropolis also provide many places where you can, quite literally, dive underwater, out of the view of the NSO assassins. This is a critical survival strategy when facing off against enemy speedboats. You should also use the various guns you find in the streets, saving on precious ammo. In the brewery in particular, using the right firearms for the job will help you fend off the waves of terrorist attacks.

Bonus 1: Commandeer Enemy Boat

1 Command the team to FIRE AT WILL. Run along the side of the house on the left and peek around the corner. Two terrorists will be waiting here, so pick them off with some accurate sharpshooting. Mount the nearby speedboat to complete the Bonus Objective (Fig. 1). Now use the turret gun to eliminate the three Tangos in the patrolling boat which looms into view. The boat is on a circular patrol path around the compound, so if you miss it the first time, it will soon come back for another pass.

PRIMARY 1: CLEAR SAFEHOUSE AREA

2 Look for enemies that are positioned on the walkway southeast of your position. Use the on-board gun to neutralize them from a safe distance. If you have problems hitting them from the speedboat, disembark and pick them off with your scope. There is another Tango located on the rooftop to the east.

Now drive south. Enemies will appear from the far bridge to the east; one of them has a powerful gun trained directly on you. Keep a safe distance and pick them off with your primary weapon or the turret gun. Another enemy will emerge from the water ahead of you a little further to the east. If he dives under water to avoid your fire, dismount the boat and take a covered position behind a vehicle or concrete strut, then scope in and take him out when he surfaces for air. Once you're ready, proceed to NAV CHARLIE.

3 You have reached the Safehouse. Take cover behind the white vehicle and pick off the two terrorists in the entrance. Another Tango will be lurking on the metal steps to the west: shoot him. More enemies will be patrolling some distance away to the northwest of your position: some in the lower walkway in front of the building, another enemy may be on the roof. Watch out for grenades. Once you have eliminated all of them, order Bravo to storm the safehouse. A terrorist will appear in the passage ahead of you: pick him off to achieve a Primary Objective.

PRIMARY 2: CLEAR THE COURTYARD

4 Leave the building and proceed toward NAV DELTA. An enemy may appear on the steps that lead to the bridge. Shoot him through the open entrance door, as it will be harder for him to hit you when you're still inside the house. Advance to the next Nav Point. On arrival, climb over the two fences and proceed cautiously to the square. The moment you get there, crouch down and neutralize the enemies in the center of the square. Crawl a little way toward the courtyard and use the wall on the left as cover (Fig. 2). Peek east around the corner of the wall to spot two more enemies, one in the courtyard below, the other on the first floor. Shoot them both. The next enemy in this zone is lying in wait in the room to the right. Either eliminate him by sniping through the window or storm through the door on the right. Go to the centre of the courtyard (NAV ECHO) and take out the final enemy on the first floor to your right (west). Bingo! You have accomplished another Primary Objective.

PRIMARY 3: NEUTRALIZE DR. MIRONOVA
CROSSTALK 1: NEUTRALIZE DR. MIRONOVA

5 Exit the courtyard in the direction of NAV FOXTROT. Climb over the fence and follow the path. An enemy will be waiting for you on the roof to the south at NAV FOXTROT. Another enemy will show up in the water below: take him out, then deal with yet another Tango firing at you from the roof to the southeast. Go up the steps in front and sneak to the bridge. One more terrorist will be aiming at you from the rooftop on the left. After you have eliminated this threat, proceed toward NAV INDIA and onto the plank. The brewery is just ahead of you. Climb onto the roof to your left and continue left along the next roof. Neutralize the enemy that is standing in front of the brewery (Fig. 3). Run right again, back over the two rooftops and across the plank. Take the steps down and proceed cautiously to the west. At the corner of the house peek to the right and take out the enemy at the turret gun. Now move to the south and kill the Tango standing at the entrance to the brewery.

6 Now advance south to the tree and climb the ladder up to the roof. Climb through the open window to reach the brewery loft: eliminate the enemy guarding the floor below. More Tangos will fire at you from the vats to the east, so take them out. Run along right to the end of the walkway and look down to the northwest where you will see a terrorist and the scientist (Fig. 4). Shoot them both to complete another Primary and Crosstalk Objective.

PRIMARY 4: CLEAR THE BREWERY
CROSSTALK 2: CLEAR THE BREWERY

7 Climb down the two ladders and kill the last remaining terrorists. The brewery is now secured and you have achieved a Primary and Crosstalk Objective.

PRIMARY 5: NEUTRALIZE KRZYSZTOF GRYC
CROSSTALK 3: NEUTRALIZE KRZYSZTOF GRYC
PRIMARY 6: DEFEND BREWERY

> TIP + TIP + TIP + TIP + TIP
>
> *Here comes the very tough part. The terrorists will stop at nothing to regain control of the brewery and will storm the building from every direction with their assault squad. Listen very closely to the advice from HQ during these next few minutes, to stem any onslaughts before the Tangos reach the building. Be extremely careful: these enemies know no fear! With their base overrun and their plan unraveling, they will attempt to destroy the chemical tanks and take you out with them. You must protect the tanks at all costs, despite the many enemies rushing in attempting to engage you at close quarters.*

The first force will come from the northwest. Run out of the brewery and grab the mounted gun. Fire at the approaching soldiers until the gun barrel is red hot! The second wave will come from the northeast. Run through to the other side of the building and again use the mounted gun at NAV KILO to repel all comers. A third assault force will rush in from the southeast. Leave the gun and take cover behind the outer walls. The fourth onslaught comes streaming in from the northwest. Cross back through to the other side of the brewery, grab the mounted gun and open fire on the enemies yet again. Once you have crushed this wave, run to the other side of the building and fire on the forces approaching that area. Meanwhile, a few die-hards will have infiltrated the building: neutralize them. More will stream down from the roof. Hide behind the vats and eliminate them. Yet more will appear from the northeast, including the NSO Leader (Fig. 5). By taking him out along with all the other terrorists, you will accomplish two further mission objectives and successfully complete the whole adventure. Bravo Zulu! Time for a little R 'n' R. You've earned it!

MULTII

3ᴿᴰ CHAPTER

SOCOM 3 offers a massive online multiplayer gaming experience with up to 32 players competing simultaneously in squad-based warfare. Opportunities for customization and improvisation abound: you can even configure your weapon to your own particular specificiations, equipping different scopes, suppressors, attachments and much more. There are many different character skins, maps, and gameplay modes to choose from, including the all-new Convoy and Control modes. What's more, the dream of driving multiple vehicles across vast maps in a SOCOM game is now sweet reality: armored assault vehicles, trucks, boats and all sorts of goodies are available for assault and transportation purposes. You'll find that how you use vehicles will play a huge part in your domination of the opposition, adding a whole new dimension to your gaming skills.

SOCOM 3 Multiplayer mode also has its own built-in challenge ladder system where you can challenge other clans directly from the game, as well as read and post comments and suggestions in the Community section. Whether deciding if it's day or night in your online world or choosing the right weapon configuration for a specific map, you now have the option to play SOCOM 3 virtually any way you want to.

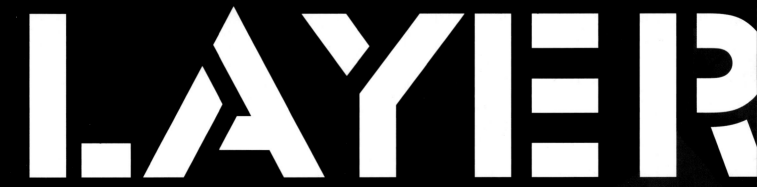

LAYER

GETTING STARTED

This is the moment you've been waiting for. You're itching to dive into the wide world of multiplayer gaming, but first there are a few tweaks and tune-ups that you really need to read up on before you jack into the SOCOM 3 network.

You'll find that you're already familiar with many of the features described in the following section, but you'll soon discover that the choices available in the single-player campaign merely hint at the array of settings available in online play. As well as the onscreen display and basic online login details, you can also expect to learn all about menus, online communities and clans.

ONSCREEN DISPLAY

The in-game onscreen display (Fig. 1) provides a wealth of information.

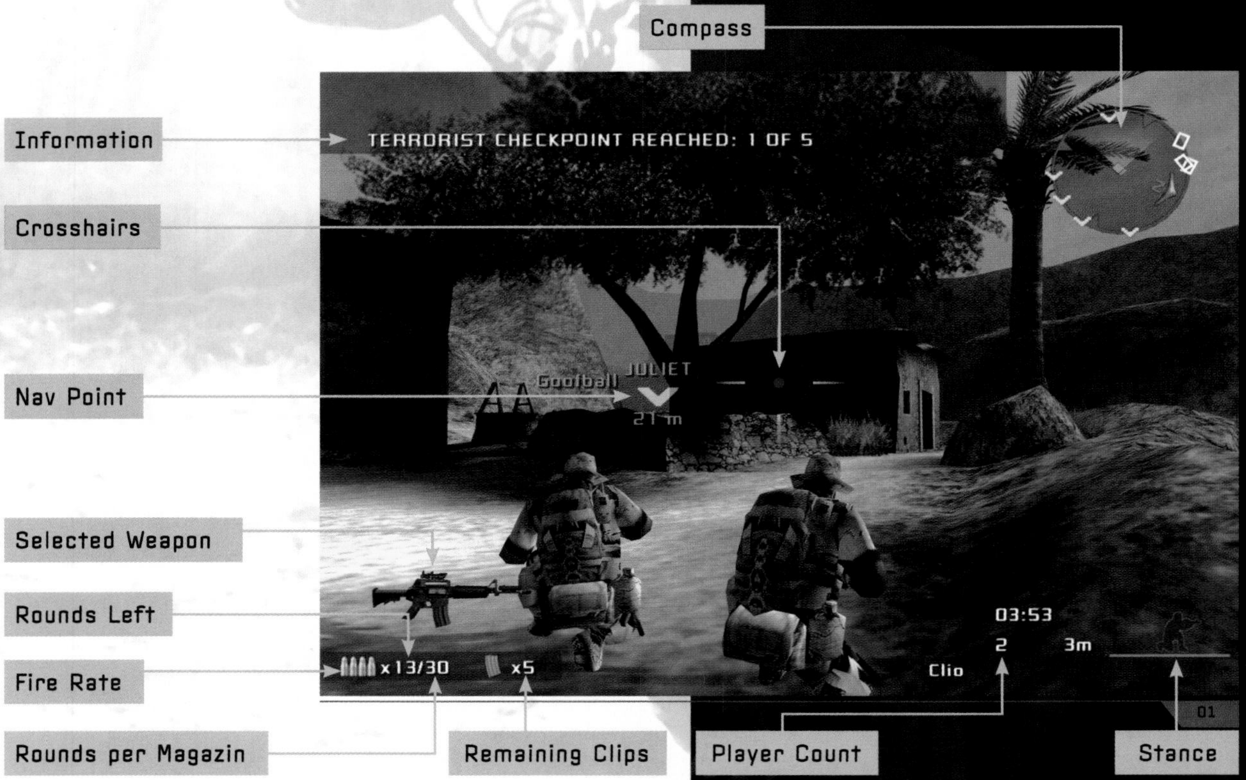

Compass

Information — TERRORIST CHECKPOINT REACHED: 1 OF 5

Crosshairs

Nav Point — JULIET 21m Goofball

Selected Weapon

Rounds Left

Fire Rate — x13/30   x5

Rounds per Magazin

Remaining Clips

03:53
2   3m
Clio

Player Count

Stance

01

STARTED

SOCOM 3
U.S. NAVY SEALS

GAME BASICS

WALKTHROUGH

MULTIPLAYER

EXTRAS

INDEX

GETTING STARTED

GAME MODES

TIPS AND
STRATEGIES

MAP ANALYSIS

ONSCREEN DISPLAY

STARTING AN
ONLINE GAME

MENUS

RANKING SYSTEM

MAXIMIZING
YOUR CHANCES

Compass: The compass rotates as you move, always showing which direction is north. An effective tool for communicating your location to your teammates, it also displays the location of key items such as vehicles (SEAL and Terrorist), bombs, hostages and VIPs (see pages 6-7 to learn more about the compass).

Crosshairs: Your crosshairs expand and contract based on your movement, depicting the effective radius of fire. When you run, the crosshairs expand, and bullets that you fire during this time could hit anywhere within the expanded crosshairs. When you stop moving, the crosshairs contract, giving you a smaller and more accurate target to aim at.

Noise Detector: You will notice that flashing red arcs appear on the outer ring of your target reticle when bullets or explosions are heard in the distance. This feature is an extremely effective way of pinpointing the direction of enemy fire. For example, if the red arc appears in the northeast section of your reticle, you will know that your opponents are attacking from that general direction, and you can then act accordingly to protect yourself.

Headset: This icon indicates who is talking over the headset and when it is possible for you to join in. If the icon is red, you can't use the headset, because another player is speaking. Wait for it to change back to yellow before trying to speak.

Countdown: This shows you how much time is remaining in the round.

Stance: Indicates whether your character is standing, crouching, prone, or swimming.

Player Count: This shows the number of players left on your team, as well as the total number of players in the room.

Player Names: When you are dead and watching other players, their names will be displayed.

Selected Weapon: This icon depicts the currently selected weapon.

Remaining Clips: This shows the number of clips or magazines that you have left for your primary weapon.

Rounds per Magazine: The number of bullets available for the currently loaded magazine in your primary weapon.

Rounds Left in Magazine: The number of bullets remaining in the currently loaded magazine in your primary weapon.

Fire Rate: This indicator shows which fire rate you have selected for your primary weapon. You can switch from single shot, two-shot burst, three-shot burst, or full auto. (Note: not all fire modes are available with all weapons, see the Weapon Stats charts on pages 25-35.)

STARTING AN ONLINE GAME

If you select Online from the OCN Main Menu without having a network configuration you will only be able to access Account Setup from the next screen. If a network configuration is available on your memory card, Fast Login will also be available (see Fig. 1).

ACCOUNT SETUP

If you've played SOCOM 1 or 2 and have already set up a network configuration, you won't have to do it again for SOCOM 3. If you need to create a network configuration, make sure that you have a Memory Card (8MB) (for PlayStation®2) and your internet settings to hand. Changes to your configuration are also made in this menu.

Logging In: When creating your profile make sure that you choose a name that you are happy to be called online, and a password that you can easily remember. Once you save your profile to your memory card, you can login and start playing online. Player names must be from 5 to 15 characters long with no spaces, and passwords must be from 4 to 15 characters long with no spaces. When creating an online name for yourself, try to use single-syllable names to make it easier for other players to communicate with you via the headset. (Refer to the game manual for detailed instructions on the login process.)

FAST LOGIN

This feature skips several steps (the Network Configuration login screen, screen name selection, etc) and takes you directly to the User Agreement page. This facilitates quick re-entry if you're disconnected from a game.

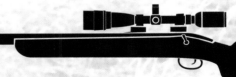

SERVER NEWS

This page notifies players when maintenance is due to be performed on the SOCOM servers, as well as detailing any other important SOCOM 3 server news.

JOINING A GAME OR ROOM

To join a room, select Briefing and select a server (Fig. 2). Once you have joined a server, you can scroll through the list of active rooms. This will show you how many players are in each room, what maps and modes are set, and various other details. Scroll down to the room of your choice and press ⊗ to join it. Note that you will not be able to chat with other players if the room has already started. Use this time to visit the Armory and select your character's skin and weapons. When you're finished, hit the Ready button to start playing.

Lobby: When you join a game or room, you will be presented with several options and tabs (Fig. 3). The first tab is Team View, which shows who is in the room and what side they are on. The second tab is Spawn Points. From here you can select where you wish to start when the game begins. Make sure you choose a spawn point that is close to where you want to go in the game. Otherwise it will take you longer to reach your desired location, and you may be killed along the way, which kind of spoils the fun. The third tab is the Armory, where you can select different skins and weapons. Take care to choose an appropriate skin and weapon for the map you will be playing on. For instance, if you're planning on doing a lot of sniping, select the ghillie suit skin, a sniper rifle and Claymore mines. The last tab tells you the map on which you will be playing.

MENUS

BRIEFING ROOM

From this screen (Fig. 1) you can join, create, or watch a game, or join a server.

AUTOPLAY

This time-saving feature (Fig. 2) ensures that you don't have to search around for a game to play. Set your filters to automatically take you to a room that is hosting exactly the type of game mode that you're looking for (ie, Breach, Extraction, Convoy, Control, etc) and the sort of map you want to fight on. You can also customize your player number requirements, toggle friendly fire on or off, specify what weapons are available, whether the game has vehicles or not, time of day, connection speed and so on.

COMMUNITY

SOCOM 3 has an online community built into the game (Fig. 3) which comprises the features outlined below.

SOCOM 3 Daily: This page features news, polls and surveys, as well as special promotions such as tournaments sponsored by the developers and Sony Computer Entertainment America.

Leaderboards: From here you can view individual, weekly and monthly leaderboards, and search them all by user name. You can also check out how well you or your friends (or rivals!) are doing.

Clan Ladders: This section enables you to view different ladders and to check out the rankings and scheduled matches for each ladder.

Message Boards: This section (Fig. 4) contains the following categories of information posted by users and available for posting by users:

- General Discussion
- Clans
- Gameplay
- Weapons
- Vehicles
- Issues/Exploits
- Tech Support

- Reading messages – Read all the latest information about the game in the SOCOM 3 News section and participate in surveys and polls.

- Posting messages – Post your comments and suggestions on the Message Boards. View and contribute to posts about many different subjects, including General Comments, Clan Info and Recruiting, and Gameplay Feedback. You can also get tech support and post about tech issues within the game. Just click on the category you wish to post in, and either reply to a post or create a new post.

Personal: In this section you can create or edit your profile, send mail to other players, or edit your account.

- Sending/Receiving Mail – You can use the game to send mail to other gamers. Simply input the name of the player that you wish to mail; they can be either offline or online. This great new feature is especially useful for setting up clan matches, letting your buddies know where to meet you, or as a means of staying in touch with your friends if you don't have access to mail via a computer.

Feedback: This feature enables you to send vital information to the developers about any bugs you might come across in the game, as well as more general feedback (ideas, comments, suggestions) about the game.

Help: View FAQs and access the online manual.

SOCOM 3
U.S. NAVY SEALS

GAME BASICS

WALKTHROUGH

MULTIPLAYER

EXTRAS

INDEX

GETTING STARTED

GAME MODES

TIPS AND STRATEGIES

MAP ANALYSIS

ONSCREEN DISPLAY

STARTING AN ONLINE GAME

MENUS

RANKING SYSTEM

MAXIMIZING YOUR CHANCES

CLANS

Clans are groups of gamers that play together and tend to form close bonds. When you're a member of a clan, you can practice running different assault strategies, fine-tune your communication skills, share your tips and tricks, and plot how you're going to dominate the rest of the competition. Which hopefully you are. Remember, there's no 'I' in 'CLAN'!

Create a Clan

To create a clan, select Clan from the menu and click Create a Clan (Fig. 5). Take care when you name your clan, as this will represent your public persona in the SOCOM 3 community.

Clan Name: Your clan name can be up to 13 characters long.

Clan Tag: Your tag is an abbreviation of your clan name. Your clan tag is displayed in yellow next to your name once you have joined a clan. This lets other players know what clan you are in. Clan tags can only be three characters long, and are displayed in brackets (for example, 'abc').

Manage Clan

Appoint New Leader: Select this feature if you want to change your clan leader. Simply click on the name of the player that you wish to appoint as the new leader.

Leave Clan: Choose this feature if you no longer wish to be a part of your current clan.

Mail Clan: This feature enables you to send a clan-wide mail. Type the subject and your message and click Send. This is a great way to inform your clan about breaking news, clan matches, upcoming tournaments and so on.

Disband Clan: If your clan is no longer active, use this feature to delete it. However, only do so if you are sure that you wish to disband, as this procedure cannot be undone. Note that everyone in your clan will also lose their clan tags.

Remove Player: If someone needs to be removed from your clan for any reason, select this option, scroll down to the player's name, and click Remove. Click Yes to confirm and the player will be deleted.

Change Clan Tag: Use this feature if you want to edit your current clan's tag. You may wish to do this if you realize that another clan has the same tag as yours, in order to avoid confusion.

Clan Roster

From this screen (Fig. 6) you can see if any of your fellow clan members are online and where they are playing. If you are the leader of your clan, you can also access the following options via the Manage Clan screen (Fig. 7).

SOCOM 3
U.S. NAVY SEALS

GAME BASICS

WALKTHROUGH

MULTIPLAYER

EXTRAS

INDEX

GETTING STARTED

GAME MODES

TIPS AND
STRATEGIES

MAP ANALYSIS

ONSCREEN DISPLAY

STARTING AN
ONLINE GAME

MENUS

RANKING SYSTEM

MAXIMIZING
YOUR CHANCES

OPTIONS

Options abound in Multiplayer Mode, enabling you to tailor your gaming experience in accordance with your personal preferences. Select MP Options to configure your online settings. The Options Menu enables you to change your general game options.

MP Options (Fig. 8)

Teammate Names: This feature enables you to toggle your teammates' names on or off. When activated, your teammates' names will appear above their heads during gameplay. Bear in mind that this could lead to an increased number of 'teamkills', however.

Receive In-Game Messages: Use this option to control whether or not you receive messages during gameplay. Feel free to disable this function if you don't like being distracted when you're in the middle of a firestorm.

Whisper Messages: Use this feature to disable all other in-game messages and prevent them from popping up on screen when you're playing.

Enable Quick Login: When this feature is turned on, you can start playing immediately from the Main Title screen.

Options (Fig. 9)

SOCOM 3 boasts some incredibly lifelike and atmospheric sound effects. If you have a surround sound system, you can use this feature to enhance your gaming experience and determine where enemy fire is coming from, or even to hear footsteps behind you.

If you have a high-definition television you can play SOCOM 3 in Progressive Scan mode (480p). This not only brightens up the screen considerably, to say the very least, it also enhances every detail and lets you use the game's widescreen function.

Audio Options

Sound Output	Surround sound users should select Dolby® Pro Logic® II. If you don't have surround sound speakers, select either Stereo or Mono.
Music Volume	Adjust the volume of the in-game music.
Sound Volume	Control the volume of the sound effects in the game.
Dialog Volume	Set the level of the in-game chat.
Headset Volume	Adjust the volume of your headset.
Movie Volume	Adjust the volume of the cutscenes.

Control

Vibrate	This turns the DUALSHOCK®2 analog controller vibration on or off. Turning it on enables you to feel when you are being shot at. Turning it off may mean that you have better control without the slight tremor.
Aim Assist	Not available in MP.
Pitch	When set to Normal, your DUALSHOCK®2 analog controller will interpret pressing up on the analog sticks as 'up', and down as 'down'. When Pitch is set to Invert, it will interpret pressing up as 'down' and pressing down as 'up'.
Presets	These are preset levels for your Look Speed, Acceleration and Dead Zone. Select this option if you want to use the default settings.
Look Speed	This affects the speed at which your character turns.
Acceleration	This setting controls how quickly your character reacts when you press a button on the DUALSHOCK®2 analog controller. The higher the setting, the quicker the response.
Dead Zone	This setting determines how far you can move the analog sticks before your character starts to move. Setting the Dead Zone too high may result in your character moving around without you even touching the controller! Setting it too low will have the opposite effect, making you feel like your character is a stone snail crawling through quicksand, i.e., pretty slow!
Restore Defaults	Puts everything back just the way you found it.

Video Options

Brightness	Adjust the brightness level.
Video Mode	Select either Interlaced or Progressive Scan 480p. Use Interlaced for non-HDTV's and Progressive 480p if you have an HDTV.
Display Mode	View the game in Full Screen or Wide Screen format. Widescreen format crops the image.
Head Bob	Turn realistic head movements on or off.
Screen Position	Use this setting to adjust your picture horizontally and vertically.

MY SETTINGS

Use these options (Fig. 10) to manage your online friendships.

Friends

This menu enables you to add or remove people from your Friends list. You will then be able to see when and where your friends are online so that you can join up with them, or snub them completely, depending on how sociable you're feeling!

Add: Add a new friend by typing their name and clicking Add Friend. You can also add a friend when you're in the middle of a game. Simply select their name and add them to your Friends list.

Remove: Remove a friend by selecting their name and clicking Remove.

Ignore

Block players that you don't wish to have any contact with.

Taunts

Create and save up to three messages to send to players during a game, but play nice!

Invitations

Choose to accept or reject invitations to join other players' Friends lists or clans. If invited, you will see the name of the player who has approached you.

RANKING SYSTEM

The ranks are divided into two primary groups, the Enlisted and the Officers, each having a unique function. The Enlisted ranks serve as a form of training, in that players will have to play several games before progressing through them, while the Officer ranks make up the skill portion of the ladder.

ENLISTED RANKS

Abbr.	Rank	Notes
SR	Seaman Recruit	0-4 games
SA	Seaman Apprentice	5-14 games
SN	Seaman	15-24 games
PO3	Petty Officer Third Class	25-39 games
PO2	Petty Officer Second Class	40-54 games
PO1	Petty Officer First Class	55-74 games
CPO	Chief Petty Officer	75-100 games - 50 wins

The ranks are all earned by playing the game: to move up in these ranks, players must complete a certain number of 'Scored' games. These games played can result in both Wins and Losses and still be tallied into the total number of games played, to encourage players to remain in the game, rather than aborting if there is a chance they might lose. Although Enlisted players can only gain ranks by increasing the number of games they play, their total Rating is still being tracked.

The final goal of the Enlisted ranks requires a bit more dedication to reach, as it shifts the focus to the number of wins rather than number of games played. Once players have reached the necessary number of games and wins, their experience on the Ladder changes, and they are now placed in the Officer ranks. When a player reaches Officer class, they can never return to the Enlisted ranks.

OFFICER RANKS

Abbr.	Rank	Grade	Notes
ENS	Ensign	Junior Grade	81-100% on Officer ladder.
LTJG	Lieutenant Junior Grade	Junior Grade	66-80% on Officer ladder.
LT	Lieutenant	Junior Grade	51-65% on Officer ladder.
LTCR	Lieutenant Commander	Mid Grade	41-50% on Officer ladder.
CDR	Commander	Mid Grade	31-40% on Officer ladder.
CAPT	Captain	Mid Grade	21-30% on Officer ladder.
RADM (LH)	Rear Admiral Lower Half	Flag	11-20% on Officer ladder.
RADM (UH)	Rear Admiral Upper Half	Flag	6-10% on Officer ladder.
VADM	Vice Admiral	Flag	2-5% on Officer ladder.
ADM	Admiral	Flag	0-1% on Officer ladder.
FADM	Fleet Admiral	Flag	Limit this to the top 10 Officer players.

The Officer ranks make up the top portion of the ladder, where gaming skill is more important than racking up the hours played. The Rating scores apply to these players, and are used to move them up and down the Officer ranks, in relation to the other Officers.

There are eleven Officer ranks, separated into percentage brackets, which place the majority of the Officers in the lower ranks, and the smallest percentage in the top ranks. Players will be constantly shifting between these ranks and positions as their Rating changes.

Certain features in this game require you to become a 'verified user' in order to achieve any of the ranking options. For further details see game manual or go to www.us.playstation.com/gamemanuals.

RANKING TIPS

Participate in full games: in the games where there are more players, there is a greater potential to earn more points.

Play in games that have multiple rounds: in games where more rounds are played, there is a multiplier applied to the player ratings. Competing in an eleven-round game will result in the greatest rating shift.

Winning against higher ranked players will result in a larger increase in your rating.

SOCOM 3 SCORING

Kills	2pts
Win Round	5pts (ALL players on the winning team are awarded, dead or alive)
Survive Round	1pt (Don't die)
Suicide	- 2pts
Friendly Kill	- 2pts (Team Kills are Friendly Kills)

COMPLETED OBJECTIVES:

Breach
Plant the bomb	1pts
Destroy the base	2pts
Defuse the bomb	1pts

Demolition
Plant the bomb	1pts
Destroy the base	2pts
Defuse the bomb	1pts

Control
Capture Nav Point	1pts

Convoy
Load Cargo Truck	1pts
Drop cargo	2pts

Escort
Escort a VIP	3pts
Kill a VIP (OFFENSE)	- 2pts
Kill a VIP (DEFENSE)	3pts

Extraction
Extract a hostage	3pts
Kill a hostage (OFFENSE)	- 2pts
Kill a hostage (DEFENSE)	- 2pts

MAXIMIZING YOUR CHANCES

RESPAWN
You can configure maps to use the Respawn feature, which enables you to play the game continuously within the allotted time. When you die, you may respawn and start again, after a short period. You can also select different spawn locations when you are dead, in case people have staked out your spawn point to shoot you before you can get your bearings ('spawn-camping'). Respawn tactics for each game mode can be found in the Game Modes section of this chapter starting on page 124.

MUTING PLAYERS/VOTING PLAYERS
If other players are being beligerent or are hampering or interfering with gameplay, you can mute them from your headset or vote them out of the game. Just tap the ◎ button to pull up a list of players and select either Vote or Mute (Fig. 1). Voting requires the majority of players to vote a person off.

HEADSET/SPLITTING CHANNELS
Effective use of the headset is vital if you want to be a successful SOCOM 3 player. You can converse with your teammates by holding the ◎ button. You can only speak for ten seconds at a time, so make sure that your communications are clear and concise. You can also split your team into two separate channels. This is useful for scenarios involving two squads, where one squad is attacking and one is defending. Hit ◎ and select Radio from the menu to choose a comms channel.

SELECTING WEAPONS/SKINS
Selecting the right skin and the appropriate weapon are crucial to your success in SOCOM 3.

Weapons
When selecting a weapon, be sure to take the following factors into consideration:

- What map you will be playing and what mode is selected. For instance, if the map is indoors, you may want to choose a weapon that is better suited to close quarters combat, such as a shotgun or a machine gun.

- If you know that you are going to be 'running and gunning', don't add too many gadgets such as scopes or pistol grips. You need to be agile and light on your feet, so overloading with accessories will only slow you down.

- Conversely, if you expect to be shooting enemies over long distances, choose an assault rifle with a high accuracy rating,

or a sniper rifle, and equip it with a high-powered scope and a pistol grip. More information on weapon selection can be found on page 25.

Skins
Make sure that you choose a skin that will give you the best cover for the environment you will be playing in. For instance, don't choose a dark outfit if you will be playing on a daytime or desert map (Fig. 2); choose a skin that will give you maximum cover and enable you to hide more effectively.

VEHICLES
SOCOM 3 supports several driveable vehicles: use them for transportation, heavy fire, roadblocks, and running people over. Learn more about vehicle controls in the Game Basics chapter on page 16.

CLAN GAMING
Inviting Players
To add players to your clan, select Invite from the Clan Menu (Fig. 3) and enter the player's name. (Make sure you know their exact name, including special characters, otherwise you may invite the wrong person to join your clan). Once you have sent the invitation, the player you invited can either accept or decline your offer. If they accept, they will appear in your clan roster, and your clan tag will be automatically added to their name. You can add a total of 31 people to your clan. Players don't have to be online for you to invite them. Once they have accepted the invitation you will receive a message informing you of their decision.

Finding/Messaging Clan Members
You can use the Clan Menu to view a list of your clan members, check if they are online and even find out what room they are playing in. You can also message your clanmates by entering their name and using the onscreen keyboard or a USB keyboard.

Clan Wars/Challenges
Once you have set up your own clan, you can challenge other clans from within the game. To do this go to the Community Menu and select the Clan Ladders option. From here, choose which ladder to join: Daily, Evening, or Weekend. You can only join two ladders. Scroll down to Ladder Info to find out the nuts and bolts of that particular ladder, such as what time to schedule matches, and what type of set-up it has (such as whether or not Friendly Fire or Equipment Limitations are activated). When you've made your decision, select a ladder and click on Join/Edit (Fig. 4).

SOCOM 3
U.S. NAVY SEALS

GAME BASICS

WALKTHROUGH

MULTIPLAYER

EXTRAS

INDEX

04

05

06

To battle with another clan, select Challenge to call up a list of clans that are available for you to fight. Pick your opponents by pressing ⊗. This will display a list of possible dates (Fig. 5). Select the date and time that you know your clan will be available. Press ⊗ and scroll up or down to change the time, remembering that the time you see on screen is the same time that your personal information is set to. By default, the time will be set to Mountain Standard Time (MST).

Now move down to Challenge and hit ⊗. If you already have a challenge pending you will see an alert, and will be unable to challenge that clan.

Room Creation
To create a room or game, click on Briefing and join a server, then select Create Game (Fig. 6). You now have the opportunity to choose several different parameters, including the number of players you wish to allow in your room, and what maps and restrictions you want. You can elect to protect your room with a password, and only give the password to the players that you'd like to join, or leave the room open for all to play. You can also set a list of maps to cycle through, have the room Ranked or Unranked, and decide whether or not you want to allow spectators.

Match Settings/Playlist
When you battle another clan, you may want to consider the following features that are available in the Playlist:

- What maps you will be playing
- The length of each map
- How many rounds it includes
- What mode each map is to be played on
- Whether the maps are day or night
- What restrictions you want to set

SOCOM 3 offers so many multiplayer options that you can create just about any game situation you can think of, keeping the gameplay fresh and interesting. Here are some examples of different match types that you can create and compete in:

- Pistols Only, No Vehicles: This format encourages patience and timing as you must rely on a pistol as your only firearm. Make every shot count and surprise the enemy with ambushes. The lack of vehicles can make for longer matches, and will increase the stealth aspect of the game.

- Snipers only, No bombs, Night-time: This configuration will all but eliminate the 'run and gun' style of play. The lack of automatic weapons creates an atmosphere of paranoia, where you never know if someone is watching you, or just about to shoot you from a distance. The focus here is on sniping of course, so make sure you choose the right scope for your rifle. You will need to weigh up the advantages (and disadvantages) of the high visibility/limited range of a Thermal Scope as opposed to the lower visibility/longer range of a High Scope. This type of game will also facilitate more freedom of movement, as you won't have to worry about stepping on, or driving over, enemy mines.

- CQC (Close Quarters Combat) Respawn: Configure this match to use only SMG's or only shotguns and select the Respawn feature. Choose a map that has a closed-in environment, such as a building complex or a claustrophobic underground area. This type of game is extremely fast paced and fun, with the emphasis firmly on staying alive in a small, confined area, and little need for vehicles. Tactics here are less important than an all-out frag-fest. However, you can think strategically to a certain extent, by choosing different respawn locations when you die in order to trick the enemy into thinking that you're going to be somewhere you're not.

GAME MODES

SOCOM 3 offers seven different Multiplayer game modes, with Control and Convoy being brand new additions to the SOCOM series. The following section provides a thorough analysis of each mode, from general information and Respawn tips (applicable when the corresponding setting is activated – see page 122 for details) to the sneakiest SEAL and Terrorist tactics.

SUPPRESSION

This is a timed mode where the objective of both teams is not necessarily to eliminate all the opposition, but rather to have at least one more player alive than the other team, when time runs out. Keep this in mind and be aware of the number of players still alive on each side during the session, as you may need to alter your strategy mid-game. Suppression mode may be basically an all-out slugfest, but it can still be approached tactically. A good strategy is to send out one assault squad to decimate the opposing crew, while keeping a second, more defensive squad in hiding. This will ensure that you have at least a handful of players still alive when time runs out.

OBJECTIVES

SEALS	TERRORISTS
Have one more player alive than the Terrorists when time runs out	Have one more player alive than the SEALs when time runs out
or Eliminate all Terrorists	or Eliminate all SEALs

TACTICS – SEALS

Feeling out the other team is the key. You may find it useful to scout enemy positions and familiarize yourself with their tactics for the first round, regardless of the outcome. Once you get an idea of where the enemy is coming from and how many of them are advancing from each location, you can better devise strategies to counter their moves. Reaching hotspots as quickly as possible is essential. The faster you get to an engagement area, the more time you will have to set up in advance and surprise the enemy.

Work as a team: split up into squads and select different spawn locations so that you cover more of the map in less time. This will also keep the Terrorists guessing as to where your team is advancing from or defending. Try to have a spotter/sniper in each

group to point out enemies before your squad moves forward. Once you've identified your targets, move in a group and attack. Remember to stay clear of your teammates' firing lanes to avoid team damage. When moving in a group, be sure to keep a distance of roughly 10-15 meters between each person to avoid a possible grenade attack taking out multiple team members.

Stay in formation and appoint a team leader. Try different configurations such as the 'wedge', where the leader takes point and team members fan out to the sides in a triangular shape behind him. This will widen your squad's field of vision and give them more time to react when approaching the enemy. In any case, you should usually have at least two players together at any given time to increase your odds when encountering lone opponents.

When advancing into enemy territory, use silenced weapons to avoid alerting the opposition too soon. Stick and move: hold key locations on the map for short periods of time, then proceed to the next. The longer you stay in one area, the better the chances of the enemy communicating your position to their teammates. Use your squads wisely and think large scale. Send one squad around each side of the map and converge at the rear, sweeping back up through the middle. This will enable your team to cover more ground and channel the Terrorists toward a central location. Once your squad clears a flank, alert your teammates so that they don't waste time combing the areas for enemies. If necessary, use vehicles to seek out the opposition and clear areas. This is a highly effective scouting tool, as you can cover much more ground in considerably less time as well as communicating enemy locations to your teammates.

Remember, to win a round you only need to have one more player alive on your team than the enemy. For example, you may notice in the middle of the round that you have eight members alive and the enemy only has four. In situations like this, it is better to play it smart: send a squad of six to track down the remaining four enemies while you keep two team members hidden or have them help you spot Tangos. Hopefully your squad of six will eliminate the Terrorists. If one of the Terrorists manages to survive, then the two members that you have kept in hiding should try to remain alive so that your team can win the round. As much as everyone may want to run out and assault the last few enemies when you outnumber them, a single grenade could still decimate your team, so be prudent and camp a defensive position. Your team will thank you in the end when you win.

TACTICS – TERRORISTS

As a Terrorist, you have several options here. Defending your base is the first. Since you will be able to equip mines, you may want to lay them at key locations and chokepoints that you think the SEALs will pass through. Familiarize yourself with the key points of entry to your base and watch them from multiple locations, hidden from view. Snipers will have a chance to shine in such circumstances.

Split your team up into small squads: four teams of four will work well; you can have a decent-sized unit watch four key locations. Be sure not to double up on too many duties, though. For instance, don't have three snipers watching one area. Each squad should have four different specialists: a sniper, a heavy gunner, a demolitions expert and an assault player. Try to coordinate these jobs with your team members prior to each round. Be patient: when the other team sees that you are digging in, they will eventually come for you. When they do, you'll be ready. Ambush them as they enter your base, popping out from behind corners to surprise them. HooYah! After you start shooting, they will most likely figure out your location and try to eliminate you. Therefore, be ready to adapt to their plan of attack on the fly. This is key in all

modes. Always keep in mind that you only need to have one more player survive on your team than the other team to win the round. Don't be afraid to run and hide. Do what you need to do to win.

If you decide to go on the offensive, try splitting the team up into two squads of eight and have them advance parallel to each other. You will inevitably encounter SEALs along the way. Be careful to avoid firing on your own teammates as they run back and forth in front of you, dodging enemy fire. This takes some getting used to, but practicing is worth the effort, and your teammates will thank you for it!

A truck full of Terrorists can be a dangerous thing. Try loading up a vehicle with your teammates and make your way toward the SEALs. Use any available mounted weaponry to eliminate the opponents that you encounter, or simply run them over. With four players on board, you can even have two of them hop out and engage foot soldiers in the area while the driver keeps driving and the gunner keeps gunning. Be watchful of snipers as they can shoot through the truck windows and take out your driver, leaving you a sitting duck.

TACTICS – RESPAWN

If you are playing with this mode set to Respawn, there are a few things to bear in mind. Remember that once you die, you can select another spawn location. You may need to do this to minimize the time it takes to get to the engagement areas. You may also need to switch spawn locations in case the enemy decides to 'camp' your spawn point. Alternatively, place team members at each of the enemy's spawn locations to suppress their advance.

BREACH

This mode requires the SEAL team to breach different areas of the map and infiltrate a Terrorist base, then plant explosives and destroy it. Terrorists, on the other hand, need to prevent this from happening: to do so, they can plant mines at breach points to deter the SEAL team from gaining access to their base. Breach missions require careful planning on both sides. Defending as a Terrorist and assaulting as a SEAL will take considerable cooperation from your teammates to achieve success.

OBJECTIVES

SEALS	TERRORISTS
Breach the defenses and use the bomb to destroy the enemy camp	Use all defenses and prevent the enemy from destroying the camp before time runs out
or Eliminate all Terrorists	or Eliminate all SEALs

TACTICS – SEALS

As a SEAL you have many options. Your main objective is to locate and pick up the bomb, then plant it at the Terrorist base to win (unless you decide instead to eliminate all Terrorists). You have to infiltrate the enemy base via breach points (such as fences, gates and walls), using C4 to blow them open. Therefore, some of your team should equip C4 before the round starts. Once inside the Terrorist base, be ready to encounter enemy resistance. Get to the target area and have your team cover you while you plant the bomb. After planting, make sure you cover the bomb so that the enemy cannot defuse it before it goes off. Try throwing Smoke grenades on and around the bomb to make it more difficult for the enemy to find the device.

There are usually multiple breach points that you can blow and enter through, so think about splitting your team up into several squads. This way you can coordinate your breaches at the same time and confuse the enemy about which one you are actually coming through. An option here is to throw a Smoke grenade at one breach point, making the enemy think that you are getting ready to come through that way, while your other squad waits in hiding near another breach point. After the first squad throws smoke, they can start firing to cause a distraction, enabling the second squad to breach the other point. Once they are inside the Terrorist base, the two squads can rendezvous. Alternatively, the first squad can delay their advance and wait a few moments. This will make the enemy think that squad two is the only one coming through. When both squads have made it inside the Terrorist base, eliminate any opponents that you meet on your way to the target area. When you reach your destination quickly plant the bomb, smoke it up and defend it against the Terrorists with all your might.

Since the Terrorist base is walled off, you and your team will need to be prepared for 'jumpers'. No, you won't be attacked by killer cardigans, these are players that jump the walls and attack as you are trying to breach. Learn each map's breach points so that you know where the Terrorists will be jumping the walls and can then assign snipers to those locations.

Planting the C4 takes a few seconds, so you may want to throw smoke or flashbang grenades or lay down some covering fire to enable your demolitions expert to safely plant the C4 at the breach point. Since the Terrorists expect your team to come through one of the breach locations, they will no doubt be waiting for you and may have snipers locked into the breach point. If this is the case, you can use smoke to blind them even if they are using thermal scopes.

TACTICS – TERRORISTS

Several different options are available to you as a Terrorist in this mode. Since you know that the SEALs must come to you, you can 'camp' or defend your base with your entire team. Assign snipers to thin out the enemy assault squad, while the rest of your team takes up key ambush positions and waits for the SEALs to arrive. Have one team camp the entrances to the bomb plant area and another wait inside to fend off any enemies that get through. The team that is camping the entrances should plant mines just outside of them to eliminate or slow down the SEALs. The team camping inside can also lay mines at the bomb plant area so that if the enemy makes it inside, they may accidentally detonate one.

Another option for Terrorists is to camp the breach points. Move your team up to the breach spots and assign even-numbered squads to guard each one. This will enable your team to stop the enemy at the front entrance. Set up snipers to scope the breach points and take out any incoming enemies, forcing their comrades to regroup and giving your team more time. Remember, the more seconds that tick away the better: if the clock runs down, the SEALs haven't planted the bomb, and you still have players alive, you will win. Note that if you have a squad camping each breach point you can hide and wait for the SEALs to plant the C4, then pop out and shoot them while they're immobilized. This may force them to move to another breach point where one of your other squads can do the same thing. Again, this takes time off the clock which is in your best interest.

Another tactic is to assemble your entire team at one breach location, plant the C4, and blow your way through. This will most likely overwhelm the enemy and enable the bomb carrier to make a run for the bomb plant area while your team engages the Terrorists. Make sure that once you have the chance, you head to the target area to help cover your teammate. Some Terrorist hideouts offer a great base location for defending, so when you manage to get inside, try setting up a position before the Terrorists come running to try and defuse the explosive.

Another tactic is to try breaching in waves: send one team of four through a breach point, let them engage the enemy inside the base for a minute or so, then send another team of four in through another breach point. Have them join up with the first team of four and engage the enemy. Wait a minute or two, then send a team of eight through either a third breach point or one of the first two, and rendezvous inside to eliminate the rest of the Terrorists.

Vehicles can play a pivotal role in this mode, enabling you to have armored cover while breaching. Use a vehicle to roll up to a breach point and block enemy fire while a teammate plants C4. Once the charge goes off, order everyone back inside the vehicle and quickly make your way to the bomb plant location. Use the trucks to block the entrance to the Terrorist base once your team is inside. This will slow the enemy reinforcements down and leave plenty of time for the bomb to detonate.

One of the keys to success in this and all game modes, is to keep the enemy guessing. Avoid repeating your set plays too many times, or your opponents will wise up and find a way to stop you: mix up your tactics on a regular basis.

If you decide to go on the offensive, jump the breach walls and assault the enemy while they are storming the gates. Apply this tactic after you have used some of the other set plays outlined above, to increase the surprise factor. Again, one of the keys to success is keeping the enemy guessing. If they think you're going to be camping your base, they will be more brazen, coming out into the open and trying to breach the gates, not realizing that your team may have jumped the walls and be about to flank them. Remember that if you do the same thing too many times in a row, chances are the enemy will get wise and find a way to stop you. Always be ready to adapt and switch it up on the fly.

Finally, keep an eye out for approaching vehicles. Set vehicle mines at all breach points in case the SEALs arrive on wheels rather than on foot. If they drive through the breach points, keep well away from the mines' blast radii. It may be prudent to assign a couple of players with RPG's to each breach point to quickly destroy any approaching vehicles.

TACTICS – RESPAWN

When playing this mode on the Respawn setting, always keep an eye on what is going on in the game when you die. If, as a Terrorist, you see that the SEALs have breached the gates and are coming in to plant the bomb, make sure you select a spawn point close to your base so that you can quickly get to the bomb plant area to either defend it or defuse the bomb. If you see that one of the gates has been breached and your team is struggling to keep the enemy at bay, you may want to choose a spawn point closer to the breached gate to help your team repel the invaders. As a SEAL, if you see that your team is taking casualties at one breach point, try spawning closer to a different one and blow through there. This will draw the Terrorists away from the other breach point and enable your comrades to hopefully get through.

DEMOLITION

The main objective for both teams in this mode is to acquire a bomb (sometimes centrally located, sometimes situated closer to one team) and plant it in the opposing team's home base. When the device explodes, the squad that planted it will win.

Be sure to guard the bomb once you have planted it, as the other team can defuse it in a matter of seconds. Keep an eye on your compass to monitor which team has the bomb and where they have planted it. When you see that your opponents have the bomb, it's often a good idea to head back to your home base and repel the would-be bomber. Alternatively, you could hide and wait for the device to be planted, then jump out and eliminate the player who planted it before defusing it, although this is a risky strategy, with little margin for error.

OBJECTIVES

SEALS	TERRORISTS
Find the bomb and destroy the enemy base with it	Find the bomb and destroy the enemy base with it
or Eliminate all Terrorists	or Eliminate all SEALs

TACTICS – SEALS

Since both team's objectives are the same here, it may be best to wait a few minutes in a safe location and watch what the opposition does before you devise your plan. If the Terrorists are assaulting, set up ambush locations throughout the area between the bomb pickup and your base: surprise the enemy when they advance toward you. If you intend to camp your base, have a sniper scoped in on the bomb plant area: he can protect your base by taking out the enemy who is attempting to plant the bomb. Plant Claymores in key locations to slow the Terrorists' advance. Even if you don't blow them or are not near enough to detonate them, the enemy will assume that you are and will either look for another way through, or try to detonate the mines with their own explosives. In any case, this will give your team more time to return to base.

Should you decide to go on the attack and try to plant the bomb, using a vehicle may work in your favor. Throw a barrage of grenades to stop the Terrorists from getting to the bomb before you while you drive to the bomb. Once you pick up the device, drive to the Terrorist bomb plant area. Armored vehicles will give you more cover and a better chance of reaching the enemy base without getting killed and without losing the bomb. Try to coordinate with a ground assault team to get to the enemy base at the same time so that they can lock down the area and clear it of mines. Park the vehicle in front of the bomber to block sniper fire while he plants the bomb Remember to always have at least one other teammate helping to fend off enemies while

the bomb is being planted. The planter can't move when setting the device and will therefore be totally vulnerable to incoming fire.

It's key to keep an eye on your compass. Check which team has the bomb: if the enemy has acquired it, run back to your base to protect it, or to defuse the device if it has already been planted.

Another strategy consists of splitting your team up into squads, advancing in staggered waves, and letting the enemy think that you are bypassing the bomb and simply going for all-out attack. Send two teams ahead at the same time to engage the enemy while two more teams sit back and wait. Once the first two teams engage, a third team should move up, acquire the bomb and advance into areas that the first two teams have cleared. The last team should shadow the bomb carrier team and be ready to defend them, or even to grab the bomb if the carrier is neutralized.

TACTICS – TERRORISTS

If your team reaches the bomb pickup point before the SEALs, try planting mines around the bomb so that they will detonate when a SEAL tries to snatch it. You can also carry the bomb away from the pickup location, drop it and plant mines around it. The SEALs will notice that the bomb has been dropped, see its location on the compass and be tempted to pick it up. You can also assign a sniper to watch from afar and to snipe any SEALs trying to grab the device.

Plant M2 vehicle mines at key chokepoints that the SEALs have to drive through. This will cut off their advance and possibly eliminate some of them, enabling you to turn the tables and attack the SEAL base. Use vehicles to transport the bomb to the enemy base, but be wary of snipers as well as mines. Snipers can shoot through the windows and kill the driver, cutting your joyride short.

Camping your base is another good plan. Divide your team into squads, then camp each entrance and wait for the enemy to advance. This will enable you to gain the upper hand by keeping your team hidden in ambush locations while the SEALs run blindly into your trap. Use walls and other objects as well as the third-person viewpoint to see around corners and anticipate the enemy advance. Lay mines inside the bomb plant area to delay the SEALs from planting the bomb, and maybe even eliminate a few while you're at it. Be sure to notify your teammates of your mine locations so that they don't accidentally detonate them.

Alternatively, split your team in two. Send an assault squad to take the bomb to the enemy base, while maintaining a defensive or camping squad at your base. This tactic will be all the more effective if your assault squad is faced with enemies that are split up into several small squads: when you gain the upper hand, the camping team can push up and help out the assault squad, thereby overwhelming the SEALs. Conversely, if the assault team is quickly decimated and the SEALs acquire the bomb, your camping team will already be in place, waiting for them to come and plant.

TACTICS – RESPAWN
As always, keep a close eye on your compass: if the enemy has the bomb, select the closest spawn point to your base to minimize the time necessary for you to get back and defend it. If your team has the bomb, choose the spawn point closest to the enemy base so that you can advance ahead of your team and clear a path for them. Always be on the lookout for 'spawn campers'. These are people that will lie in wait at your spawn point and kill you as soon as you appear. Should you fall victim to these tricksters, choose another spawn location and make your way back to the first spawn point to surprise and eliminate the spawn campers. If the bomb has not yet been acquired by either team, you should try to spawn close to the bomb and pick it up. The team that has the bomb usually controls the pace of play.

CONTROL

This mode is all about controlling different areas of the map. When you reach a control point, you can claim it for your side by placing a beacon. Once you have placed your beacon it can't be removed. However, the other team can also plant a beacon at the same control point. The objective is to mark all of the control points before the other team does. To maximize your chances, it's a good idea to move to each control point in a group and leave at least one man behind to defend each Nav Point that you have marked: this way, it will be more difficult for the enemy to plant a beacon on your territory.

OBJECTIVES

SEALs	TERRORISTS
Mark all checkpoints before the other team	Mark all checkpoints before the other team
or Eliminate all Terrorists	or Eliminate all SEALs

TACTICS – SEALS AND TERRORISTS
Set out in vehicles crammed with as many players as they can hold. Make your way to the nearest control point and deploy Smoke grenades. Note if there is smoke or an enemy beacon planted at the control point already: if there is, mark your territory, then immediately head for a further Nav Point with your entire squad; if not, leave at least one man behind to defend it. Using the vehicles to advance to the control points is the key. The driver should select one passenger to exit the vehicle at each control point, then drive on to the next one. This will enable your team to quickly capture the most points in the least amount of time. Continue to drop passengers off at each control point while staying in contact with your team to see which points have come under fire. In any case, you should always keep a player in the gunner position of the vehicle to eliminate any enemies that you encounter on your way.

Players that capture control points should communicate with the rest of their team to notify them when they need help defending an area. If the enemy has not captured a point that you have control of, you should focus on defending that position. Avoid having too many players camping control points though, as you will need teammates to be out capturing any remaining points.

Try breaking your team up into as many squads as there are available spawn points. This will enable you to quickly reach more control points than the enemy. Have your squads spawn at different locations to maximize your speed. Every second counts: the more you delay, the more time the enemy has to make their way to any control points they haven't taken; the more ground your team covers, the better your chances.

GAME BASICS

WALKTHROUGH

MULTIPLAYER

EXTRAS

INDEX

GETTING STARTED

GAME MODES

TIPS AND STRATEGIES

MAP ANALYSIS

SUPPRESSION

BREACH

DEMOLITION

CONTROL

CONVOY

ESCORT

EXTRACTION

Another tactic is to try and control two points before the enemy does. Hold these points with at least four players each while the rest of your team heads out to take the remaining points. This will enable your team to fend off the enemy from those two points and give your team more time to capture the others. Set up snipers in hidden locations with clear shots at the control point plant areas. Wait for the enemy to get close and deploy smoke, then take your shot. It can also be very effective to plant mines or Claymores in and around the control points that your enemy has not yet taken. This will again delay your opponents and give your team more time to gain control of the remaining points.

Remember this mode is all about speed and time. The team that controls all of the points first, wins. As mentioned above, this can be achieved in many ways, by either driving to all of the control points as quickly as possible, or by preventing the enemy from reaching them ahead of you. As with all modes, you can also win the round by eliminating the entire enemy team. Use vehicles to run them down and to scout out their location and relay the details back to your snipers.

TACTICS – RESPAWN

When you die, note which control points need to be taken for your team and select the spawn point closest to them. This will give your team a better chance of capturing all of the targets before your enemy does. If you know one of your points is being attacked, pick a spawn point closer to that control point so that you can get there quickly and help defend it. As always, watch for spawn campers.

CONVOY

In this mode, Terrorists have to load up cargo vehicles and make their way to an extraction point. When they dismount and approach the cargo an icon will appear, enabling the Terrorists to load the cargo onto the truck. Once they've loaded up, the squad moves out to the next loading zone and repeats the process. If the Terrorists make it to the drop zone with a loaded vehicle, their team wins. The SEALs team will try to stop the convoy and destroy the cargo vehicles. If both cargo trucks are destroyed, that team will win.

OBJECTIVES

SEALS	TERRORISTS
Destroy both convoy vehicles	Pick up the cargo and deliver it to the extraction area within the allotted time
or Prevent the Terrorists from unloading their cargo within the allotted time	or Eliminate all SEALs
or Eliminate all Terrorists	

TACTICS – SEALS

Your main goal is to destroy the incoming Terrorist convoy. One way to do this is to commandeer Terrorist vehicles in order to weaken them. Prepare traps at the Terrorists' loading zones, for example by parking your vehicles so that they have to go around them (giving you a chance to hit them with RPGs) or by planting vehicle mines. You'll want to set up snipers at these locations as well to target the drivers and the Terrorists that are trying to load up. Furthermore, don't hesitate to plant mines here, as the Terrorists have to get out of their vehicles to load the cargo. RPGs work best on the cargo trucks (as opposed to the support transport) as they are not so heavily armored.

Keep in mind that the Terrorists may split up and drive one cargo vehicle to one loading zone and one to another, so you may need to divide your team accordingly. It's often a good idea to send a team to the final drop zone, as if the Terrorists can't get there, they can't win. Feel free to consolidate your position at the final drop zone and force the Terrorists to engage your entire team. Plant vehicle mines in the path of the cargo truck to prevent it from reaching the drop zone. Consider parking several of your own vehicles in a line to stop the Terrorist convoy in its tracks. This will give you and your team more time to destroy the cargo trucks. You may want to position a couple of snipers in the distance to take down anyone on foot. It will take the Terrorists some time to load up all of their cargo and make their way to the final drop zone, so find a good spot to snipe the driver, forcing another player to get out and take over his position.

Remember that the Terrorists have to load the vehicles on foot at each zone. Position a few players with silenced weapons under cover nearby to pick them off as they try to lift the cargo. This will, at the very least, shave some seconds off the clock. If you are having trouble destroying the convoy vehicles, delaying your opponents as much as possible is a viable strategy.

TACTICS – TERRORISTS

Your mission is to either eliminate the SEALs, or load up the convoy vehicles at each zone and deliver your cargo to the drop point. An effective way of doing this is to pile your entire team into vehicles and make your way to the first loading zone. Be sure to have a few team members equip C4 to breach any areas that are blocking the convoy's path. Use the vehicles that are equipped with mounted weaponry to fend off any attackers. When you reach your first destination, have one of your team dismount and load the cargo. Once it's on board, make haste to the next loading zone and repeat the process. When you've loaded all of the cargo, drive to the drop zone to unload it. Be on the lookout for vehicle mines as you go. It's a good idea to park smaller vehicles such as armored assault vehicles around the cargo vehicles while your squad is loading the truck, in case of an RPG attack. This will possibly sacrifice one of your armored assault vehicle, but your cargo vehicle will hopefully remain intact, with the added bonus that the enemy has now revealed their position!

Try splitting the convoy into two groups; take one truck to the first loading zone and the other to the second. This will enable you to load the cargo at both areas more quickly (but with less support). When both vehicles are loaded up, charge to the drop zone and unload immediately. Alternatively, mix your strategies up: the SEALs can't defend against your tactics if they don't know what to expect.

Another approach consists of sending groups out to secure each loading zone until your convoy gets there. This is very effective as the enemy won't have a chance to plant vehicle mines or set up snipers at these zones, leaving you with a safe environment in which to load your cargo. Your advance party can drive the faster vehicles on ahead of the main convoy to swiftly reach each loading zone. Then, once all the cargo is loaded, they can escort the convoy to the final drop zone. In any case, be careful not to leave any of the cargo vehicles unattended.

Time is not on your side in this mode. Should you and your team fail to unload the cargo at the final drop zone within the allotted time, you will lose the round. Always be conscious of how much time is left, and how far you have left to go.

ESCORT

In this scenario, SEALs or Terrorists are charged with escorting three unarmed VIPs through hostile territory to extraction zones. To win the round, the offensive team must either extract at least two VIPs, or eliminate the entire defending team. As for the defenders, they must either kill at least two VIPs to prevent a successful extraction, or eliminate all of the offensive team. A good tip for the offensive team is to split the VIPs up and move them to the extraction zones separately. This way your group is less likely to be eliminated by a single strike. The defending team should concentrate on neutralizing the VIPs rather than trying to kill all of the opposing team, as it's much quicker.

OBJECTIVES

OFFENSIVE TEAM	DEFENSIVE TEAM
Move at least two VIPs into the extraction zone before time runs out	Kill all three VIPs
or Eliminate opposing team	or Prevent at least two VIPs from being extracted within the time allotted
	or Eliminate opposing team

TACTICS – OFFENSIVE TEAM

There are several options for the offensive team in this mode. The first of course is to escort the VIPs to safety. This can be done quickly by acquiring a vehicle with at least three vacant seats. If one offenisve team member tells all three VIPs to follow him and then jumps into the driver's seat, the VIPs will also enter the vehicle. This is a great way to protect them from random enemy fire as well as get them quickly to the extraction zone. Try to have a gunner on the vehicle to eliminate any Tangos along the way and clear your path to the extraction zone. Chances are they will be waiting for you. Watch for vehicle mines and have snipers zoom in and check the area before you get there. Once you reach the extraction zone, dismount: the VIPs will follow suit and be extracted.

Another strategy you can employ is to round up the VIPs and move them to an easily defendable area. From this secure location, you can fend off the enemies as they come to kill the VIPs. All you have to do then is ambush the Tangos while keeping the VIPs secure. Once you've thinned out the defensive team, you can proceed with the extraction. Move quickly to the extraction point and get the VIPs to safety. Keep a close eye on the clock: you will lose the round if time runs out and the VIPs have not been extracted. Be conscious of the fact that the opposing team may opt to 'camp' the extraction zone and wait for you, knowing that your team will lose if the VIPs are not extracted.

As with the other modes, make sure you frequently switch your tactics and strategies to confuse the enemy. If you try to extract the VIPs too many times at the same point, the opponent will be waiting for you. You can also use this to your advantage, however, by taking the VIPs to the same extraction point a few times in a row, then changing to another location. Always keep 'em guessing.

Alternatively, try splitting up the VIPs: take them in different directions and meet up at the same extraction point. Note that you can't escort two VIPs to one extraction zone and one to another. If all three VIPs are alive, they must all be in the same extraction zone. If one of the VIPs dies, you can still extract the remaining two VIPs.

TACTICS – DEFENSIVE TEAM

This mode favors the defensive team. Your main objective is to prevent the VIPs from being extracted. You can do this one of two ways: kill two of the VIPs, or make sure the offensive team doesn't move the VIPs to the extraction zone before time expires. The best way to win is to split your team up into as many groups as there are extraction points. Send one group to each extraction point and set up a defensive position. The offensive team has to come to you anyway, in order to extract the VIPs. The clock is also on your side, as if time runs out and the offensive team has not extracted the VIPs you will win the round.

Be aware that the offensive team may arrive in vehicles. To prepare for this eventuality, plant vehicle mines at the entrances to all extraction points. It's also a good idea to plant PMN anti-personnel mines at all extraction points. Hide them in the long grass or other locations that the enemy may not see. That way, when they lead the VIPs to the extraction zone, they will step on the mines, killing the VIPs and possibly themselves. Clean-up on aisle 5!

To increase your chances of success, have a sniper or two watch over each extraction zone and pick off any VIPs that make their way in. You can also have snipers looking out toward where the opposing team will be coming from. This way, you can snipe them on their way to the extraction zone as well as communicate their position and how many of them there are. If a sniper calls out that the entire offensive team is moving toward one extraction point and you have a team camping another extraction point, you should all converge on the location that the opposing team is moving to.

Whenever possible, try creating vehicle road blocks to stop the offensive team from easily accessing the extraction zones in their own vehicles. This will also give you and your defensive team a nice barrier to hide behind. Make shooting the VIPs your priority. Chances are that the enemy will move all three of the VIPs in a group: this will enable your team to use explosives or RPGs to wipe them out.

TACTICS – RESPAWN

As a member of the offensive team, check if your squad has control of the VIPs. If it doesn't, you'll want to select the spawn point closest to the VIPs so you can grab them and move them to safety. If your team already has control of the VIPs, select the spawn point closest to the extraction zone to help get them to safety. As a member of the defensive team, you will want to spawn near the extraction zones as this is where the offensive team will be headed. Try and get intel on where the opponents were last seen so that you don't spawn near the wrong extraction zone. Whenever you respawn, don't forget that you are free to select new weapons, so be sure to communicate with your teammates and choose the weapons that you'll need as the game progresses.

EXTRACTION

In this mode, the SEALs or Terrorists try to rescue and extract at least two hostages, while the others do all they can to prevent them from escaping. If the defending team happens to kill one of the hostages, it will be recorded as a rescued hostage for the extraction team. When playing as part of the extraction team, it's a good idea to send a scout squad ahead to take out any enemies that may be blocking your path to the extraction zone. As part of the defending team, a good tactic is to split your team into multiple squads and defend each extraction point, making it difficult for the extraction team to save the hostages. If no hostages are rescued and there are still players left alive on each side, the round will result in a tie.

OBJECTIVES

OFFENSIVE TEAM	DEFENSIVE TEAM
Locate and move at least two hostages to the extraction zone	Prevent the opposing team from rescuing the hostages within the allotted time
or Get the defensive team to kill two hostages by mistake	or Eliminate the entire offensive team
or Eliminate all opponents	

TACTICS – OFFENSIVE TEAM

Your main objective is to extract the hostages that are being held at the enemy base. You can also win the round by eliminating the entire defensive team. Your opponents will probably be guarding their hostages fiercely, so be prepared to encounter ambushes and well-defended areas. Move in squads or small teams and infiltrate the enemy base. Make sure some of your teammates carry C4 as there may be breach points to demolish. Scout out the area, as the defensive team may have placed the hostages near one of these points in order to prevent you from breaching it. If there are hostages on the other side of a breach point and you blow it with C4, you will injure or possibly even kill the hostages and lose the round.

Once you've made your way into the enemy base, try and locate the hostages. When you find out where they are, you will need to clinically dispatch the opponents and gain control of the hostages to extract them. Throw a flashbang grenade to stun and disorient any member of the defensive team that may be camping the hostages. While they are blinded, breach into the area and eliminate them carefully to avoid hitting their prisoners in the crossfire. Once you've gained control of the hostages, it is your job to safely lead them to the extraction zone. Escort at least two hostages to the extraction zone to win the round, or eliminate all members of the opposing team. If time runs out, the round will result in a draw.

You may wish to send in a distraction team. Assemble a group to breach the opposing base and engage the enemies in a firefight. This will distract them and make them think that you are foregoing the extraction of the prisoners, enabling the rest of your team to move in behind them, grab the captives and quickly take them to the extraction zone. Be careful, the defensive team will get a message on their screen telling them that you have gained control of a hostage and they will advance to the last known position of their quarry. Try using vehicles to quickly extract the hostages while keeping them protected.

TACTICS – DEFENSIVE TEAM

Your team has three prisoners that they need to protect from the offensive team. At the start of the round, you should gain control of the hostages, find a safe place to hide them and set up a perimeter. The second floor of a building or similar location is great for this. Use anti-personnel and vehicle mines to block off any entrances and chokepoints. Assign players to watch key chokepoints and breach points to stop the offensive team from advancing. Also keep a team close to the captives to prevent the enemy from extracting them. Place the hostages in between you and where you think you will be encountering your opponent. Putting them in the line of fire will force the enemy to ease off the trigger so as not to injure or kill the hostages. If they kill all three hostages you will win the round. Conversely, if *you* kill all of the hostages the offensive team will win the round.

You can also place hostages at breach points to prevent the opposing team from breaching certain areas for fear of hurting the prisoners. If the offensive team kills a hostage, they will have one minute deducted from the clock. If you kill a hostage, the opposing team will be credited with rescuing that hostage.

Try splitting your team up into two groups: an assault team and a defense team. The assault team should rush out and meet the offensive team before they even get a chance to enter your base, while the defense team can set up camp and prevent the hostages from being extracted if the others happen to get past your assault team. You could also set your assault squad up inside your base and wait for the opponent to ambush them when they breach in: your defensive squad would still be there to prevent a member of the offensive team from sneaking in and extracting the hostages.

You may want to herd the hostages into a vehicle and just drive them around. Your opponent will be wary of firing on the vehicle for fear of killing the hostages and losing the round. It will also give the rest of your team ample time to attack the enemy while you keep the hostages safe from extraction: the offensive team will be concentrating on how to get the hostages out of the vehicle, and thus pay less attention to the oncoming assault.

TACTICS – RESPAWN

Pay attention to the scenario before you die so that you can come back at the spawn location closest to your mission objective. Members of the offensive team will want to take note of the hostage situation and spawn either closer to the extraction zone if the hostages are on their way to being extracted, or nearer to the enemy base if their team needs help acquiring the hostages. As for the defensive team, they will tend to spawn nearer to the hostages to guard them, or to retrieve them from the offensive team. Don't forget that respawning is the perfect opportunity to change weapons, depending on whether or not the offensive team is inside the base. Members of the defensive team could opt respectively for a close quarters combat weapon such as a shotgun, or for extra mines, for example.

TIPS AND STRATEGIES

Want to improve your multiplayer skills?
Well, there are many ways to achieve that goal.
You could of course spend hours of trial and error,
observing other players, or even thinking really
hard... But there's a much more efficient method
that's also a lot more fun: just read the following
pages! They're packed with juicy tips and
strategies that can take you from noob to
ringer in no time flat!

GENERAL TIPS

ADJUST YOUR CONTROLLER
Make sure you select the controller preset with which you are
most comfortable. Some presets are better suited to sniping,
while others are more conducive to fast action, running and
gunning. Once you've chosen a preset configuration, take the
time to fine-tune settings such as Look Speed, Acceleration and
Dead Zone. You may need to play a few rounds with different
settings before you find what works best for you.

SELECTING A CHARACTER
Before you begin a game, you will be presented with a selection
of playable characters. Each character has a different outfit and
preset weapon loadout. Be sure to choose the character that
has the outfit best suited for the map and environment you will
be playing in. For instance, if you're going to be playing a map
with desert terrain, choose a character with a light-colored outfit,
rather than something dark that will stick out like a sore thumb.
In short, choose a character with the best camouflage for the
surroundings, that will make you less visible to the enemy.

SELECTING EQUIPMENT
It's best to know what map you will be playing before you select
your equipment so that you can choose the right kit (weapons
and accessories) for the specific map. If the map is small and
predominantly indoor-based, with the emphasis on close quarters
combat, you should select a weapon that functions optimally
in that situation (such as a shotgun or sub-machine gun). If the
map is large and requires you to cover a lot of meters, avoid
encumbering yourself with too many add-ons such as scopes
and pistol grips. If the map is fairly open with little cover, then
it will be of scant use to equip a silencer. Conversely, if there
is abundant cover, choose the suppressor that best suits your
surroundings so that you can snipe away to your hearts content
and remain undetected. Finally, always coordinate with your
team to ensure that you are equipped with a varied selection of
weapons. For instance, don't start a game with *everyone* on your
side toting sniper rifles.

WATCH AND LEARN
Before throwing yourself into the intense fray of a multiplayer
battle, take a few minutes to watch a series of rounds via the
Spectator mode. This enables you to study a game that is already
in progress by cycling through all the players, as well as observing
from fixed camera viewpoints. It's a great way to find out where
people are meeting each other, or to scope out good sniping
positions and suitable places to set mines or throw grenades.
It's also a fantastic way to learn tactics by observing other more
experienced players on the battlefield.

BASIC MOVEMENT
When advancing to different areas, be sure to use the cover of
your surroundings (walls, trees, brush, hills...) to get from point
A to point B undetected. Move from one area of cover to another
and stop at each point to survey the landscape and eliminate
any possible threats. Try to fan out from your teammates while
advancing or holding, so that a single grenade or explosive blast
can't take out everyone in one fell swoop.

Remember, the enemy can't shoot you if they can't see you. If you
have to cross open water, use the new dive feature to swim underwater
and avoid detection (all the more vital as you are a sitting duck in the
water, unable to fire your weapon). When running, don't always follow
a straight line, as this will make it easier for a sniper to get a better fix
on you. Avoid wide open spaces whenever possible, as players are
attracted to movement and will notice you. If you are under fire, try
jumping and/or moving from side to side to avoid the bullets.

When it's not possible to use stealth to move from one point to
another, avoid standing still for too long: stationary targets are easier
to hit than moving ones.

When moving through enemy territory, watch for mines at key
chokepoints and areas of interest such as bridges, tunnels, bomb
pickup points, etc. Snipers may also be watching these areas
closely, so carefully scan the horizon before moving forward.

TRATEGIES

SOCOM3
U.S. NAVY SEALS

GAME BASICS

WALKTHROUGH

MULTIPLAYER

EXTRAS

INDEX

GETTING STARTED

GAME MODES

TIPS AND
STRATEGIES

MAP ANALYSIS

GENERAL TIPS

WEAPON TIPS

VEHICLE TIPS

RUNNING AND
GUNNING

CAMPING TIPS

SNIPING TIPS

TEAMWORK

CLAN TIPS

Make good use of the third-person view: it enables you to peek around corners. To use this trick, walk up to the corner of a building and face it, then rotate the right analog stick to view the area in front of you without breaking cover. This works great for ambushing: if you know that the enemy will be passing a certain building, make your way there, stand at the corner and wait for them to come to you. Once you see them, you can sidle out from behind cover and surprise them with a bullet.

The standing and crouching positions each have their own advantages and disadvantages when it comes to movement: the standing position offers more stability in the sense that your character will not move unless you direct him to; the crouching position implies that your character will move from upright to crouching when he stops, which can sometimes have an adverse effect on your targeting of enemies. So basically, remember this: if you are not moving, you are better off crouching or going prone; if you are going to be on the move and dodging back and forth, you will achieve more consistency with the standing position. In this case, try using the strafe controls to fine-tune your targeting. Sometimes it's easier to strafe slightly to the left or right instead of actually turning your character. This is also quite helpful in close quarters gunfights. Instead of standing still and turning to aim and shoot at your enemy, use the strafe controls to sidestep back and forth and keep your target in the crosshairs while remaining a moving (and therefore less vulnerable) target yourself.

USING THE COMPASS

Use the compass to make your way from your spawn point to the necessary mission objectives and to locate vehicles, VIPs, bombs, hostages, extraction points and more. You can also use the compass to find out where your team members are: when a team member speaks, you will see an icon on the compass showing you where they are speaking from. Additionally, the compass displays various points of interest, such as ALPHA, BRAVO, CHARLIE, DELTA and so on. Feel free to use these points as landmarks to let your team know the location of trouble hotspots, or where you're headed.

USING THE HUD (HEAD-UP DISPLAY)

The HUD is a valuable part of the game, providing all of the information that you need to help you make key decisions. Among other things, the HUD enables you to:

• View how many players are still alive and how many are dead.

• View which weapon you have selected.

• Choose which weapons you want to set as your hotswap items.

• See how many bullets are available in each clip, and how many clips you have left.

The HUD also shows vital information (such as who killed who, which team is winning, which team has acquired a bomb or breached an area) and many other important facts (such as how much time is left in the round, which position you are currently in – standing, crouching, or prone).

Your crosshairs are multi-functional: they spread apart when you run, and contract when you stand still. As bullets fired at a given time can hit anywhere within the crosshairs, this means that your accuracy naturally decreases when you are moving. Note that the crosshairs also serve as a sort of sonar, via the Noise Detector. When bullets are fired in your vicinity, you will see a red arc flash on the targeting reticle in the direction of the fire. This gives you a general idea of where a firefight is taking place, or more importantly, where the next bullet is coming from.

WEAPON TIPS

PRACTICE

To become proficient with different weapons, you will need to practice with them all. Some weapons are more accurate than others but have less effective range. Some have longer range, but less accuracy. Some have more power at short distances and some have a faster rate of fire than others. You will need to practice with each weapon to see which ones you like the feel of in different situations. One of the most important factors that you should take into account is recoil, i.e., how high your weapon kicks up into the air after firing. You can compensate for this disorientating effect by firing in short controlled bursts. You can also add a pistol grip attachment which will steady your weapon and reduce recoil when you are standing or crouching. In any case, try only shooting three or four bullets at a time before re-targeting the enemy: this will lessen the recoil factor and enable you to place more bullets on target.

Before starting a game, make sure that you choose the right accessories for your weapon as well as the right gear. For instance, in a close quarters combat scenario, there's no need to add a scope to your sub-machine gun. If you are a sniper, you may not need grenades but you might want to choose some Claymores to protect your hiding place. If you are going to be setting up ambushes, be sure to equip a suppressor to mask your location when firing at the enemy. All these things will play a part in your success in the game. If you make a mistake and choose inadequate weapons and gear at the start of a game, you can always change them when you die. Coordinate with your team and see what kind of gear or firepower they need you to equip in order to help complete the mission.

SHOOTING

When you come into contact with an enemy, shoot them! Remember, they will shoot back (unless they're in the kitchen grabbing a snack!), so accuracy is a factor. You are much more accurate when stationary, so take cover and fire from an area where the enemy can't see you. Again, use a silencer/suppressor if you want to attain a high level of stealth. When firing from a concealed position, peek out and fire off a few rounds at the enemy before ducking back behind cover. If your quarry presents a suitably stationary and oblivious target, take your time to line up a headshot.

Lead your targets: when enemies are running, they won't be at the location you aimed at when the bullet actually gets there. Make sure that if your opponent is running you aim a little bit ahead of them before you fire. You may need to experiment with how far to lead a target as different weapons will have different results.

Each weapon has one or more of the following fire modes: single shot, two-shot burst, three-shot burst and full auto. While the full auto mode is great for close quarters combat, it can be inaccurate when you hold the trigger down for an extended period of time. Use the single, two-shot or three-shot burst modes for the highest degree of accuracy.

Keep a close eye on the amount of ammo that you have left. The last thing that you want to happen is to run out of ammo in the middle of a firefight. Reload whenever you get the chance. When you're in a gunfight, fire off a few rounds before taking cover, wait for your enemy to run out of ammo, then while he is reloading (and thus unable to fire), break cover and attack him. If you find yourself out of ammo, check corpses for dropped clips. If you know you're going to be in several firefights throughout the course of a round, be sure to choose Double Ammo when visiting the Armory.

Be patient; make your shots count. It's useless to fire off a couple of rounds at an enemy right before he or she runs out of view. It's better to follow them and wait for the chance to get the right shot in. Don't just fire blindly. If you see an enemy pass in front of you and they don't see you, wait a few seconds to see if they have any teammates with them. They may be traveling in packs, so it's better to wait until they all pass before you start to fire.

When you get into a firefight, check out your enemy's equipment. If they are toting a shotgun, you know that particular weapon has a limited range, so instead of getting into a close quarters firefight, move back to minimize the effectiveness of *their* weapon, while you maximize the effectiveness of yours.

GRENADES/EXPLOSIVES

Grenades can be bounced off surfaces such as walls. Try deflecting grenades off windowsills to deliver them closer to targets that might otherwise be unreachable. You can use this technique to damage or even neutralize enemies that are hiding around a corner. Note that grenades are pressure sensitive: the harder you press R1, the further you will throw the grenade. You can also throw grenades much further when standing up as opposed to when crouching. As with all weapons, avoid tossing grenades of any kind at your own teammates.

There are several different types of explosive device available in SOCOM 3 and each serves its own unique purpose:

- An HE grenade delivers a high explosive charge that works best in confined spaces as opposed to outdoor areas.

- Frag grenades explode in a burst of shrapnel. While this grenade is also effective at close quarters, it is most potent in an outdoor setting.

- Smoke grenades can serve many purposes. For example, throw a smoke grenade at the entrance or exit of a bridge or tunnel to mask your team's advance. If you know there is a sniper watching you, pop a smoke grenade either as a diversion in the opposite direction, or to blind the sniper while you advance. Smoke is also effective in close quarters combat situations: try using it to confuse the enemy and force them out of certain areas. Smoke grenades are great for covering items and objects as well as players. For instance, use a Smoke grenade after you plant a bomb at an enemy base: the time it takes for the terrorists to find the bomb in the smoke cloud could buy you the few seconds you need for the bomb to detonate. Unleash a synchronized Smoke and Flash attack to confuse, stun and blind opponents.

- Flash grenades produce a blinding flare and a deafening blast, temporarily disorienting targets. Use Flash grenades to stun enemies in close proximity to vital hostages or VIPs: explosive ordinance such as HE or Frag grenades could injure or eliminate friendlies as well as hostiles, so it's best to use a Flash/Smoke combination for entry into well-guarded areas containing vital mission targets that must be kept alive.

- RPG's are shoulder-fired Rocket-Propelled Grenades. These high-velocity projectiles can penetrate armored vehicles, so use them sparingly and precisely. They can also destroy breach points, which is especially handy when your team doesn't have any C4 on hand.

- Claymores are explosive mines that detonate outwardly from where you place them and can be triggered remotely. When you plant a Claymore, it will detonate away from you; in other words, make sure that you position it in the relevant direction. Try to set Claymores at the bottom of hills when you are sniping so that you can quickly switch to the detonator and neutralize any advancing enemy forces before they find you.

- Mines are available for taking out personnel and vehicles. When planting vehicle mines, take care to place them where the vehicles will actually run over them. The car or truck tires must make solid contact with the mines in order for them to detonate. Furthermore, don't place vehicle mines in the middle of the road as your target may simply drive harmlessly over. Plant personnel mines in key chokepoints on the map or at entrances to sensitive areas. Alternatively, use them to protect yourself when sniping or camping in certain areas. Mines may even serve as a sort of detection device: putting a mine at the only entrance to a building will usually let you know when someone is coming in (whether the mine neutralized the intruder, or was safely detonated). The following are all good places to plant personnel mines: corpses, bushes, dark corners, building entrances, close to water or on ledges that enemies might climb over, even on a bomb after you plant it, to prevent the enemy from successfully defusing it. Always inform your team of the exact location of any mines you might be placing. The last thing you want to do is to blow up one of your own teammates with a mine that was meant for the opposition.

ACCESSORIES

SOCOM 3 offers the possibility of customizing your weapons. With several dozen weapons and add-ons, the potential combinations are in the hundreds. You will soon realize that the equipment you choose is absolutely critical. If you're looking for a thorough description of each piece of gear, turn to page 36 of the Game Basics chapter. By applying the information you find there to the requirements of the battle you're about to fight, you'll quickly learn how to change mere stats into gold.

VEHICLE TIPS

- The vehicles in SOCOM 3 play an integral part in helping you to successfully complete your mission. (A list of all vehicles can be found in the Game Basics chapter on pages 39-41.) Indeed, vehicles enable you to quickly transport multiple team members (relatively) safely to important locations. And they're loads of fun too! Not only will you be able to get almost a third of your team to your desired location faster than if you were running, but most modes of transport also offer heavy mounted-weaponry to disperse any threats you may encounter along the way.

- Use vehicles for cover by parking them at key locations and ducking behind them. However, be warned: bullets can pass through most vehicles, so it's still possible for you to take a hit through the metal..

- You can use any land vehicle to effectively run down enemies in your path. This tactic works great when you are the only person in the transportation, without a gunner. If you are not proficient at driving, use the headset to ask someone else to drive for you while you man the turret gun. Oh, and you might as well request a driver that knows where they are going and how to steer while you're at it!

- It's best to dismount if you need to fire on someone, rather than trying to shoot them with the mounted weaponry. The mounted guns offer great firepower, but leave you immobilized and easy prey for enemy fire. Jump out, go prone, and shoot from underneath the vehicle.

- Use vehicles to create new chokepoints and prevent enemy vehicles from passing a certain area, or when you want to set up an ambush.

- Make sure to avoid driving land-based vehicles into the water as this will immediately destroy them.

- To make sharp turns, slap the left analog stick down and in the direction you wish to turn. For instance, if you want to make a sharp right turn, move the left analog stick down and to the right. Practice your driving as you may be called upon to transport your team in a firefight. Get the feel for driving the trucks and boats as they each have their own physics. Some will skid out more than others when making sharp turns, depending on the composition of the surface that you are driving on. For instance, you will slide through turns more often on dirt roads than you will on pavement. You can also use the third-person view to pan around and see what's going on up ahead or behind you. This can be a very effective way to foil an upcoming ambush.

RUNNING AND GUNNING

By definition, 'running and gunning' is when you forego stealth for an all-out offensive attack. Grab an accurate, semi-lightweight rifle, make your way to any one of the various meeting points and get ready for a firefight. Choose your weapon based on the map and side that you will be playing on. If you will be engaging in close quarters combat in an indoor setting, it is best to choose a weapon with a high rate of fire, such as a sub machine gun, or something with a large damage radius, such as a shotgun. If you're going to be out in wide open spaces, choose something with a bit more range, such as a rifle.

Before you start, decide whether or not you will need to hotswap to a pistol to avoid reload times or if you think you will need to clear an area ahead of you with grenades. Set your hotswap selection to your main rifle and either your pistol or grenades. Think about adding a pistol grip to your rifle as this will help steady your weapon and improve your accuracy when standing or crouching.

Eventually you will encounter the enemy. You may find yourself in a position where the two of you are ducking in and out of cover and popping shots off at each other. In situations like this, have your grenades set to your hotswap button so that you can easily switch from your rifle to a grenade and flush the enemy out from his or her hiding place, giving you a chance to eliminate them as they run for cover.

Be sure to select Double Ammo from the Armory if you plan on 'running and gunning'. The last thing you want to happen is to run out of ammo and have to switch to a pistol.

During gunfights, it is inevitable that someone is going to run out of ammo and need to reload. One of the keys to winning a firefight is to make sure that your opponent runs out of ammo before you do. A simple trick to ensure this happens is to use short, controlled bursts of fire. Even if you have your weapon fire mode set to full auto, don't just mash down the trigger and fire every bullet you have. Use a tapping or pumping action to squeeze off between two and four shots at a time. This will conserve ammo as well as improve your accuracy immensely.

Another trick is to get your enemy to fire off shots at you blindly (thinking they are going to hit you), thus causing them to waste ammo and forcing them to reload. Do this by peeking out from behind various objects such as walls, trees, vehicles, etc. Run out, jump out, and do whatever it takes to get them to fire off more rounds than necessary, leaving you the opportunity to rush up and attack them, when they can't retaliate.

Suppressors are not usually necessary in running and gunning situations. However, a suppressor will enable you to squeeze off a few more rounds at someone before they realize that they are even being shot at. Know your surroundings and chokepoints and make a decision as to whether or not you will need to equip your weapon with a silencer. Remember that suppressors will lessen the power and effective range of your rifle.

While on the run, you may encounter more than one enemy. When grenades are not an option, try to position yourself so that enemies are in front of each other, thus minimizing their effective lanes of fire. Grenades are usually the best option for quickly eliminating multiple threats, but some scenarios may either prevent you from discharging them (as in hostage or VIP situations), or you simply might not have any left. Make sure that you call for help over the headset when encountering multiple enemies. This will let your teammates know where the opposition is congregating and how many of them there are, provided that you give a clear description of your location and situation. Saying something like "I've got three on me at DELTA" is a great way to concisely vocalize your situation. On the other hand, don't say things like "Help!" or "They're over here". Such cries won't do your teammates any good as they give no indication of your location.

Even though you're running and gunning, don't just shoot at everything you see right off the bat. If you encounter an enemy that runs from one building to another, instead of firing off a couple of shots to see if you can hit him, wait and see if someone else is with him. He may be traveling with a buddy who could be just a few steps behind him. If you fire at the first enemy, the second will be able to spot you easily and take you down. Instead, wait to see if there is more than one hostile, then sneek up on them from behind to surprise them. When you get into gunfights, use cover to duck in and out: you'll minimize damage to yourself and make the enemy expend his ammo.

CAMPING TIPS

'Camping' is when you opt to 'hang back' or ambush the enemy instead of assaulting or running and gunning. This is a highly effective tactic in several situations and missions.

Let's say that your mission is to plant a bomb at an enemy base. We'll assume that your enemy has several times previously acquired the bomb before you did and advanced it to your position each round. You may decide to 'camp' your base: this will make it more difficult for the enemy to gain access and plant the bomb.

Make sure you survey the lay of the land before you devise your camping strategy. Scope out all of the entrances to the base so that you and your teammates have each one covered. There are several ways to effectively camp an area. One is to assign a group of players armed with heavy machine guns that enable them to lay down a virtual wall of bullets to prevent enemy access to guard each entrance. They may also choose to set up a crossfire with their heavy weapons. This will protect your team with a near-impenetrable forcefield. Be wary of the enemy targeting you from behind a wall with their third-person camera view and strafing out from their cover to shoot you. Keep mobile. To do so, assume a crouching position but avoid going prone (as it makes you an easier target). As a general rule, try to set up crossfires at the end of long hallways, tunnels, valleys, or even on opposing hilltops. You will soon realise that this is a great way to protect territory as well as VIPs and hostages.

Mines and Claymores are very effective weapons for campers. They enable a minimal force to lock down a large area. Plant them at all entrances and chokepoints that the enemy might use to gain access to your base. When you plant these types of explosives, be sure to hide them as best you can. Try placing them in doorjams, under bushes, on corpses, on the corners of

buildings and anywhere else you can think of. If your opponents see your explosive ordinance, they will of course try to destroy it with a grenade. Wait for them to pull the pin and pop out and shoot them while they can't fire back at you.

A camper's best friend is surprise. Set up ambushes: let the enemy think they managed to infiltrate your base, then jump out and eliminate them before they know what hit them. Use silenced weapons: this way, if a group of enemies reach your base, you can fire at them from concealed positions, confusing them and giving you more time to crush them. Try setting up silenced crossfires to really put a dent in the assaulting forces.

When camping, make good use of your environment: this means choosing the best camouflage for your surroundings. Once you've selected the right character for the map terrain, find a good place to hide, somewhere that offers you a great view of attacking forces while giving them little or no view of you. The third-person view works great for this: tilt the camera down to look over walls or hills; tilt it left or right to peek around corners.

If you camp every round, chances are the enemy is going to get wise to your scam, so take some time to find yourself a handful of camping areas. Being able to switch from one place to another from round to round will offer you the chance to outwit your enemies by keeping them guessing as to what you and your team are doing.

Camping is a team effort. Sure, you can camp a few rounds and even pick off a few enemies, but you can't protect an entire base yourself against an entire enemy attack squad. Try to coordinate with your teammates prior to a round to see if anyone will join in and help your cause.

SNIPING TIPS

Having a crack sniper on your team can be a valuable asset. One sniper can single-handedly hold back an entire squad while simultaneously thinning the herd and calling out enemy positions. Be sure to select the sniper camouflage or Guille Suit that will best conceal your body from the enemy.

The M87ELR and M82A1A are the two most sniper rifles in the entire game: you only need to hit someone once in the torso (or head, of course) to kill them. These weapons are great for sniping people on the move as well as those that are hiding and exposing just their head or part of their torso. Other sniper rifles are accurate and have good range but do not kill with one shot.

Before you begin sniping, be sure to attach a suitable scope to your weapon or it may turn out to be completely useless. The High Scope works wonders, however some low light or night missions may require you to choose a Thermal Scope, which offers high visibility at medium range and displays a brightly colored outline of the target, but is not so useful at long range.

Select your rifle based on the type of situations you think you may encounter. For instance, if you will be covering a large area from the top of a hill, you may want to select a one-shot weapon since your enemy will most likely move around a lot in open areas. Conversely, you may want to choose a silenced sniper rifle to conceal your location, giving you time to take more than one shot, and enabling you to stay in position instead of relocating because someone heard or saw you fire.

Snipers don't usually need to carry extra ammo. Instead, think about equipping Claymores or grenades. These are ideal to booby trap the area around you.

While sniping, aim for the head whenever possible, but remember that you are more likely to hit your target if you aim for the chest. This works fine when using a one-shot weapon, but will only damage a target if using a normal sniper rifle.

When moving from one location to another, be sure to set your pistol as your secondary hotswap weapon. You can't run and gun when toting a sniper rifle. When moving from point A to point B, switch to your pistol in case you come into contact with enemy forces.

Being a sniper carries with it several responsibilities such as being the spotter for your team. Many times while sniping, you will not be able to actually make the shot (because the enemy runs between two buildings, for example). In these cases, it is your responsibility to inform your team of the location of the enemy soldiers that you spotted. Again, do not just say, "I see two up ahead." This does your team no good as they have no idea where "up ahead" is in relation to their current position. Be sure to accurately and concisely call out enemy positions: "two hostiles spotted at DELTA" is a great way of letting your team know what may lie ahead, giving them time to prepare a strategy to advance on the enemy location.

If you decide to be a sniper, you'll need to find a good place to shoot from. Sit out a match and watch for a few rounds to find out where opposing forces have a tendency to run to. Feel free to attach a Bipod to your rifle for increased stability and accuracy. Once you've found yourself a nice little niche to hide in, go prone, be patient, verify your target, take careful aim and then fire. Beforehand, surround your position with either mines or Claymores to ensure your safety: as stated previously, your pistol can't compete against an automatic rifle, so covering your 'six' with explosives is a great way to protect yourself.

Another good strategy to keep in mind when you're a sniper is to take to high ground. You are much more efficient when shooting from an elevated position. Most enemies will not even look up when getting shot at, which can afford you extra time to land another shot. Lofty positions also offer a reduced line of sight for the enemy. Of course, try to make your shots count: once an opponent hears the boom of a high-powered sniper rifle, chances are he or she will scurry for cover. Additionally, avoid going to the same locations every time. The enemy will get wise, and pick up a rifle of their own to suppress you. Find a few locations that offer you good vantage points, and switch between them often. Even if the positions are just a few feet away from each other, it may give you enough time to identify the enemy and eliminate them. When taking the shot, be sure to slightly 'lead' the enemy to anticipate when they will enter your crosshairs. If you miss your shot and lose the enemy, inform your team via the headset of your foe's last known position.

Play the same map from both sides to familiarize yourself with all the best sniping spots. This can prove very helpful when you battle another sniper, as it enables you to anticipate your rival's most likely movements: let him get set, then take your shot.

One final tip is to use water to your advantage. You can crouch near the water's edge and lean to one side, almost completely submerging your character, and making them virtually invisible. This may afford you the time you need to fire off another round while the enemy is still trying to locate your position.

SOCOM3
U.S. NAVY SEALS

GAME BASICS

WALKTHROUGH

MULTIPLAYER

EXTRAS

INDEX

GETTING STARTED

GAME MODES

TIPS AND
STRATEGIES

MAP ANALYSIS

TEAMWORK

THE BASICS

Teamwork is vital to your mission success. One-man armies don't win matches. Communication is the key to organizing an effective force and making the most of your assets and time. Calling out enemy locations as well as your own locations will enable you and your team to not only effectively flush out the opposition, but also guard against friendly fire. Use the headset to inform your team of areas that you have checked when looking for the last enemy so as not to waste time searching areas that have already been covered.

Team members should have positions or duties assigned to them. For instance, it is of no use to have six snipers. Make sure everyone gears up with the appropriate weapons and understands the general plan of attack (or defense). Set certain groups to spawn at different spawn points to more effectively cover the entire map. Remember, your impressive personal stats won't do your team any good if you lose the match, so stay focused on the mission and take one for the team if and when necessary.

Always check your HUD to see how many members of your team are still alive and how many enemies remain. This will help you to organize a search party if necessary to hunt down the last man. Watch your teammates: when someone on your team dies, do a quick scan around the map to see if you can find their name before it fades out. This will give you a general idea of where that person went down and where to expect a possible enemy advance.

Be sure to inform your team of any areas where you have placed mines or Claymores so that they don't accidentally detonate them. When moving as a group, be sure to keep a good distance between you and your squad as a single grenade can kill the whole party in one fell swoop. Keep to a tight formation, but still far enough apart from each other to avoid an explosion. Also be aware that if you are the last person in a group, you will need to watch the team's back.

Work with your team to coordinate attacks such as breaching a room. Have one player open the door while another tosses in a flashbang grenade, then order everyone else to storm the room while the enemy is stunned or blinded. When camping, make sure you don't have more players than you need covering a certain area. Too many people in one area can make for problems, and friendly fire kills. If you only need one person watching an entrance, then only use one. Simple.

Adapt to your enemy. You may enter into a game and find that for the first few rounds, your team's tactics work perfectly. However, your opponent will eventually figure out your strategy and find a way to counter it. When this happens, you will need to adapt and change your strategy as well. Try having a few plans to switch to if one of your plays gets figured out by the enemy. If you see that they are all sniping, then you should rush. If you see that they are all rushing, then camp and ambush. Always keep an eye on what the enemy is doing from round to round to best decide on your team's course of action.

Team movement is essential to keeping your own players alive. For instance, when you have more than one teammate heading down a tunnel, don't stick too close to the person in front, to avoid the possibility of the enemy shooting right through the person in front of you and hitting you in the process. Stagger your formation, and advance down the hallway with teammates on either side of the wall. That way your team will have an unobstructed line of fire if an enemy is encountered, as well as less chance of being wiped out simultaneously.

It's always a good idea to run with a group. Even if it's just one other person, two people have a better chance at surviving a firefight against one person.

WINGMEN

Running with a wingman will increase your chances of surviving a firefight with a single enemy. Take turns leading: you lead one round, your wingman leads the next. This way the leader can take the route that they think is best, knowing that their back is covered. This works great in small groups and offers a chance to let inexperienced players try their hand at leadership.

Use a wingman as a distraction. Have him take a large, loud weapon and stand out in a semi-open area and fire away. This should attract the enemy while you sit in hiding with a silenced weapon or a sniper rifle. When the enemy comes to investigate the shooting, you can pick him off from a concealed position.

You can also use this tactic to gain access to an area or entrance that is being watched by the enemy. Have your wingman create a disturbance with loud fire or movement. Then, when the fighters guarding the entrance move to engage him, sneak through. Many times your wingman might have to give his life for you to proceed and complete the mission, so make sure their sacrifice isn't in vain.

SQUADS

SOCOM 3 offers enormous battlefields and room for 16 vs 16 players. You are free to divide your team up into many different configurations depending on the map, mode and opponent. For instance, if you are playing a Suppression mode, you can split your team up into three squads: two squads of four and one squad of eight. Send each team of four around to the sides of the map and the main squad up through the middle. This will enable your smaller squads to get into flanking positions, skirt around the enemy and come up behind them. Alternatively, try splitting your clan up into two teams of eight for a powerful pair of breaching teams. Coordinate with each other to blow breaches and charge in simultaneously. Experiment with various squad formations: you could also have four squads of four and send two squads out in different directions to attack, while the other two squads stay back and defend different areas of your base.

Squads need leaders that coordinate breaches and assaults on the fly. For instance, if you have one squad of four to breach two points that you know the enemy is covering tightly, send a squad member to one breach point to cause a distraction such as throwing a Smoke grenade. This will make the enemy think that you are going to try to breach on that side when in reality, the remaining three members of your squad will be waiting to rush in at the other breach point. The squad leader may also decide to break up the squad into two wingman teams in certain situations, such as two wingman pairs breaching through two different areas, then meeting back up in the center once they've broken through.

You can use your squads to set up positions. Try setting up a forward assault squad that is spread across the map almost in a search line so that no one can get past them. Have your defensive line set up in similar positions, but further back, near to your base. Make sure everyone knows everyone else's positions so that if someone goes down on the forward line, the defense will know where enemies may be advancing from. If the forward line loses a man, they should spread out, fill in for that person and reform the line.

There are many different ways to disperse your team in any given match. You will need to decide which format is best for each map and each mode. Different modes will require different groupings

of players. Be aware of these elements of the game so that you can prepare for upcoming matches in your weekly training and practice sessions.

SPORTSMANLIKE CONDUCT

When you're playing in a match and things don't go your way, it's easy to blame the game or your team, or even accuse the other side, but the truth is, most of the time you will have to take your share of the responsibility. Take your loss like a soldier and learn from it: you will fail from time to time and you need to look back at where you went wrong and practice ways to make it right.

Do's and don'ts: Don't finish up a match and go back into the lobby accusing the other team of cheating: this will only start a fight and tarnish your clan's reputation. Don't eliminate someone, then stand over their body and shoot them over and over again. Don't taunt players too much after beating them: sometimes you will play matches just for fun or with other clans that you know will be lighthearted about it, but for the most part, making a taunt after landing a shot will only antagonize the other team.

CLAN TIPS

OWN CLAN?

Starting your own clan? Be sure that you have the spare time to devote to it. Most clans have their own websites, forums, logos and more. Take it as far as you like, but check that you can make the time for your clan members. Don't accept matches if you won't be able to attend them as this will only result in a loss.

RECRUITING

You will need to find good players for your clan once you're ready. Try looking on some of the major SOCOM forums. Most of them have specific areas that you can post in and use to recruit members for your team, but don't take just anyone that comes along.

If you want to create a great clan, you need to screen your tryouts. If you are an older group, then you'll want to set an age limit such as '18 and over'. If you're a younger group and you want all of your buddies in the clan because you all have the same schedule, then set your restrictions accordingly. Think about the kind of clan you want to create before you start looking for players. If you want to have a clan that will strictly dominate the competition, then recruit only the best shooters you can find. Watch out though, you are bound to get some 'children' with attitudes in your group. If you want to create a clan that has fun, doesn't worry about winning every match, and just wants to have a good time with good friends, then screen your recruits accordingly. Let the candidates play with you and your clanmates, and see how they fit in before you invite them to join.

Make sure you specify at what time your clan will be playing and inform your recruits that if they are not going to be available during these times, then they should not apply. Set up a free forum (message board) for you and your team members to communicate with each other. You can also use it to keep your clan informed about upcoming matches and planned events.

PRACTICE

We all need to practice, no matter how good we are. Don't necessarily think of practice in the literal sense of the word, think of it more as a training session. Individual clan members can practice on their own time. Schedule weekly team practice or training sessions and get the whole clan together to run through newly created strategies or to practice something that you got beat on in a previous match.

Sometimes practice is a great way to boost your clan's morale. Just getting together with your clanmates will build friendships and camaraderie that will enhance your abilities on the battlefield. Use practice sessions to train for upcoming matches and have your clanmates help devise tactics that you may not have previously thought of. Run through various options and strategies so that you have something to fall back on if a planned play doesn't work so well in a match.

CHAIN OF COMMAND

Every organization needs a chain of command: use a ranking system to assign ranks and duties to your clanmates. This will guarantee that everyone knows who to listen to in life or death situations. You don't want your entire team yelling their heads off in the middle of a match, with no one knowing what to do or who to listen to. Your chain of command should be solid and well defined, so that every single team member knows who will be giving the orders and who will be following them.

Make sure that you have a fall back: this way, if your leader goes down in a match, you'll have a second in command to take over his duties.

Running a clan is a lot of work. Try to assign some of the jobs to your clanmates. For instance, have someone in charge of setting up matches. This way, you won't have 20 people setting up 20 different matches for the same night. Try putting someone in charge of recruiting: if they bring you qualified candidates, you'll have the time to concentrate on other things.

REWARDS

Most people want to be noticed for the things they do and the contributions they make. Set up a reward system that allows your members to move up in rank by helping out the clan, or bestow awards on them for outstanding play on the battlefield. This will encourage your members to want to excel in battle and for your clan.

Don't make it easy for your members to attain these ranks and awards, but don't make it too difficult either. Find the balance that stimulates your partners without discouraging them. Keep an eye on everyone and have your members report outstanding behavior to you if you cannot keep a watchful eye yourself.

STANDARDS

Set your standards ahead of time and don't stray from them. If you want to create a clan that upholds the highest sporting conduct, then hold yourself to it. Have your members watch each other when playing in public rooms to ensure that they are showing your clan's name in the best light. The last thing you want is to have a loose cannon running around in public cursing, berating other players, or being rude in general. This will reflect negatively on you and your entire clan.

If someone gets out of line, you should have rules set forward ahead of time so that you can point to them and decide on an acceptable punishment such as not letting the transgressor play in the next match.

Make sure that your players show up for events. If they tell you they will be there and they don't turn up, impose an appropriate penalty. Stick to your guns and your team will respect you for it.

MAP ANALYSIS

In this section you will find detailed Multiplayer maps. You will notice that each map is featured several times, with each version depicting one of the different times, with each version depicting one of the different game modes that can be played on the specific map. Unique icons are used for each mode, to enable you to locate them at a glance.

HARVESTER

SUPPRESSION

BREACH

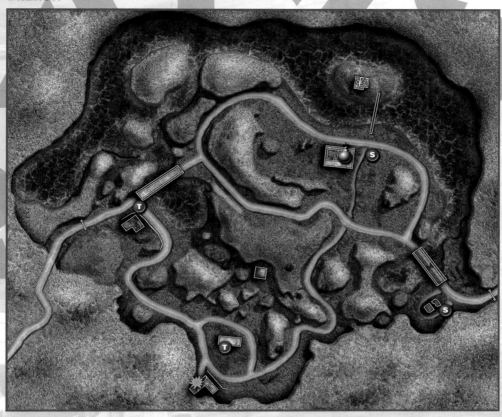

DEMOLITION

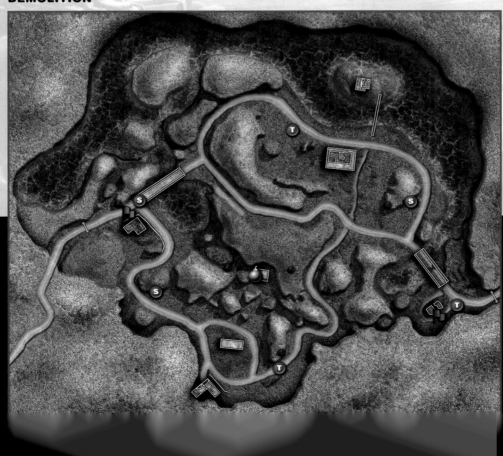

CONTROL

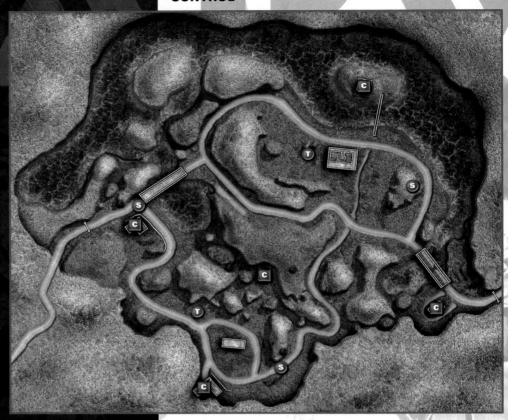

CONVOY

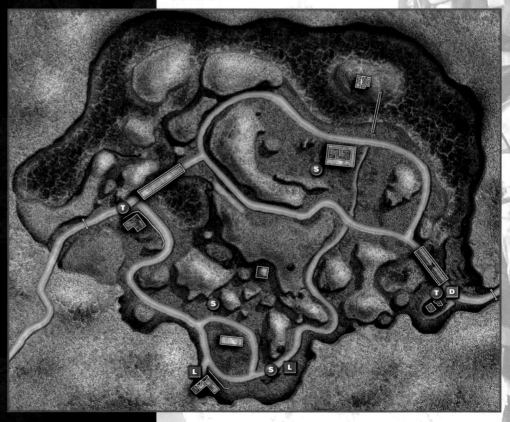

ESCORT

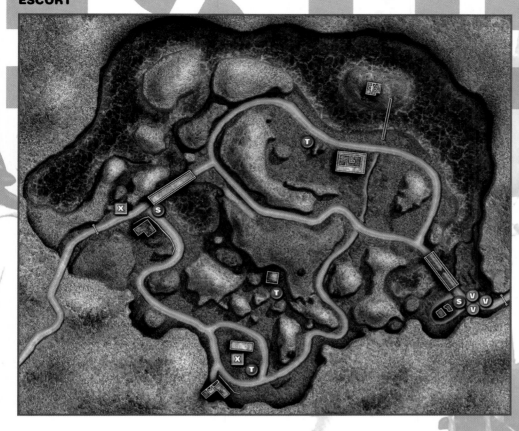

EXTRACTION

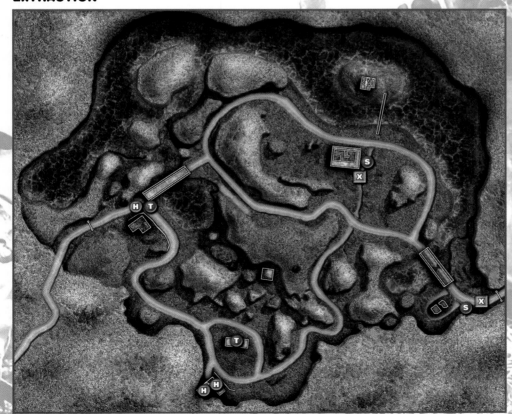

SOCOM3
U.S. NAVY SEALS

GAME BASICS

WALKTHROUGH

MULTIPLAYER

EXTRAS

INDEX

GETTING STARTED

GAME MODES

TIPS AND
STRATEGIES

MAP ANALYSIS

HARVESTER

CRUCIBLE

KILLING FIELDS

CITADEL

DEVILS ROAD

BONEYARD

TIDAL FURY

ANTENORA

STORM FRONT

FAULT

WATERWORKS

BLACKWOODS

SUPPRESSION

SOCOM3
U.S. NAVY SEALS

GAME BASICS

WALKTHROUGH

MULTIPLAYER

EXTRAS

INDEX

GETTING STARTED

GAME MODES

TIPS AND
STRATEGIES

MAP ANALYSIS

HARVESTER

CRUCIBLE

KILLING FIELDS

CITADEL

DEVILS ROAD

BONEYARD

TIDAL FURY

ANTENORA

STORM FRONT

FAULT

WATERWORKS

BLACKWOODS

DEMOLITION

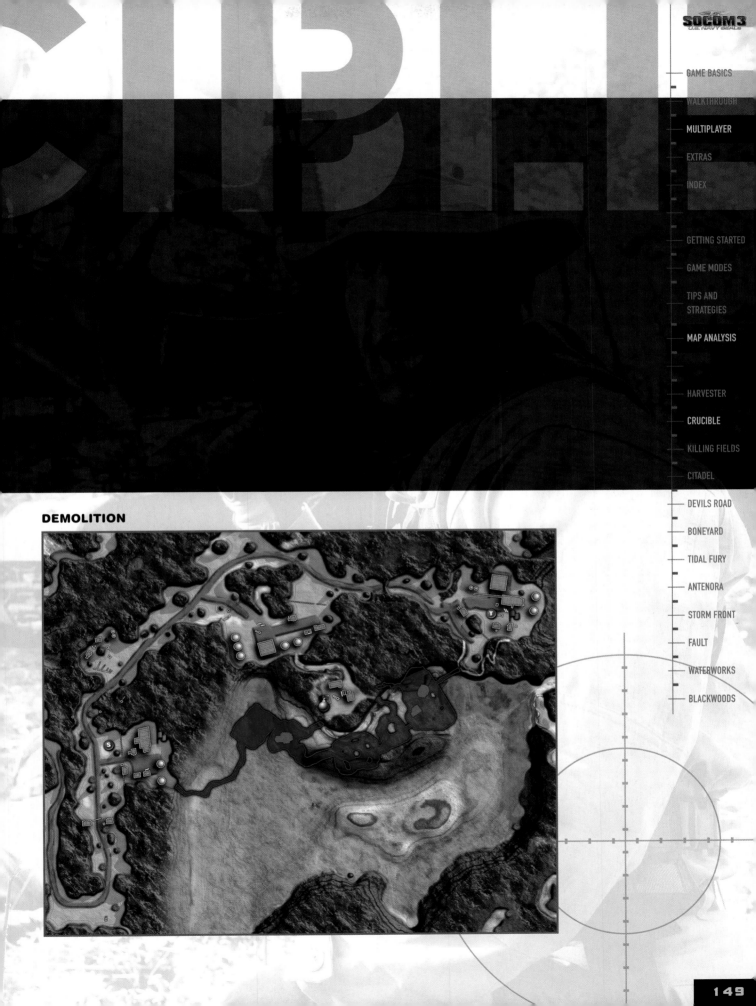

CONTROL

CONVOY

ESCORT

SUPPRESSION

DEMOLITION

CONTROL

CONVOY

ESCORT

CITADEL

SUPPRESSION

BREACH

DEMOLITION

CONTROL

ESCORT

EXTRACTION

DEVILS ROAD

SUPPRESSION

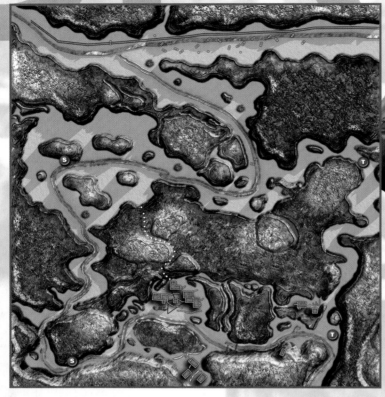

CONTROL

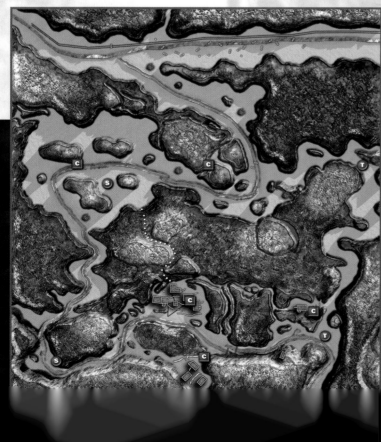

CONVOY

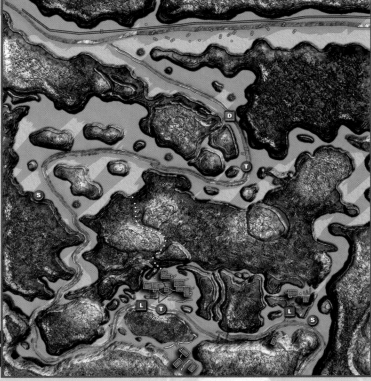

EXTRACTION

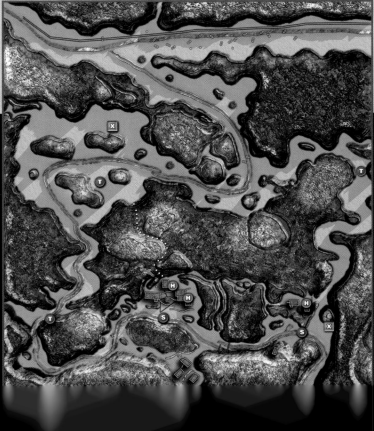

SUPPRESSION

BREACH

EXTRACTION

TIDAL FURY

SUPPRESSION

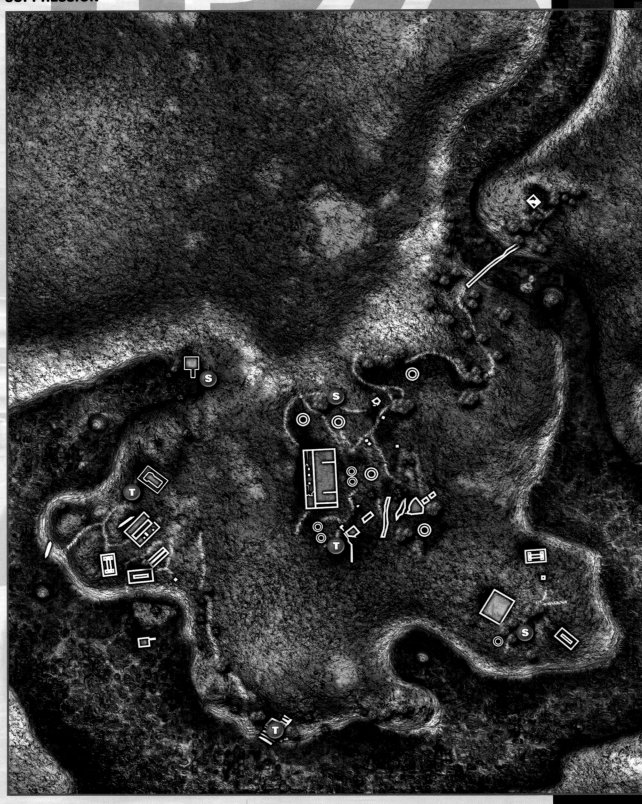

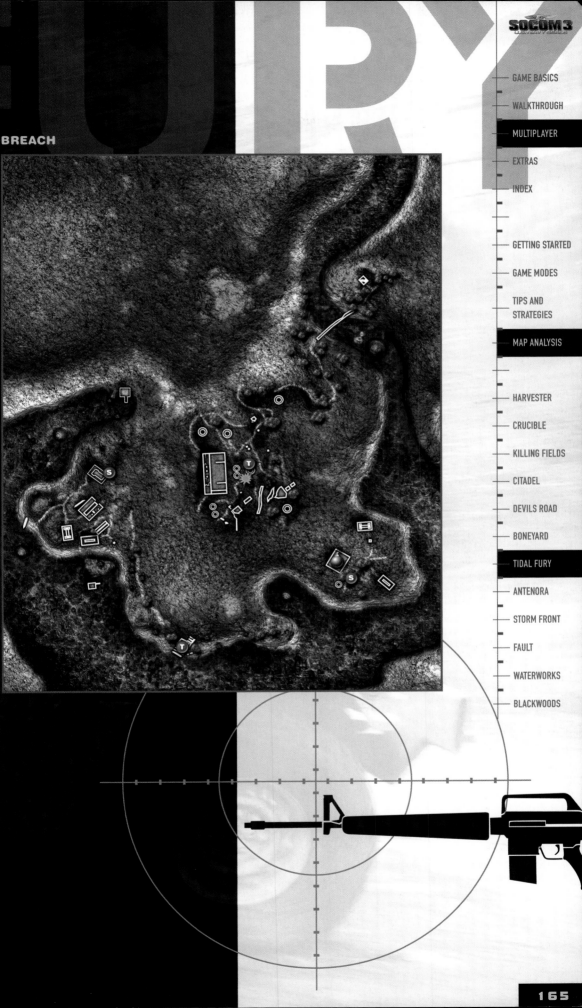

CONTROL

EXTRACTION

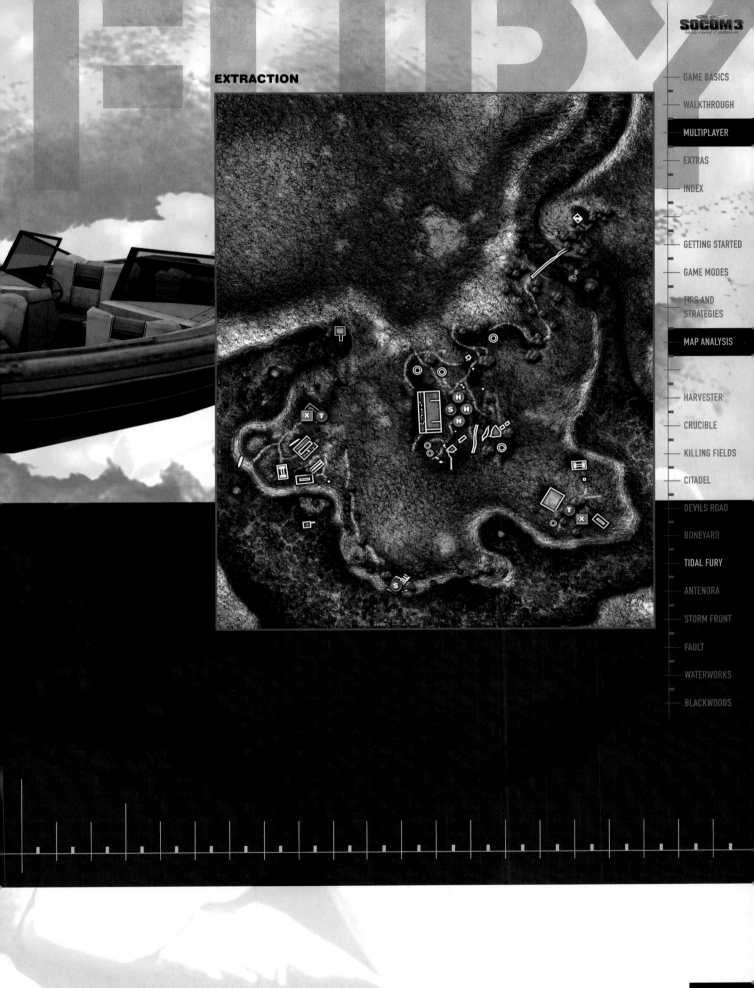

ANTENORA

SUPPRESSION

BREACH

CONTROL

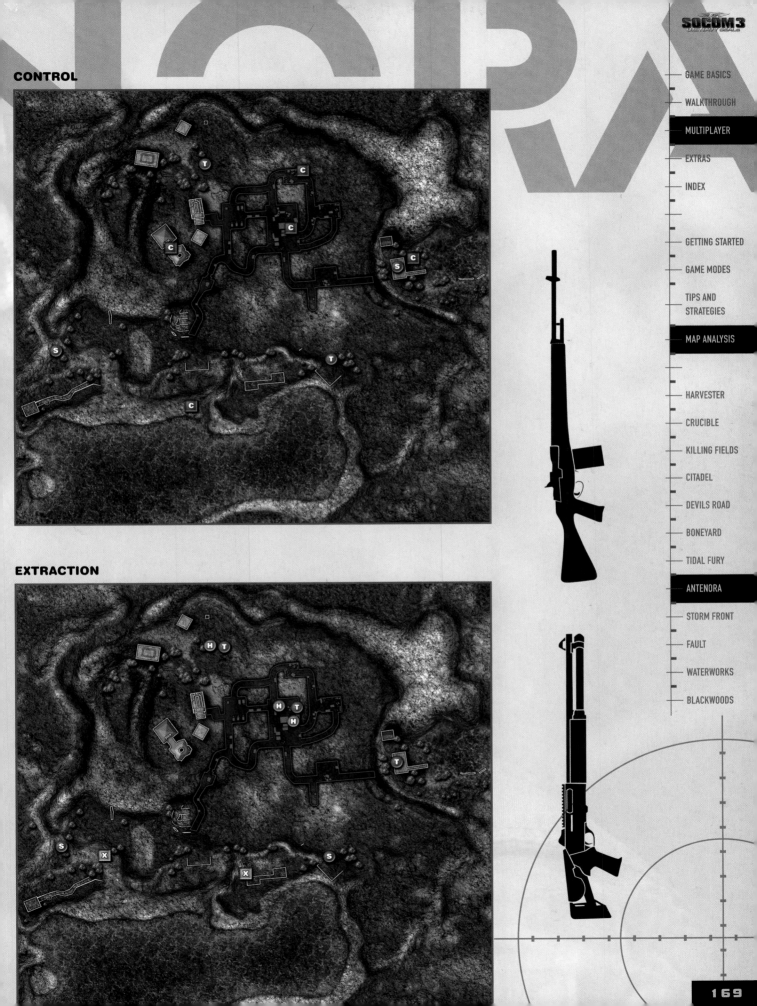

EXTRACTION

STORM FRONT

SUPPRESSION

DEMOLITION

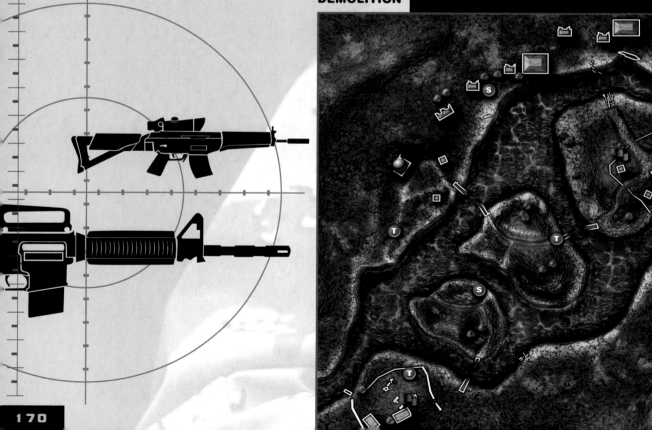

CONTROL

EXTRACTION

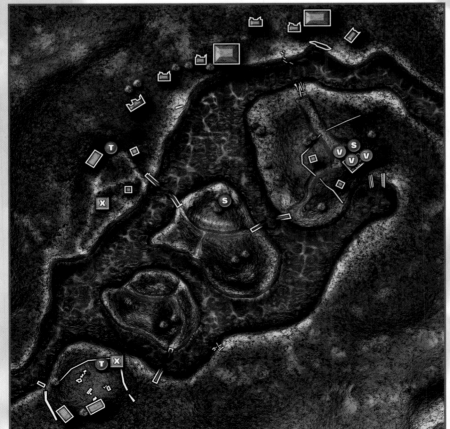

FAULT

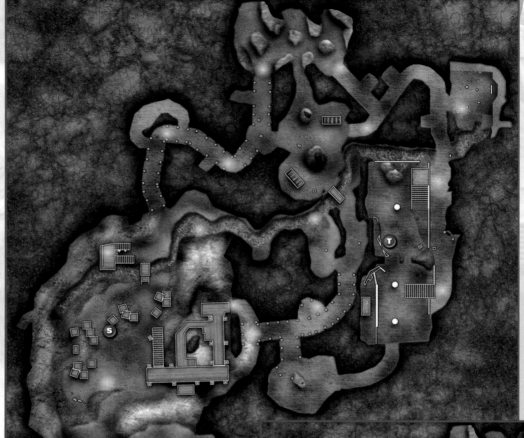

BN

DEMOLITION

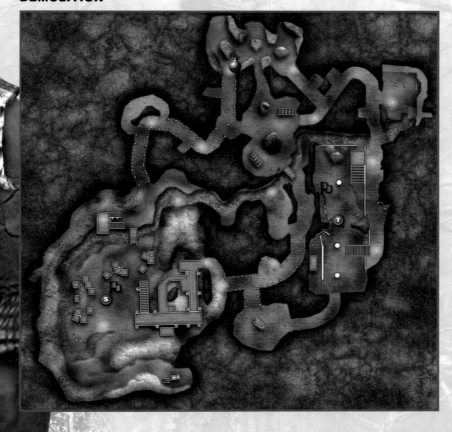

CONTROL

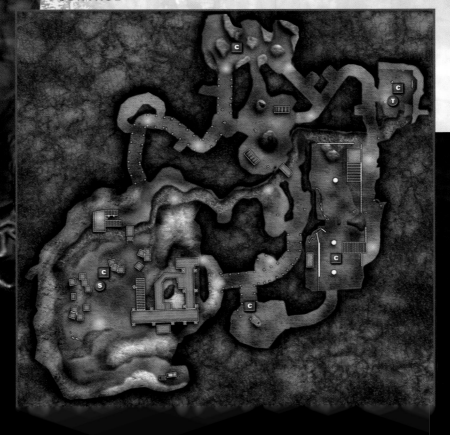

SUPPRESSION

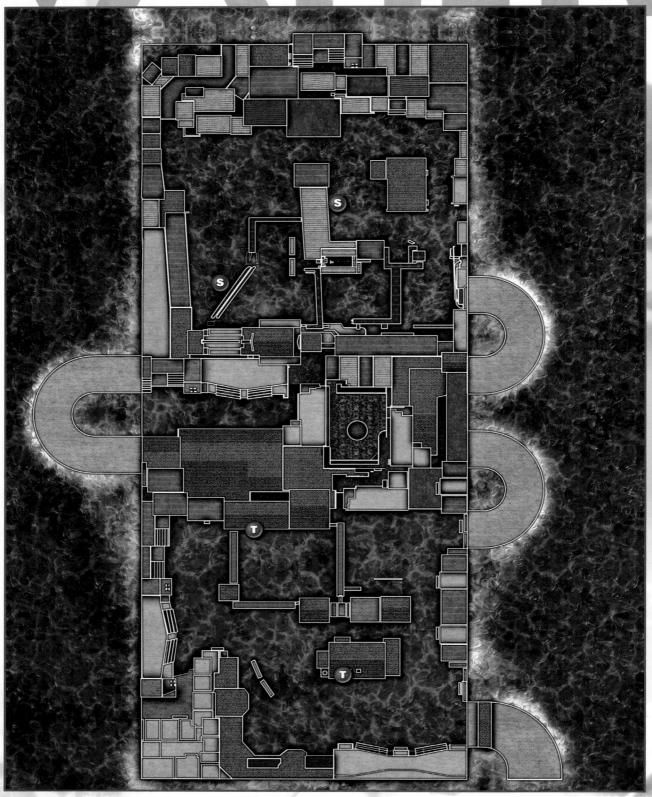

BREACH

DEMOLITION

CONTROL

ESCORT

BLACKWOODS

SUPPRESSION

MOLITION

CONTROL

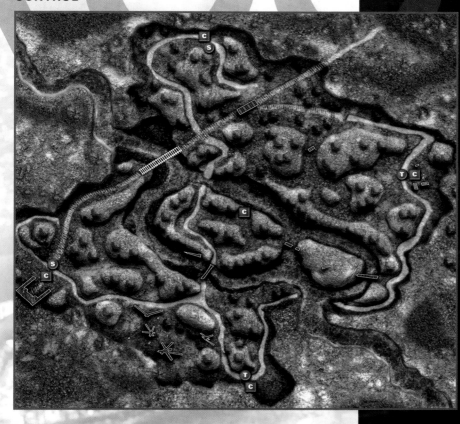

EXTRACTION

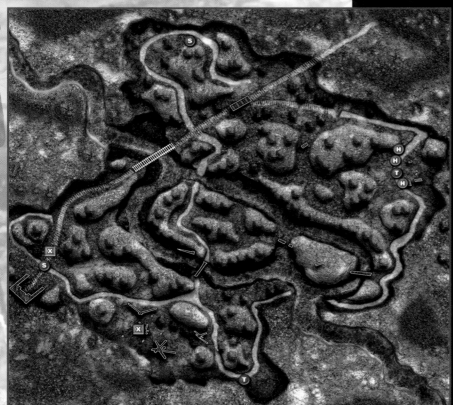

GAME BAS

WALKTHRE

MULTIPLAY

EXTRAS

INDEX

GETTING S

GAME MOD

TIPS AND
STRATEGIE

MAP ANAL

HARVESTE

CRUCIBLE

KILLING FI

CITADEL

DEVILS RO

BONEYARD

TIDAL FUR

ANTENORA

STORM FR

FAULT

WATERWO

BLACKWOO

◻ You've never heard of Piggyback? That shows how covert our operations have been. Although we are leader in the European market and have been publishing official game guides for seven years, we have managed to stay off your radar for all of that time.

◻ How did we ensure that you knew nothing about our exclusive European guides to Metal Gear Solid®, Metal Gear Solid®2 – Sons of Liberty™, Metal Gear Solid® 3: Snake Eater™? How were these missions kept secret from you? How did we ensure you were unaware that we had published the exclusive European guides to Final Fantasy® VIII, Final Fantasy® IX, Final Fantasy® X, Final Fantasy® X-2 and Final Fantasy® Crystal Chronicles™?

◻ Over the last seven years we've been working on handpicked, stealth operations. Our elite teams have been surreptitiously developing technologies, structural aids, camouflage techniques, quality control procedures and online expertise – all in order to publish precision guides for you.

Because we have focused on an average of just four guides each year since 1998, our R&D vets have become experts in precision and detail. They have developed structural aids such as our back cover foldout, quick search index, color coded index and 3-level tab system. These tools ensure you find the data you require immediately in our guides. ▣

Our layout artists have carefully applied choice camouflage, through creative use of official artwork, to ensure that our guides are a natural, seamless extension of the game property they represent. Unobserved examples include our guides to Silent Hill™, Silent Hill™ 2 and Silent Hill 4: The Room®.

In our guide to SOCOM 3: US NAVY SEALs you may notice our use of subtle support techniques; we clearly link our maps to our Walkthrough text, our screenshots (secret technology) relate unmistakably to the Walkthrough text through the use of numbered (Fig.) markers. The maps are given an added dimension by listing the keys to all icons in the back cover foldout. All of these mechanisms are then subjected to furtive quality assurance processes. This then enables you to access maximum, reliable information at all times! Some of these methods are new to this title, others were developed during operations on our guides to Gran Turismo™ 3 A-spec, Gran Turismo™ 4, Kingdom Hearts and the Legend of Zelda™ – the Windwaker ▣

It is only a matter of time before the code to any stealth technology, no matter how good, is decrypted. All of our techniques, developed in secret over seven years, during operations on precision titles, got us noticed by some highly informed US gamers. As such, and due to their popular demand, Piggyback published its first guides in the US market in November 2004 when we released Jak 3™ - The Official Guide and Halo® 2 – The Official Guide. You can access free download page samples to each at www.piggybackinetractive.com. ▣

piggybackinteraactive

EXTRAS

4ᵀᴴ CHAPTER

You've finished the game, and saved the world, but you've only just begun to scratch the surface of all that SOCOM 3 has to offer. In the following chapter, we outline every single extra that you can expect to find in the game, including the Crosstalk unlockables that directly affect missions in the game SOCOM Fireteam Bravo for the PSP™ (PlayStation® Portable).

Warning: there may be 'spoilers' contained within the following pages, so if you like to keep your gaming surprises, well, surprising, look away now, and come back later!

EXTRAS

BONUS OBJECTIVES

Each mission has several extra objectives that are only revealed when you reach a certain location, or perform a particular act. It's entirely possible to complete a mission without even being aware of its hidden Bonus Objectives. They only appear on the Mission Objective list in the TacMap (highlighted in dark blue) once they have been completed (Fig. 1).

Below you will find a list of all Bonus Objectives, sorted on a mission-by-mission basis, and including a brief summary of any impact that completing the objective will have on the rest of the mission, or on subsequent missions. Page references are also included, to enable you to locate details about each Bonus Objective in the Walkthrough.

NORTH AFRICA: GLOBAL FURY

FLASHPOINT
Board SOC-R (page 48)
Impact: Use the SOC-R to safely cross the river, taking out enemies as you go.

Eliminate Village Opposition (page 49)
Impact: Securing the area before entering, enables you to safely pass through the village without taking hostile fire.

DEEP STRIKE
Stop Runaway Vehicle (page 52)
Impact: Prevents the NAPF fighters from escaping and turning up elsewhere later on.

ESCALATION
Obtain Delivery Ledger 1 (page 59)
Impact: The ledgers contain vital information about SSM missile sites that will be used in the next mission.

RIPOSTE'S PRIMER
Prevent Further Launches (page 62)
Impact: More CHA peacekeeping troops will survive to help you on your next mission.

IN THE BALANCE
No CHA Points Overrun (page 66)
Impact: CHA reinforcements will arrive to help out during the attack on the NAPF base, and there will be fewer enemies in the following mission.

DAY OF RECKONING
Obtain Intel (page 71)
Impact: The intel will help you to locate Mahmood's hideout in the next mission.

WAKE OF THE FALLEN
Capture Surrendering NAPF Troops (page 74)
Impact: None, although the soldiers you spare will be very pleased!

SOUTH ASIA: CHAINED LIGHTING

NAUTICAL SALVAGE
Obtain Intel (page 78)
Impact: Will help you to find the Breakneck.

Overhear Arms Shipment (page 79)
Impact: Gain vital intel about a shipment of arms on its way to terrorist group Al-Shakoosh. Unlocks Destroy Arms Shipment objective in the Friend or Foe mission.

Obtain Shipping Manifest (page 79)
Impact: Provides more valuable information about the Breakneck's cargo.

FRIEND OR FOE
Destroy Arms Shipment (page 84)
Impact: You will prevent the arms shipment from reaching its destination.

Obtain Intel (page 85)
Impact: Gain vital information about where the Fist and Fire stores its weapons.

HEART OF THE FIST
Capture Ibrahim Abbas (page 88)
Impact: You take Fist and Fire's second-in-command out of the loop.

Find Terrorist Contact List (page 89)
Impact: Reveal valuable intel about Al-Shakoosh contacts.

Destroy Speedboat (page 89)
Impact: You will prevent the raiders from escaping in the speedboat.

POLAND: WINTER'S TEMPEST

NIGHTCRAWLER
Keep Guards Unsuspicious (page 92)
Impact: When you return to this area during a later mission, the guards will be more relaxed, and therefore easier to sneak up on.

STATE SECURITY
No Bonus Objective.

RETRIBUTION
Restrain Arms Dealer (page 102)
Impact: The captured dealer will provide intel on the NSO's black market sources for small arms.

WATERLOGGED
No Terrorists Engaged (page 106)
Impact: In the following mission, terrorist patrols will let their guard down and be easier to surprise.

BREWED CHAOS
Commandeer Enemy Boat (page 110)
Impact: You can use the boat to move quickly around the area and take out as many enemies as possible at the start of the mission.

CROSSTALK OBJECTIVES

In addition to Bonus Objectives, most missions in the game also feature Crosstalk Objectives. As with Bonus Objectives, these are not essential to completion of the game, but achieving them will generally have a favorable impact on SOCOM Fireteam Bravo for the PSP™ (PlayStation® Portable). Crosstalk data can be uploaded from PSP™ (PlayStation® Portable) to PlayStation®2 and vice versa by connecting the two with a USB cable and synchronizing their data on the Extras screen under Crosstalk.

A complete list of all Crosstalk messages and 'unlockables' can be viewed via the Crosstalk option in the Extras section of the Profile Menu (Fig. 1). Below, you will find details of all Crosstalk Objectives in the PS2 game, as well as an outline of the impact that completing an objective has on SOCOM Fireteam Bravo missions on the PSP™ (PlayStation® Portable).

NORTH AFRICA: GLOBAL FURY

FLASHPOINT
No Crosstalk Objective.

DEEP STRIKE
Destroy Transmitter (page 53)
SOCOM Fireteam Bravo Impact: Enemy forces in the Isolated Angel mission will have access to fewer reinforcements.

ESCALATION
Rescue Allied Prisoners (page 58)
SOCOM Fireteam Bravo Impact: One of the rescued prisoners imparts knowledge of Moline's exact location, making Moline easier to capture in the Short Fuse mission.

Obtain Troop Manifest (page 59)
SOCOM Fireteam Bravo Impact: SOCOM can pinpoint the insurgent forces on the TacMap in the Short Fuse mission.

Obtain Delivery Ledger 2 (page 59)
SOCOM Fireteam Bravo Impact: The team can find and destroy the cache of small arms in the Powderkeg mission.

RIPOSTE'S PRIMER
Prevent Further Launches (page 62)
SOCOM Fireteam Bravo Impact: A shipment of heavy weapons will now be available for the team in the Powderkeg mission.

IN THE BALANCE
No CHA Points Overrun (page 66)
SOCOM Fireteam Bravo Impact: Fewer enemy soldiers in base camp during the Lethal Crossing mission.

DAY OF RECKONING
Obtain Intel (page 71)
SOCOM Fireteam Bravo Impact: SOCOM can pinpoint NAPF Lieutenant's location on the TacMap in the Desert Siege mission.

WAKE OF THE FALLEN
Capture Surrendering NAPF Soldiers (page 74)
SOCOM Fireteam Bravo Impact: Stop the forces from regrouping at the Kasbah in the Desert Siege mission.

Complete Mission (page 75)
SOCOM Fireteam Bravo Impact: The CLL will guard the tenement building more fiercely in the Undertow mission.

SOUTH ASIA: CHAINED LIGHTING

NAUTICAL SALVAGE
Overhear Arms Shipment (page 79)
SOCOM Fireteam Bravo Impact: Heavy weapons will be available in the Songbird mission.

Recon Warehouse (page 79)
SOCOM Fireteam Bravo Impact: SOCOM learns more about CLL weaponry and is able to act on the information in the Powderkeg mission.

Complete Mission (page 79)
SOCOM Fireteam Bravo Impact: SOCOM learns enemy tactics and behavior, and determines the possible location of arms caches in the Clean Sweep mission.

SOCOM3
U.S. NAVY SEALS

GAME BASICS

WALKTHROUGH

MULTIPLAYER

EXTRAS

INDEX

BONUS OBJECTIVES

CROSSTALK

UNLOCKABLES

FRIEND OR FOE

Destroy Arms Shipment (page 84)
SOCOM Fireteam Bravo Impact: SOCOM prevents enemy obtaining heavy weapons or grenades in the Songbird mission.

No Non-Combatants Killed (page 85)
SOCOM Fireteam Bravo Impact: Magpie will be a more aggressive ally in the Songbird mission.

Liberate Village (page 84)
SOCOM Fireteam Bravo Impact: Anarchists in the Village Recon mission are demoralized and easier to defeat.

Obtain Intel (page 85)
SOCOM Fireteam Bravo Impact: SOCOM gains intel on where the Fist and Fire stashes its weapons, and can now access the weapons storage area in the Biohazard mission.

HEART OF THE FIST

Capture Ibrahim Abbas (page 88)
SOCOM Fireteam Bravo Impact: SOCOM can analyze tactics and evade enemy fire more easily in the Biohazard mission.

Capture Hari Raman (page 89)
SOCOM Fireteam Bravo Impact: SOCOM gains intel about Al-Shakoosh's combat tactics, making it easier to evade their attacks in the Under Fire mission.

POLAND: WINTER'S TEMPEST

NIGHTCRAWLER
Create a Diversion (page 92)
SOCOM Fireteam Bravo Impact: Chilean anarchists will be demoralized in the Undertow mission.

Bug the House (page 93)
SOCOM Fireteam Bravo Impact: Learn the location of the hard drive in the Undermining Authority mission.

STATE SECURITY
First Lady Uninjured (page 96)
SOCOM Fireteam Bravo Impact: More hostages will have to be rescued in the Supply and Demand mission.

Mission Success (page 97)
SOCOM Fireteam Bravo Impact: Chilean VP will now wear a flak vest in the Undertow mission, making him more likely to survive a gunshot wound.

RETRIBUTION
Disable Generators (page 101-102)
SOCOM Fireteam Bravo Impact: SOCOM can mark the location of the generators in the Undermining Authority mission.

Restrain Arms Dealer (page 102)
SOCOM Fireteam Bravo Impact: Learn the location of terrorist arms caches in the Powderkeg mission.

Find Terrorist Contact List (page 89)
SOCOM Fireteam Bravo Impact: Al-Shakoosh leader's location is pinpointed in the Under Fire mission.

Destroy Speedboat (page 89)
SOCOM Fireteam Bravo Impact: Terrorists will not arrive to protect the leader in the Biohazard mission.

Locate the Breakneck Cargo (page 89)
SOCOM Fireteam Bravo Impact: Terrorists will not be able to get their hands on heavy weapons and grenades in the Under Fire mission.

Secure Breackneck Captain (page 89)
SOCOM Fireteam Bravo Impact: Location of a Fist and Fire heavy arms cache marked in the Songbird mission.

Secure Breackneck First Mate (page 89)
SOCOM Fireteam Bravo Impact: The location of a Fist and Fire comms antenna will be marked in the Under Fire mission.

WATERLOGGED
No Terrorists Engaged (page 106)
SOCOM Fireteam Bravo Impact: The NSO will be easier to defeat in the Undermining Authority mission.

BREWED CHAOS
Neutralize Dr. Mironova (page 110)
SOCOM Fireteam Bravo Impact: The NSO will defend the dairy in the Chemical Reaction mission more aggressively.

Clear the Brewery (page 111)
SOCOM Fireteam Bravo Impact: Can now pinpoint the CLL leader on the TacMap in the Clean Sweep mission.

Neutralize Krzsyztof Gryc (page 111)
SOCOM Fireteam Bravo Impact: Obtain location of NSO cell leader in the Chemical Reaction mission.

UNLOCKABLES

SOCOM 3 has a wealth of unlockable goodies and secrets that help to enhance both the single-player and multiplayer modes, as well as SOCOM Fireteam Bravo for the PSP™ (PlayStation Portable), via the Crosstalk function. Complete details about all possible unlockables are provided in the Extras section of the OCN Main Menu (Fig. 1).

Below you will find a recap of all unlockables in one handy chart. The way it works is simple: when a cell is highlighted, it means that the feature it refers to in the horizontal list (for example 'CAPTAIN difficulty') can be unlocked by completing the corresponding task in the vertical list (in this example, 'Game completed on COMMANDER').

01

OVERVIEW

FEATURES UNLOCKED

Features columns:
- CAPTAIN difficulty *1
- ADMIRAL difficulty *1
- SEAL weapons (SP) *2
- Terrorist weapons (SP) *3
- SBS weapons (SP) *4
- GROM weapons (SP) *5
- IW-80 A2 Assault Rifle (SP and MP)
- STG-77 Assault Rifle (SP and MP)
- Medium Scope (SP and MP)
- Front Grip (SP and MP)
- ZX25 Airburst Grenade Launcher (SP only)
- North Africa - KILLJOY (SEAL) *6
- North Africa - SEAL Ghillie Suit *7
- North Africa - Al-Kamil Sarwat (terrorist) *8
- North Africa - Terrorist Ghillie Suit *9
- South Asia - CHOPPER (SEAL) *10
- South Asia - SEAL Ghillie Suit *11
- South Asia - Hari Raman (terrorist) *12
- South Asia - Terrorist Ghillie Suit *13
- Poland – COLDKILL (SEAL) *14
- Poland - SEAL Ghillie Suit *15
- Poland - Dr. Basia Mironova (terrorist) *16
- Poland - Terrorist Ghillie Suit *17
- North Africa intro cinema *18
- South Asia intro cinema *18
- Poland intro cinema *18
- 'Making of' music documentary *18
- Credits *19
- Music pack #1 *20
- Music pack #2 *21

1. SOCOM 3

Row labels:
- Game completed on ENSIGN
- Game completed on LIEUTENANT
- Game completed on COMMANDER
- Game completed on CAPTAIN
- Game completed on ADMIRAL
- Training mission completed
- North Africa completed on ENSIGN
- North Africa completed on LIEUTENANT
- North Africa completed on COMMANDER
- North Africa completed on CAPTAIN
- North Africa completed on ADMIRAL
- South Asia completed on ENSIGN
- South Asia completed on LIEUTENANT
- South Asia completed on COMMANDER
- South Asia completed on CAPTAIN
- South Asia completed on ADMIRAL
- Poland completed on ENSIGN
- Poland completed on LIEUTENANT
- Poland completed on COMMANDER
- Poland completed on CAPTAIN
- Poland completed on ADMIRAL

2. SOCOM Fireteam Bravo
- North Africa completed on any difficulty
- South Asia completed on any difficulty
- Poland completed on any difficulty

Legend: Difficulty | Weapons & Equipment | Multiplayer Characters | Movies | Music

Note: MP is Multiplayer, SP is Single-Player

WHAT IT ALL MEANS

You will notice that each unlockable listed at the top of the chart has a numbered asterisk next to it: below you will find a detailed explanation of each specific unlockable.

1. SOCOM 3 single-player missions can be played on the respective difficulty level.

2. The following SEAL weapons are made available in Training and all single-player missions.

- MARK 23
- HK5
- M8
- M14
- M16A2
- M4A1
- M4-90
- 12 Gauge Pump
- M40A1
- M87ELR
- M60E 3
- MK .48

- AT-4
- C4
- HE Grenade
- M67 Grenade
- SMOKE Grenade
- FLASHBANG Grenade
- Claymore

3. The following terrorist weapons are made available in Training and all single-player missions.

- MODEL 1B
- F57
- DE .50
- F90
- 9mm Sub
- AG-94
- RA-14
- AK-47
- 552
- TA 12 Gauge
- M82A1A
- SASR
- RTK-74
- RPG-7

- C4
- HE Grenade
- M67 Grenade
- SMOKE Grenade
- FLASHBANG Grenade
- PMN Mine

4. The following SBS weapons are made available in Training and all single-player missions.

- 9mm Pistol
- HK7
- L96AW

5. The following GROM weapons are made available in Training and all single-player missions.

- 226
- HK36
- SR-25

6. KILLJOY can be selected in multiplayer North Africa maps.

7. SEAL Desert Ghillie Suit can be selected in multiplayer North Africa maps.

8. Al-Kamil Sarwat can be selected in multiplayer North Africa maps.

9. Terrorist Desert Ghillie Suit can be selected in multiplayer North Africa maps.

10. CHOPPER can be selected in multiplayer South Asia maps.

11. SEAL Jungle Ghillie Suit can be selected in multiplayer South Asia maps.

12. Hari Raman can be selected in multiplayer South Asia maps.

13. Terrorist Jungle Ghillie Suit can be selected in multiplayer South Asia maps.

14. COLDKILL can be selected in multiplayer Poland maps.

15. SEAL Winter Ghillie Suit can be selected in multiplayer Poland maps.

16. Dr. Mironova can be selected in multiplayer Poland maps.

17. Terrorist Winter Ghillie Suit can be selected in multiplayer Poland maps.

18. Movies can be viewed at any time.

19. Game credits can be viewed at any time.

20. First half of the SOCOM 3 music tracks are available in the Jukebox.

21. Second half of the SOCOM 3 music tracks are available in the Jukebox.

EXTRAS

INDEX

A TO Z

Below you will find page references for all of the key topics in the guide, including all Primary, Secondary, Bonus and Crosstalk Objectives, to help you access the information that you want as quickly as possible. The list is color coded, with multiplayer pages highlighted in **blue**, map references highlighted in **green**, and references to the Extras chapter highlighted in **red**.

SOCOM 3
U.S. NAVY SEALS

GAME BASICS

WALKTHROUGH

MULTIPLAYER

EXTRAS

INDEX